Praise for the second edition

You can't have an agile company without agile leadership. Most 'traditional' leaders, however, struggle to make the transition. It is not that they lack the desire. Rather, agile practices upend so many of the hard-won instincts honed by leaders over years of experience. *The Agile Leader* is a well-researched, thoughtful guide for those wanting to make the leap. Like any good leadership coach, Simon Hayward reminds us we must first look to ourselves, before asking others to follow. BILL WINTERS, CEO, STANDARD CHARTERED BANK

In these turbulent times, thousands of companies are attempting agile transformations in order to survive. The primary cause of failure is a lack of agile leadership, which Simon Hayward's book addresses forcefully. Reading it may save your company. JEFF SUTHERLAND, CO-CREATOR OF SCRUM, CREATOR OF SCRUM@SCALE, AND SIGNATORY OF THE AGILE MANIFESTO

In his thought-provoking and necessary new book, Simon Hayward shares his deep understanding and sharp analysis of how organizations can and must embrace change, at speed and scale, to achieve growth. Leaders who follow his wise prescription for agility – acting as both disruptor and enabler, fostering a culture of collaboration and respect, building trust, and always staying close to customers – can emerge not only as trailblazers in their industries but also as catalysts of shared success for all stakeholders. JULIE SWEET, CEO, ACCENTURE

Digital is both disrupting and revolutionizing the way we work. Adopting a more agile style of leadership enables leaders to reshape organizations so people can flourish in a future augmented by new technology. The insights in this book will help leaders to transform the nature of work by enabling people to learn and adapt at speed, leading to greater efficiency. PAUL DAUGHERTY, GROUP CHIEF EXECUTIVE – TECHNOLOGY, AND CTO, ACCENTURE; CO-AUTHOR, *HUMAN + MACHINE*

In a world that's getting faster, we need to move quickly, learn and adapt. This book provides a blueprint for a more agile style of leadership to help you focus on customers and stay ahead in a highly competitive and unpredictable environment. Highly recommended. PETER PRITCHARD, GROUP CEO, PETS AT HOME

In this book, Simon Hayward breaks down the complex subject of agile leadership into a series of steps that any organization can take. For Yodel, introducing a more agile and connected style of leadership was key to becoming more centred on customers, creating cultural change, and turning our business around. We kept things simple, turned managers into agile leaders, and got colleagues on board with new ways of working. The difference is incredible, and Simon's thinking has been a big part of that. MIKE HANCOX, CEO, YODEL

The Agile Leader lays out a clear plan for CEOs and their teams to embrace new ways of working that will unlock the agile potential in their organizations. I would recommend this book to any leader who wants to improve their organization's clarity of thinking and speed of decision making. It describes how leaders at all levels can create a climate for agility and diversity to flourish, leading to greater innovation and improved customer experiences. CHRISTIE SMITH, GLOBAL LEAD, TALENT AND ORGANIZATION, ACCENTURE

This book describes how getting the right mix of leadership and teamwork wins every time. Whether we are running a global business or a famous football club, the need for agile leadership has never been so acute. Great leaders build confidence, change the rules, and focus on the priorities that will make the difference. I can't recommend this book too highly. COLLETTE ROCHE, CHIEF OPERATING OFFICER, MANCHESTER UNITED FOOTBALL CLUB

Agility is a must in a world that is constantly changing. This book is full of practical advice and covers everything you need to think about to transform your organization into an agile business. I found the agile leadership paradox that Simon Hayward sets out really helped me to think about how I adapt my leadership style to become both an enabler and a disruptor. PENNY JAMES, CEO, DIRECT LINE GROUP

The rapid disruption brought about by the pandemic demonstrated to me the clear advantage of agile leadership. During those months, I kept the first edition of this book close to hand. In this new edition, Simon Hayward provides more inspiration and timely advice for leaders to draw from on the journey ahead. DAVID HORNE, MANAGING DIRECTOR, LNER

Praise for the first edition

We need to disrupt existing business models to drive growth in our unpredictable world. This book can help leaders to think differently, to agitate for change and to take others on a transformation journey. It highlights the importance of culture, behaviour, and ways of working. KEVIN COSTELLO, CEO, HAYMARKET MEDIA GROUP

To be agile, you need to try to test things. Not everything you try is going to work. Fail small, fail fast and learn quickly. *The Agile Leader* demonstrates that agility is not just about creating things. It's also about ruthless prioritization, managing risk and knowing when to stop. This book helps leaders to make choices that define their business success on a day-to-day basis. If you're not moving forward and innovating and changing things, then your competitors will be. HUMPHREY COBBOLD, CEO, PUREGYM

In *The Agile Leader*, Simon Hayward develops the approach to building an agile organization that he introduced in his first book, *Connected Leadership*. He looks at how many successful organizations are led by their customers, working with them to constantly innovate and improve, for mutual benefit. He also focuses on the importance of simplifying business processes and breaking down silos to encourage collaboration. In an uncertain climate, businesses need to be adaptable, flexible and always evolving. As well as spotting opportunities for growth, we need to make decisions quickly to seize these opportunities. We have adopted many of the principles of agile leadership at Pentland Brands to future-proof our own organization. ANDY RUBIN, CHAIR, PENTLAND BRANDS

With disruption happening in every industry and customer behaviour changing all the time, agility has become a highly prized leadership skill. By reacting with agility to changing customer needs and focusing effort where it will have greatest impact, this book shows where leaders can gain quick wins as well as achieving long-term, sustainable success. ROGER WHITESIDE, CEO, GREGGS

This book explains very clearly just what makes agile leadership different to traditional leadership. Making the shift towards a more agile style of leadership can be a huge challenge. Simon Hayward offers a range of insights and advice to help you make that shift in a sustainable way. MARK ALLEN, FORMER CEO, DAIRY CREST

The digital explosion has had a huge impact on every industry. It has disrupted traditional ways of working. This book highlights the importance of customer focus, learning and collaboration in becoming increasingly innovative and agile. By adopting the principles of agile leadership you can stay ahead of the competition. CAROLINE RUSH CBE, CEO, BRITISH FASHION COUNCIL

A thoughtful read for leaders and aspiring leaders on the balance between reflection and action needed for transforming, or even just surviving, in an age of digital overload. BEN PAGE, CHIEF EXECUTIVE, IPSOS MORI

We live in a fast-moving world. This book recognizes that as a leader, you are on a constant journey. You cannot stand still. You need to stay abreast of new ideas and developments, to learn from others, to seek out opportunities and react to them. There is no finishing post. Being truly agile is about constantly evolving. VANDA MURRAY OBE, CHAIRMAN, FENNER

Technology is accelerating the pace of change. It increases customer expectations. *The Agile Leader* offers valuable advice to leaders who want to embrace that change and to place customers at the heart of their business. It highlights the importance of developing a clear vision, purpose and framework so leaders can empower others to go ahead and work in more agile ways, and to react to customer needs and new opportunities. ANGELA SPINDLER, FORMER CEO, N BROWN

This is a really timely and thoughtful book for any leader thinking about how not just to survive, but to thrive, in our fast-changing world. It's a powerful sequel to Simon Hayward's *Connected Leadership*, really bringing agile leadership to life through a series of compelling interviews and case studies, alongside lots of practical hints and tips. ALISON NIMMO CBE, FORMER CEO, THE CROWN ESTATE

This book demonstrates that by embracing agile leadership you can drive innovation and improved productivity. It will be relevant to managers and leaders across all organizations as it promotes having fewer hierarchical structures, and recommends collaboration and devolved decision making. This encourages a clearer focus on customer needs and will enable more agile working by removing bureaucracy and encouraging empowerment. CAMPBELL FITCH, GOVERNOR, GLASGOW CALEDONIAN UNIVERSITY

This book is full of useful tips to help leaders succeed in a digital world. Drawing on his extensive research and real-world case studies, Simon Hayward demonstrates how leaders can, indeed have to, adapt to rapidly changing circumstances. JACQUELINE MOYSE, HEAD OF ORGANIZATIONAL DEVELOPMENT, MANDARIN ORIENTAL HOTEL GROUP

This is an inspiring book which is both thought-provoking and full of practical solutions and insight to help you to be an agile leader in a fast-moving environment. HENNY BRAUND, CHIEF EXECUTIVE, ANTHONY NOLAN

In *The Agile Leader*, Simon Hayward identifies the biggest barriers to agility and explains very clearly how to overcome these. By distilling robust research into valuable insights, he offers guidance to leaders who want to develop their own capabilities in order to drive business-wide transformation. A very practical guide which can change the way you work and help you to influence wider ways of working across your organization. MARK BROWN, VICE PRESIDENT, GLOBAL TALENT MANAGEMENT, FRESENIUS MEDICAL CARE

This book provides leaders with a blueprint for creating a more agile organization. It identifies the barriers to agility and suggests some specific ways to overcome them. This is a very useful guide to streamlining your business in a complex world. RICHARD PROSSER, CHAIRMAN, AUDLEY TRAVEL AND TUSKER DIRECT

In *The Agile Leader*, Simon Hayward distils a great deal of research and real-world experience into a very practical and insightful guide. Illuminating case studies deliver some real 'light-bulb' moments. Building on *Connected Leadership*, this book provides a roadmap for developing a more agile business and describes how to take people with you on a journey of transformation. It explains why collaboration and connection between colleagues, customers and key business stakeholders is critical to ensuring your business can evolve and thrive. ALAN BODDY, EXECUTIVE DIRECTOR OF OPERATIONS, LIVIN

Many start-ups begin life as very agile businesses but find it difficult to hold on to that agility as they grow. *The Agile Leader* shows how businesses can continue to evolve, adapt and innovate, no matter how big they become. TONY FOGGETT, CEO, CODE

Once again, Simon Hayward has managed to produce a book that is informative, challenging and a good read. PROFESSOR CATHERINE CASSELL, DEAN, BIRMINGHAM BUSINESS SCHOOL

In this book, Dr Simon Hayward draws on well-documented research into agility, complexity and distributed leadership. He distils this into some very practical advice to help managers and leaders deal with the everyday challenges of working in an unpredictable and fast-paced environment. PROFESSOR FIONA DEVINE OBE FAcSS FRSA, HEAD OF ALLIANCE MANCHESTER BUSINESS SCHOOL, UNIVERSITY OF MANCHESTER

I have worked with Simon Hayward in various different formats and have found his insights on leadership to be enormously valuable. PROFESSOR DAME NANCY ROTHWELL, PRESIDENT AND VICE-CHANCELLOR, THE UNIVERSITY OF MANCHESTER

How to lead effectively in this fast-moving chaotic world? In this fine book, Dr Simon Hayward argues convincingly that today, agility is a crucial element of effective leadership. Packed with research findings and practical advice, this book should be recommended reading for current and future leaders, as well as students of management theory. PROFESSOR JOHN PERKINS CBE, FORMER CHIEF SCIENTIFIC ADVISER, DEPARTMENT FOR BUSINESS, INNOVATION AND SKILLS, HER MAJESTY'S GOVERNMENT

Dr Simon Hayward condenses a wealth of research and case-study material into a highly readable guide to agile leadership. He explains how leaders can develop their own capabilities, build more agile teams and play a part in creating agile cultures that support organizational transformation. PROFESSOR MIKE BRESNEN, HEAD OF DEPARTMENT OF PEOPLE AND PERFORMANCE, MANCHESTER METROPOLITAN UNIVERSITY BUSINESS SCHOOL

The Agile Leader

How to create an agile business in the digital age

SECOND EDITION

Simon Hayward

KoganPage

First published in Great Britain and the United States in 2018 by Kogan Page Limited
Second edition published in 2021

2nd Floor, 45 Gee Street	122 W 27th St, 10th Floor	4737/23 Ansari Road
London	New York, NY 10001	Daryaganj
EC1V 3RS	USA	New Delhi 110002
United Kingdom		India

www.koganpage.com

Kogan Page books are printed on paper from sustainable forests.

© Simon Hayward, 2018, 2021

The right of Simon Hayward to be identified as the author of this work has been asserted by him in accordance with the Copyright, Designs and Patents Act 1988.

ISBNs

Hardback   978 1 3986 0072 0
Paperback   978 1 3986 0071 3
eBook   978 1 3986 0073 7

British Library Cataloguing-in-Publication Data

A CIP record for this book is available from the British Library.

Library of Congress Cataloging-in-Publication Data

Names: Hayward, Simon J., author.
Title: The agile leader : how to create an agile business in the digital
  age / Simon Hayward.
Description: Second edition. | New York, NY : Kogan Page, 2021. | Includes
  bibliographical references and index.
Identifiers: LCCN 2021012214 (print) | LCCN 2021012215 (ebook) | ISBN
  9781398600713 (paperback) | ISBN 9781398600720 (hardback) | ISBN
  9781398600737 (ebook)
Subjects: LCSH: Leadership–Psychological aspects. | Organizational change.
  | Teams in the workplace. | Management–Technological innovations.
Classification: LCC HD57.7 .H39134 2021 (print) | LCC HD57.7 (ebook) |
  DDC 658.4/092–dc23

Typeset by Integra Software Services, Pondicherry
Print production managed by Jellyfish
Printed and bound by CPI Group (UK) Ltd, Croydon CR0 4YY

Contents

About the author

Dr Simon Hayward is an international thought leader, valued by many client organizations as a trusted adviser and partner. He is founder and CEO of Cirrus, a leadership consultancy now part of Accenture, and an Honorary Professor at Alliance Manchester Business School. He has a wealth of strategic leadership experience gained over 30 years. He has developed leadership strategy and leadership development programmes with client organizations across Europe, Asia and North America.

Simon's first book, *Connected Leadership*, was published by FT Publishing in 2016 and was shortlisted as Management Book of the Year in 2017 by the Chartered Management Institute and the British Library. It has been translated into Chinese and Arabic. Simon has also had chapters published in the *Palgrave Handbook of Leadership in Transforming Asia* (2017), which explored connected leadership in the Asian context, and the *Sage Handbook of Qualitative Business and Management Research Methods* (2017). Simon is a regular media commentator, featuring in leading publications including the *Financial Times*, *The Sunday Times*, *The Times*, *Management Today*, *Human Resources* and *The Guardian*, as well as on Sky News and the BBC. He is also a regular conference speaker. The first edition of *The Agile Leader* has been translated into Korean, Chinese, Russian, Vietnamese, Hungarian and adapted for use by EBSCO and Skillsoft.

Simon has a DBA and MBA from Alliance Manchester Business School and an MA (Hons) in English from Oxford University. He is a Fellow of the Chartered Management Institute and a Fellow of the Royal Society of Arts, a member of the British Academy of Management and the Chartered Institute of Marketing.

Cirrus was recognized as the Best HR and Learning and Development Consultancy by the Chartered Institute of Personnel and Development in its 2017 awards. Cirrus has won many other awards for its work with clients in leadership and engagement, including the International Business Award for best small/medium professional services company in 2020.

He led Academee, a successful leadership development business, to be recognized as the fifth Best Workplace in the UK by the *Financial Times*, and one of *The Sunday Times* 100 Best Workplaces in 2007. The company also won a special Business Excellence Award for People and People Results before being acquired by Marsh & McLennan Companies in 2008.

Simon has been recognized by the World of Learning Awards, British Gas/*Daily Express* Tomorrow's People Awards and Entrepreneur of the Year awards. His work with clients has been recognized by the People Management Awards, Management Consultancies Association Awards, HR Excellence Awards, *Personnel Today* Awards and the Hotel Catering Personnel and Training Awards.

Simon is a keen runner and a fundraiser for cancer charities. He is a Vice-President and Chairman of Fundraising at the East Cheshire Hospice. He lives in Cheshire, UK, with his wife Clare and has three sons.

Foreword to the second edition
The leaders of the future

We are about to enter a period of enormous change, in how we work, where we work and how we cope with the challenges of a world recession which may last longer than any we have had in living memory. The age of robotics, of electric cars, of new energy sources, of less globalization and more digitalization and the challenges of climate change for business and governments is our future. These changes, and many more to come, will require agile leaders, people capable of making quick and effective decisions in an ever-changing world. We know the management of change is not easy, as Machiavelli wrote in *The Prince*:

> It should be borne in mind that there is nothing more difficult to arrange, more doubtful of success, and more dangerous to carry through than initiating change...The innovator makes enemies of all those who prospered under the old order, and only lukewarm support is forthcoming from those who would prosper under the new.

We need leaders who are agile decision makers, who are disruptive thinkers, who take people with them, who are collaborators and most importantly have a 'sense of purpose'. We need of course leaders who have a vision of the future but also can take the decisive action to achieve the agreed organizational goals. As the old Japanese proverb goes: 'vision without action is a daydream, action without vision is a nightmare'. We also need business leaders of the future to create a culture of wellbeing and psychological safety in the workplace – this requires more managers with greater social and interpersonal skills to manage people working more remotely, who find it difficult coping with change, engaging them in the decision-making process and making people feel valued and trusted. Mark Twain summarized this in a sentence: 'Keep away from people who try to belittle your ambitions. Small people always do that, but the really great make you feel that you, too, can somehow become great.'

This book highlights all the qualities of agile and future leaders, from barriers to agility, to the importance of disruptive/innovate behaviour but in the context of a learning culture, to decisiveness in decision making and to creating a safe culture amidst a maelstrom of change. During the Covid period we have seen a lack of political leadership in many countries, with significantly less agile behaviour, which had consequences for controlling the virus and for the lives of many. Business, on the other hand, showed greater agility in embracing remote working, in the use of technology to continue to build teams and to deliver their products and services. But with the recession upon us and technology advancing at an ever-faster pace, the agility of our business leaders will become a business imperative. This book has many of the answers to how we might achieve the successful management of change over the next decade and should be read by all people in a leadership role in the private as well as the public sector. Remember, as the old adage goes, 'If you always do what you always did – you'll always get what you always got!'

Professor Sir Cary Cooper,
Alliance Manchester Business School,
University of Manchester, UK

Foreword to the first edition

It is an honour to be writing this foreword for Simon Hayward's book on agile leadership. I first met Simon when we worked together at Manchester Business School. As a Dean of a business school I am proud that our universities make an important contribution to cutting-edge thinking about leadership. In business schools we create new knowledge to help us critically make sense of the key global, grand challenges that face our economies and societies. What delights me about Simon's work is his ability to take that thought-leadership and translate it into an accessible and interesting commentary, alongside a useful set of tools.

Leaders reside in an increasingly challenging world. Being sufficiently agile in the complex, digital environments we inhabit is both desirable and necessary. Having spent a career working in business schools and watching how the preoccupations of managers and leaders change over the years, I know full well that the challenges that Simon identifies in this book are at the forefront of the thinking of many of the leaders we seek to develop.

The demands upon leaders have become increasingly sophisticated in recent years. As technological developments proceed at a sometimes alarming rate, the importance of human connections becomes even more crucial in the effective leadership and management of others. As Simon points out, we need to be disruptors as well as enablers, building trust and making decisions in thoughtful ways.

Simon's first book introduced us to the notion of connected leadership and offered a step-by-step roadmap to how we, as leaders, could enhance leadership within our own organizations. I remember reading that book and reflecting upon my own practice. Not only did it challenge my own preconceptions about how to make things work, it also gave me ideas about how to negotiate some of the everyday leadership dilemmas I encounter.

In this book the focus is agility. Once again Simon has managed to produce a text that is both informative, challenging and a good read. In writing this book, Simon draws on well-documented research into distributed leadership, authentic leadership and complexity leadership, creating a powerful framework for leaders to use to create the optimal conditions for agile working to flourish.

I invite you to join with me in learning about agile leadership and, perhaps more importantly, thinking about how we can develop our own agile leadership skills.

Professor Catherine Cassell,
Dean, Birmingham Business School,
University of Birmingham, UK

Preface

Creating greater organizational agility is one of the top concerns of chief executives with whom I speak around the world. This is especially true in the context of accelerated digital transformation, Covid-19 disruption, and continued socio-political uncertainty. To increase organizational agility requires agile leaders, who pioneer agility and create the climate for agile ways of working to flourish. In these pages you will gain what I believe is a rounded view of the specific ways in which to develop agile leaders in practical terms.

In Part One I describe what agile leadership means, both as an individual leader and as an organizational capability. In Part Two I explore key agile leadership practices, with how you can adopt them to enable agile working. In Part Three I widen this out with a description of how to create an agile organization and how this relates to our wider society.

This book builds on my work on Connected Leadership, which is based on research into what leadership factors help or hinder the transition to being more agile and customer centric. It explores in more depth the whole area of agile leadership. This book is self-contained, so you do not need to have read *Connected Leadership* (Hayward, 2016) beforehand, but if you have, you will appreciate the wider context for this book, which focuses on being an agile leader in the digital, post-Covid world in which we live. I have identified the eight leadership attributes that enable agile working to flourish at an enterprise level, as well as at departmental and team levels.

So, how can you get most value from this book? There are perhaps four main groups of readers for whom this book will be helpful: senior leaders in long-established or more recently formed organizations; middle or junior leaders in similar organizations; students of leadership; and practitioners of leadership development.

If you are a chief executive or senior leader in a large established organization, this book gives you a blueprint for creating a more agile organization, as well as a broader appreciation of how challenging this will be. If you are a senior leader in a start-up or smaller organization, you can probably implement all the content of this book more quickly, as you will probably be doing some of it already. For junior or middle managers, this book gives you both a clear route to developing more agile ways of working in your area and how to play your part in the wider organizational transformation to being agile.

For students of leadership this book provides an easy-to-read introduction to leadership in an agile context, as well as giving you a broad understanding of the key aspects of leadership that are most important in shifting ways of working to embrace agile. For leadership development practitioners, this book provides a holistic approach to agile leadership, highlighting the ways it is different to more conventional leadership. Developing agile ways of working at an enterprise level is a real challenge and needs a significant shift in both mindset and behaviour from leaders if it is to be sustainable. This book shows you how.

I would welcome feedback from readers from all groups, so please let me know what you think via email at simonhayward62@gmail.com. I look forward to hearing from you, so I can share this insight more widely, and so that we can continue to build practical insight into becoming agile leaders in this digital age of disruption. Thank you.

Reference

Hayward, S (2016) *Connected Leadership,* FT Publishing, Pearson, London

Acknowledgements

I would like to thank the team at Kogan Page for their commitment and professionalism during the publishing process, and especially to Geraldine Collard for her editorial support throughout this project. Thanks also to Jane O'Hara and Alicia Leon, my colleagues at Cirrus, who have helped enormously with research for this book. Thank you.

I would like to thank the many leaders and professionals who have contributed to the research for this book through providing case studies, ideas and quotations. In particular I would like to thank: Angela Spindler, former CEO, N Brown; Bruce Charlesworth, chief medical officer, Health, RB; Carl Moore, COO, Yodel; Caroline Rush, CEO, British Fashion Council; Catriona Marshall, former CEO, HobbyCraft; Dan Hill, visiting professor at UCL Bartlett; Dave Dyson, former CEO and Graham Baxter, former COO, Three UK; David Wilson, global head of culture and organizational development, Standard Chartered Bank; Drew Moss, head of leadership development, DLA Piper; James McClure, GM Northern Europe, Airbnb; Julia Hitzbleck, Social Innovation Venture Design, Bayer; Kevin Costello, CEO, Haymarket Media Group; Michael Lambert, formerly head of development, CDL; Nancy Rothwell, vice chancellor and president, University of Manchester; Peter Pritchard, Group CEO, Pets at Home; Rose Lewis, founder, Collider; Sally Hopson, CEO, Sofology; Tanith Dodge, former HR director, Value Retail. Thank you – it has been an inspiration to get your insights and to draw on your wide-ranging experience.

My sincere thanks go to everyone at Cirrus who has helped with ideas and feedback on the manuscript, and for helping me to take time for researching and writing this book.

Thank you to all of the Cirrus clients with whom I and my colleagues have worked in recent years – your collaboration and counsel has been and continues to be incredibly helpful in achieving clarity on what actually works in practice.

I would like to acknowledge the various authors and researchers whose work I have drawn on in my own research. They are all cited in the book, so that you the reader can follow up in more detail where you wish. I have sought to combine excellent research into all things agile with my own leadership research, which started through my doctoral programme at the Alliance

Manchester Business School in 2010, and with my experience working with some of the world's leading organizations over the last three decades.

Thank you also to the excellent research team I have been working with at Alliance Manchester Business School – Professor David Holman, Professor Robin Martin, Professor Sheena Johnson, Dr Sara Willis and Dr Kara Ng. I have enjoyed the international research journey so far, and here is to the next phase.

Finally, thank you to my family and friends for their patience and for putting up with so many weekends and evenings of me stuck in the study. Thank you, Clare, my wonderful wife, and Harry, Max and Freddie, my wonderful sons. Your patience and encouragement have helped me enormously.

PART ONE

Agile leadership and organizations

CHAPTER ONE

What is agile leadership?

Agility is a rapid whole-body movement with change of velocity or direction in response to a stimulus. SHEPPARD ET AL (2006)

Introduction

What great leaders do has changed. Time has changed. Digital and pandemic disruption is reducing the time we have to adapt or die. To create and lead organizations capable of succeeding in this environment we need to adapt our leadership approach – to become agile, both as a leader and as an organization. In fact, without agile leaders we cannot have agile organizations. Agile leaders create the vision and the environment where agile teams create innovation and drive constant improvement. To succeed in such complex times, we need to enable our teams to embrace agile ways of working and challenge the status quo. Being an agile leader means being an enabler and a disruptor at the same time – this is the agile leadership paradox, which we will explore as we go.

QUESTIONS TO ASK YOURSELF

In this chapter you may find it helpful to consider the following questions as you read, to help you extract the key insights for yourself as a leader:

- How well have you led others through recent changes in our world?
- Do you think in an agile way?
- Are you more comfortable as a leader being an enabler or a disruptor? How can you achieve a helpful balance?

Leading in a digital disrupted world

Agile leaders are connected leaders. They know how to connect with their team, customers, colleagues and wider stakeholders. They also know how to interpret societal trends that are shaping a new reality around us. The Covid-19 pandemic changed how we work and interact, accelerating digitization and political uncertainty. This creates novel opportunities and raises the threat of obsolescence across products and whole sectors. In this new reality, agile leaders and their teams make choices that define their business success or the achievement of their goals on a day-to-day basis.

At the time of writing this second edition, the effects of the Covid-19 pandemic had been seismic: millions ill and dead, massive unemployment and significant economic disruption. The pandemic also had a major impact on work, with workforce dislocation as well as new levels of flexibility in how we work, and changes to the flow of goods and services across national and regional boundaries challenging global business operations. Such disruption requires a new approach to leadership, one which the agile approach is well suited to provide.

On top of this, technology, and what we can do with it, is transforming human behaviour and how we communicate across sectors and geographies. The explosion of internet connectivity and artificial intelligence is raising questions about who, or what, is in control. It feels like time and space are shrinking and the time we have as leaders to think and respond to changes around us is in danger of diminishing in parallel. The pace at which we can now operate is an amazing achievement driven by mobile technology, the internet, innovative apps and intelligent systems. In this context, we need to create new ways of working that reflect the changing world outside and inside our organizations and enable us to respond to unexpected opportunities and threats with speed and accuracy.

In this digital post-Covid-19 world, where customer experience expectations (and the quality of internal operating models to deliver them) are rising at an ever-faster rate, we need to learn to create an environment for our organizations that can embrace uncertainty and flourish by working in ways we had not even heard of five years ago. For some this will continue to be more incremental change in response to competitive forces, whereas for others it involves wholesale reinvention. The software company moves into hardware, for example. The telecoms company becomes a digital company. The retailer becomes a service provider. The car manufacturer becomes a tech giant. We are all too aware of the 'Uber moments' happening around us, where competitors change the rules and structure of our market – Uber has disrupted the taxi market around the world, using an app to change how we travel in cities. Covid-19 has disrupted Uber in a way it probably had not anticipated – disrupting the disruptor.

In this book I am using the term 'disruption' in line with the *Oxford English Dictionary* (2017) definition: 'disturbance or problems which interrupt an event, activity or process'. This captures the sense of interruption, of challenging established norms, and the level of change needed to flourish in this digital age. I am using the term 'agile' to embrace a whole approach to being 'able to move quickly and easily' (*OED*, 2017). To quote from my first book (Hayward, 2016):

> Organizational agility presents something of a paradox. You must be able to identify and respond quickly to emerging threats and challenges while at the same time having a firm vision of your strategic plans and coordinated activity to execute them. This paradox is at the heart of connected leadership, with its stable foundations and flexible and evolving ways of working. Creating an organization that is 'able to move quickly and easily' needs a strong spine and supple muscles.

Whether we face an Uber moment or not, if we are not evolving at least as quickly as our environment, we are likely to be caught out. A 2020 forecast from IDC estimates that there will be 56 billion internet-connected devices by 2025 (IDC, 2020). These intelligent devices are sensing and responding to data about everything from our heart rates, the movement of goods in supply chains, to volcano temperatures. As this exponential growth in connectivity continues, we are in the middle of a shift where human interaction will no longer be needed for systems around the world to connect, adapt and decide on future actions. In this context the potential for chaos is increasing and the ability for human control decreasing.

Covid-19 has demonstrated how for many of us the risk of an Uber moment in our industry is just around the corner, and it is better to be evolving as quickly as we can rather than waiting for change to be forced upon us. Online retailing, for example, has been an unforgiving battleground over the last decade or so, with many traditional retailers struggling to embrace a digital business model when they are rooted in more 'bricks-and-mortar' or paper-based operations. The Covid-19 pandemic accelerated the shift to digital retail in 2020 in a matter of weeks. Consumer expectations are being raised daily by innovations driven by the clever use of technology, such as same-day delivery with online shopping, in-play betting during sporting events, virtual reality gaming experiences, and online sizing for clothing when we can try the garment on and see what it looks like before buying.

Here is how Angela Spindler, ex-CEO of N Brown, the successful UK online clothing retailer, describes the shift it has seen over the last few years. N Brown has moved from being a traditional business that printed catalogues to a digital business trading through a range of brand websites. Angela describes how things changed quickly in the online clothing retail market:

> The big difference in the pace of change has been the connectivity of consumers, fuelled by technology, both to each other, the market and the world. This both introduces and accelerates the pace of change and the expectations that consumers have. They know far more about pretty much everything, and it's at their fingertips, quite literally.

Many of the people and most of the systems have changed in the last few years at N Brown as it has moved quickly to a digitally led retail model. The results have been impressive, but the journey has been painful at times, with changes in business platform, people, and ways of working. In April 2020 another fashion retailer, clothing giant Primark, went from making £650 million in sales a month to nothing as the coronavirus pandemic forced it to close its stores in Europe and the United States (BBC, 2020). The company also wrote down the value of its clothing stock by £284 million at that time. Primark had done well without an online presence, but when the coronavirus struck it was unable to respond effectively in the short term.

This book is a guide for leaders to think and act in an agile way so that you can create an environment where organizational agility can flourish and you can stay relevant even when the rules change, sometimes gradually, sometimes overnight. I will draw on research that is both current and robust, as well as nearly 30 years of working with many international corporate clients to create new leadership practices to transform the way their organizations operate. I will use my own research and that of leading experts in their fields, from both academic and practitioner research sources, so that you can understand what the experts are reporting and interpret this in relation to your own organization. I will explore how agile software development processes work, focusing on Scrum, and what we can learn from them as business leaders. I will also use case studies to explore what various leading organizations are doing to deepen their levels of agility and include extracts from interviews I held with participants in my research. I will provide tools to help you apply this to your own organization, whether you are the CEO or an aspiring CEO.

Most of the organizations I have studied or worked with are seeking to succeed in a context of ever-increasing disruption. This includes the effects of the coronavirus pandemic, digital transformation of whole industries, the upsurge in populist politics, increasing levels of protectionism, the break-up between the United Kingdom and the European Union, religious conflict and social division in parallel with the hyper-connected world that social media and digital communications have brought. This disruption creates opportunities for major commercial or service delivery advancement. Seizing these opportunities is often fraught with risk, but not seizing them can be riskier still. In this unpredictable world, agile leadership has never been more relevant.

Connected leaders

In my book *Connected Leadership* (Hayward, 2016) I described a fresh approach to leadership that is relevant to this context. There are five attributes that are most prominent in describing how organizations make the transition to be an agile and customer-driven organization in this digital age. Figure 1.1 shows the five factors, with the two at the bottom providing a foundational framework that enables the top three to flourish.

FIGURE 1.1 Connected leadership factors

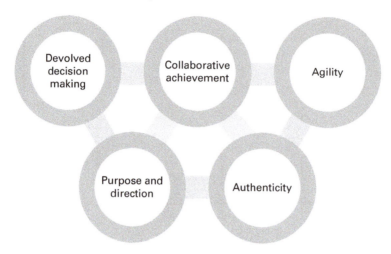

Source: Hayward (2016)

As you can see, agility is an element of connected leadership, and the one on which this book is focused. As we dig deeper into what agile leadership looks like in practice, it is helpful to remember that it is part of the wider connected leadership framework, which is the product of several years of research and in line with most authoritative leadership research today.

So, what are connected leaders like? Firstly, they lead with a deep sense of societal purpose and clarity about the organization's strategic direction, to create belief in the future. People in (and outside) the organization buy into what they are doing together and why it is significant. Secondly, connected leaders are authentic, open, and driven by values that inspire confidence and commitment from others. They have open and transparent relationships with colleagues to build trust and a positive culture around them. The third factor is these leaders believe in others, and actively devolve decision making as close to the customer as possible to create empowered teams able to deliver in line with the organization's direction and purpose. Fourthly, they encourage collaboration across the organization, with people working together within and between teams to achieve shared outcomes and break down silos. Finally, connected leaders are agile, enabling others to adapt to changing circumstances through experimentation, learning and constant improvement. Through these connections they are creating an agile organization, able to adapt easily to changing circumstances.

The agile leader paradox

All the factors above are helpful in becoming an agile leader and are proving to be highly effective in organizations around the world that are using them to change their leadership approach; I will explore this later in this chapter. In the context of agile leadership, we need to add another aspect of leadership that is directly relevant to the acceleration of change around us. Leaders need to be disruptors as well as enablers, able to shake up thinking, embrace ideas from different environments, link unrelated pieces of information, see new possibilities and challenge the status quo. My wife, Clare, for example, has an eye for houses. She has a knack of looking at what I regard as an unappealing and unsuitable property and seeing what it could be. She sees new possibilities, looking beyond the walls, the colours and the furniture to envisage how the house could be. She is also good at making the dream into a reality, explaining her vision to the architect, and getting the builders organized, creating a new home that bears little relation to the original edifice. We are fortunate that at least one of us is good at this. She challenges preconceptions and refuses to see things as others do, and through this disruptive mindset she creates new possibilities, engaging others to make it a reality.

As the effects of the pandemic and digitization continue to accelerate in all areas of life, we need to embrace a leadership paradox: great leaders connect people, customers and nations, and yet they also challenge the status quo, disrupt thinking and break well-established norms such as the regulation of taxis in our cities or the time-to-market for fashion garments around the world.

To be **agile** leaders we need to be both enablers and disruptors, creating a joined-up organization and at the same time challenging how it operates at the most fundamental level. We need to embrace both sides of the agile leadership paradox – the need to enable and the need to disrupt – creating cohesion, yet questioning the assumptions that underpin it. This paradox is typical of the balancing acts leaders need to make to be effective in the 21st century, which is now commonly described as being volatile, uncertain, complex and ambiguous (VUCA). Originally used in the US military, VUCA (Stiehm and Townsend, 2002) has become a shorthand for the changeable environment in which we now operate, and the need to think in a more adaptive way, not relying on tried and tested methods to respond effectively to it. Our context is increasingly complex, and this complexity calls for a more nuanced approach to leadership, balancing competing factors to adapt and at the same time continue to deliver.

On the enabler side, agile leaders are creating organizations that can respond quickly to changing economic conditions, customer demands and competitor behaviour. People would rather work for a cause than a company, according to research (Cirrus/Ipsos, 2017), and agile leaders work hard at creating a 'cause' that our multigenerational workforce can buy into. They also work hard at empowering their people, giving them confidence to respond effectively within a coherent framework, so that decisions are made as close to the customer as possible. They are building a connected organization, able to move as a whole with ease, however significant the changes going on around them. At the same time these leaders are identifying the need for pivotal changes that redefine the foundational elements of organizational identity. They are looking for opportunities to reinvent their operating model to create or anticipate 'Uber moments' in their industry. They are encouraging new ways of thinking, behaving and reacting to events among their colleagues – developing a shared disruptive mindset. They are looking for moments of disruption.

The disruption of the Covid-19 pandemic has created significant variability in working practices around the world, which we can use to increase the level of agile thinking in our organizations. If we can 'capitalize on the tensions that stem from implicitly paradoxical relationships' we can increase levels of agile thinking among our people and 'create a state of [greater] agility or flexibility' (Hill *et al*, 2017). Disruption to the stable patterns of work presents the opportunity to accelerate unexpected thinking and enable our people to embrace new ways of working.

Now more than ever, post-Covid-19, we need to embrace this paradox – to hold at the same time the need to create connected, team-based ways of working as well as re-imagining how we work, how we provide a unique customer experience, how we survive. This is in line with extensive research by McKinsey involving over 1,000 companies, which highlights the need to combine stability with speed. McKinsey describes companies that have this combination as agile, with only 12 per cent of the companies in the study demonstrating both characteristics strongly (McKinsey, 2015). Interestingly, those 12 per cent had higher average organizational health and performance than the rest of the sample.

To take it to another level of detail, it is helpful to define what are the main characteristics of enablers and disruptors. If we need to embrace both

FIGURE 1.2 The agile leadership paradox

Enabler		**Disruptor**
• Clear purpose and direction		• Looking out
• Create a safe place		• Close to customers
• Trusted and trusting		• Ruthlessly prioritize
• Coach for improvement		• Challenge the status quo
• Devolve decision making		• Bold and determined
• Collaborative		

styles to be agile leaders and build and sustain agile organizations, we need to know what they look like in practice. I will explore these points throughout the book, but here is an initial summary to give you a flavour in Figure 1.2.

Enablers tend to provide clarity of purpose and direction to their colleagues, which helps to ensure aligned priorities across the organization. Enablers encourage experimentation and learning by creating a safe environment in which to make mistakes. They tend to be trusted by their customers and their colleagues, who might describe them as being 'authentic' or 'genuine'. They coach others, empowering them to get on and do a great job, and to collaborate with people across diverse areas. They are also socially adept, able to engage others on a transformation journey, using their natural curiosity and compassion to create a strong personal connection with a wider group of people.

Disruptors, on the other hand, tend to be looking outwards, reading the evolving customer experience landscape, often using big data to understand trends in buying patterns in their marketplace. They choose to spend time with customers, to listen to what they say they want and don't want, to pick up underlying trends or gaps to fill. They then give these insights priority. They will often challenge the status quo, risking ejection from their organization if it is not able to accommodate this. I remember, for example, challenging a chairman in the early stages of my career and the resulting fallout ended up in my leaving the business and moving into consulting, where I was better suited, as it turns out. Disruptors like to cut through bureaucracy and re-imagine the operating model, busting silos and challenging tribal thinking. They are often creative, bold and optimistic about the possibilities the future holds, and expect colleagues to adapt quickly to changes in the external environment. They also often have a determination to achieve a breakthrough, to achieve the mission in hand rather than be limited by the constraints of what they would see as 'old ways of working'. This can in turn inspire others to take risks and achieve real innovation.

An agile leader needs to do both. By combining these counter-intuitive leadership approaches, leaders can create in their teams and organizations the strength and movement needed to be truly agile. Reading this section through, where do you think you are more effective currently? At the end of this chapter there is a simple questionnaire in Table 1.1 you can use to see where your preferences and capabilities lie. This will help you read the rest of this book with some personal insight into your current strengths, to which you can play. Similarly, the questionnaire results can help identify where you need either to develop greater strength, or work with colleagues who are stronger in that characteristic so that you can complement each other. Remember, however, that a strength overdone can become a problem as well.

CASE STUDY   Airbnb: disruption, connection and focus through the good times and the bad

Airbnb is regarded as a classic 'disruptor'. Founded in 2008 and headquartered in San Francisco, the business is also founded on the concept of 'connection' – building a community which connects people to each other and to experiences across almost 200 countries. It has disrupted the market for short-term and holiday accommodation. Airbnb's distinctive business model combines with clear purpose and values to give it a unique market position which is difficult to emulate.

Although Airbnb is often described as a tech company, its original vision was to evolve from being a platform for overnight stays into a comprehensive travel company. Technology is regarded as an essential enabler. In 2017, an article in *The Economist* attributed much of Airbnb's success to its strong, values-based culture. Potential employees are assessed on their values and performance reviews are also values-based.

Airbnb was a pioneer of the 'sharing economy' – economic activity which takes place in online communities via peer-to-peer-based connections. Chip Conley, a strategic adviser to Airbnb and former head of global hospitality and strategy, told *Adweek* in 2016 that Airbnb had transformed the hospitality industry by following three rules of innovation: innovation doesn't happen without foreshadowing [clues about the future]; innovators address a human need that isn't being met; over time, the establishment embraces innovation that was once disruptive (Conley, 2019).

Another factor in Airbnb's success is its balance of local and global activity. Globally, it has a clear set of operating principles and an excellent online platform. Locally, hosts create individual experiences.

Brian Chesky, Airbnb's co-founder and CEO, has spoken frequently about the importance of values such as trust and authenticity. Community and connections are at the heart of the Airbnb philosophy. Chesky has always viewed himself as the head of a community, and the company hosts conventions and online forums where feedback from hosts is encouraged and acted upon. For example, engineers and developers listen to feedback from hosts on these forums to implement changes to the website. Airbnb has taken the principles of 'agile' – collaboration, continuous improvement, rapid and flexible response to change – and applied them widely across its organization for the benefit of customers.

Leaders at Airbnb have always invested a great deal of time and energy in building connections with hosts, who are regarded as partners. They aim to encourage all hosts to participate in the business as fully as they can and encourage this in a variety of ways. Clear expectations are set around timings and deliverables from both parties. Regular, open communication is encouraged. Airbnb leaders frequently stay in Airbnb accommodation to meet hosts and experience accommodation first-hand.

The Covid-19 pandemic was particularly disruptive for Airbnb. 'We spent 12 years building Airbnb business and lost almost all of it in a matter of four to six weeks,' Chesky told CNBC in June 2020 (Bosa, 2020).

The business responded to the challenges of the pandemic swiftly and decisively. For example, it relaxed its policy on refunds – something which many customers appreciated but many hosts were less happy about. Reflecting on this decision, Airbnb investor and board member Alfred Lin observed that although everything had not been handled perfectly, 'it was about speed and being directionally right' (Griffith, 2020).

Significant lay-offs were also announced. This represented a particular challenge for a company built on belonging and human connection, and whose mission was to 'create a world where anyone can belong anywhere'.

Chesky communicated frequently and at length with employees and hosts. He described many of his messages, particularly those announcing widespread redundancies, as 'difficult'. He invited questions and addressed many of the concerns raised. He aimed to communicate in an open and transparent way, demonstrating empathy to employees, hosts and customers.

From an operational point of view, it was time for ruthless prioritization, which I will explore in more detail later. The business had started to expand into experiences, transport and hotels, but pulled back to focus on its core business. In an open letter to all employees, Chesky said, 'This crisis has sharpened our focus to get back to our roots, back to the basics, back to what is truly special about Airbnb.'

Crises present a particular challenge for organizations such as Airbnb which are built on strong values of trust, sharing and inclusivity – values which helped to make Airbnb such a success story. It is difficult to keep your stakeholders on board when you're asking them to accept difficult messages such as reduced income and job losses. However, Airbnb demonstrated that it could retain its focus on these core values while embracing disruption and continuing to adapt in the face of seismic change. This approach helped Airbnb to retain its reputation as an innovative market leader, recovering more quickly than the rest of the beleaguered travel industry.

What can we learn from Airbnb?

- **Communicate with openness, transparency and empathy.** This helps stakeholders to feel engaged throughout your organization's journey.

- **The importance of wider collaboration.** Airbnb partners with hosts, guests and other partners in innovative ways.

- **Prioritize ruthlessly.** Focus on doing a few things brilliantly rather than spreading your efforts over many activities you could do less well.

- **Agility is the means not the end.** Being agile helps you to get where you want to go, to react with speed and decisiveness.

- **Operate globally and locally.** Have a clear sense of purpose, values and direction at the centre and encourage local employees and partners to tailor solutions to local needs.

- **Technology is simply an enabler.** Airbnb is in the business of giving people great experiences, not in the business of being a search engine.

Agility

So, what is agility? If we think of our favourite sports player, yoga teacher or dancer, we can recognize some of the characteristics that make them able to move and change direction so easily. They typically train hard to have balance, the ability to change pace, and strength in their limbs and core to coordinate their bodies in motion. In a sporting context, agile players move quickly and easily in response to their competitor's actions, seeking advantage and defending their position. Because of their training and innate ability, they move faster and with more precision than their opponents. Studying agility in athletes, Sheppard *et al* (2006) defined agility as being 'a rapid whole-body movement with change of velocity or direction in response to a stimulus'.

If we apply this definition to leaders in organizations, there are some interesting parallels. Movement often needs to be rapid, which is likely to be a challenge for leaders in large, bureaucratic institutions with strict governance and a complex myriad of legacy systems and working practices. It involves the whole body, not just the bits of the organization that operate more easily in agile ways, such as the software development teams. Agility involves a change in velocity or direction, which may mean accelerating or decelerating key projects, or pivoting into a new market or product category as gaps emerge. Agility is in response to a stimulus, a cognitive act such as seizing an opportunity when a pandemic occurs or a competitor trips up or to negate a competitive threat like a price war.

In this description we can see that there are two aspects of agility that are essential and complementary: situational awareness, which is the cognitive act of reading the situation and making sense of what it means for you; and the physical act of 'whole-body movement', shifting the enterprise so that you can compete more effectively. If we think about elite sports men and women, they can read the situation more quickly and accurately than their opponents, which gives them the edge. It may be that they move to counter an opponent's attack a moment sooner than others (who might otherwise be equally fit). They read the way opponents are moving their feet or leaning their body and interpret it quickly so that they can then respond sooner and negate the attacking move.

This 'read and act' ability is helpful as we think about what it means to be an agile leader. Reading the situation is based on our perception as we sense or anticipate the stimulus, and then our interpretation of the stimulus and making a choice about what to do. Acting is about execution as we initiate the response through others (Cox, 2002).

Speed of processing is key to how agile we are – top sports performers differ from the rest in their ability to use more clues earlier in reading an opponent's movement and the execution of a manoeuvre. If we want to be agile leaders, we need to develop our ability to anticipate what our customers want or our competitors are doing, and make effective choices about how to respond, often without much time or detailed information. In research published in the *Harvard Business Review*, Botelho *et al* (2017) identified that CEOs who excelled at adapting quickly to changing circumstances, where there was no playbook to fall back on, were 6.7 times more likely to succeed than those who lacked this attribute.

Once we are thinking in an agile way we can behave in an agile way, but this takes a lot of effort. Top athletes get to the top through extensive and intensive training, dedication, sacrifice, intolerance of toxic inputs, and expert coaching and data to inform the journey. We will explore these as we go through the book, as the same applies to becoming a top leader.

> Once we are thinking agile we can behave in an agile way.

The physical aspects of agility (Sheppard and Young, 2006) include the following five characteristics:

1 Balance – coordinating our senses and activity to maintain a position.
2 Strength – to overcome resistance.
3 Speed – moving all parts of the body quickly.
4 Coordination – control of the different parts of the body.
5 Endurance – stamina to sustain movement over time.

These physical characteristics are like the five organizational agility characteristics identified by Lin *et al* (2006) in their meta-analysis of organizational agility. They identified responsiveness, which they described as identifying changes and responding quickly. They highlighted flexibility, which is achieving new goals with existing facilities and resources; competency (the ability to achieve your goals); and quickness, which is carrying out the activity in the shortest possible time. They added coordination, which is integrating these principles in a coherent system and competitive capabilities. So, the similarities between athletic and organizational agility are significant.

The main addition to our thinking from this list is the emphasis on 'competency', which is self-evident in a way, but worth calling out. We do need core capability to achieve our goals if we are to be agile. I love running, for example. I've run a few marathons; it is unlikely however that I could have been an outstanding gymnast. My competency to rotate with ease on parallel bars, to somersault over the horse, or to hang in balance on the rings is low. So, I must face up to the conclusion that however hard I might have worked I did not have the fundamental competency to become a top-class gymnast. If agility is, at least in part, about achieving our goals more quickly and effectively, then we need the essential capability to accomplish those goals as part of the mix.

The outcomes from agility are varied. Graham Baxter, ex-COO of Three (UK), summed it up nicely in our research when he described their experience of shifting to more agile ways of working between 2014 and 2019:

> The outcomes we were getting included more engaged staff, because they felt part of something significant, they had a line of sight between what they were doing and what we were delivering as a business, and they were getting more empowerment. We also got things delivered faster, at lower cost, more aligned to the objectives of the organization. Also, from a longer-term perspective, it meant that we could evolve our organization to meet new challenges, so we did not become out of date.

Graham describes the business benefits as well as the personal benefits for the people in Three that were achieved with the move towards more agile ways of working. Both were important and tended to reinforce each other as motivation increased and drove improved business performance.

Different stimuli

Going back to the sporting definition of agility we have been using, agility is most required 'in response to a stimulus', and there are different types of stimulus we often face as leaders in 21st-century organizations. They sit on a spectrum defined at one end by in-the-moment, short-term, tactical changes, such as those in local consumer buying patterns in fashion, and at the other end by structural and strategic changes, what are often called 'Uber moments'. The Covid-19 pandemic accelerated some of these changes, such as the switch to digital and virtual working. We need different types of agile response to these ends of the spectrum – our choices as leaders will determine the outcome of our response. (Of course, you may also have the opportunity to create an 'Uber moment', and we will explore how to stay attuned to this possibility later.)

For frequent minor changes like consumer buying patterns, we need to choose to build an organization that can adapt locally without losing our core strength and efficiency of supply. Inditex is a good example of an agile organization with both speed and stability. The company is the largest fashion group in the world, operating in 93 countries, and its flagship fascia is Zara. Inditex works on short cycles, with in-season adjustments based on customer buying patterns and local demand management. New styles are often prototyped in less than a week and it can take as little as 15 days for new garments to go from design and production to store shelves. This allows the company to change stock in individual stores based on local consumer demand on a week-by-week basis, staying in tune with fashion trends in the moment.

Conversely, for 'Uber moments' we need to choose to build an organization that can reinvent itself quickly and effectively, responding to structural changes in our market by adopting new operating or commercial models without losing our core purpose, values and direction. In 2007, for example, Waterstones (a leading bookseller in the UK) came close to failure when Amazon's Kindle was launched. Had it closed its stores, many of the traditional stockholding bookshops in the UK would also have disappeared as publishers would have had to rationalize supply. Back then, Waterstones had a model that presented a single uniform bookshop across the UK. You walked into a Waterstones and found the same books in Middlesbrough, London or Edinburgh. Given the stimulus from Amazon, Waterstones took the bold decision to give individual shop managers the autonomy to do what was best for their customers, to make the right choices for each individual shop. So, store managers and their teams started ordering what was popular and created an environment that suited their market. The result was customers coming back in their droves.

The approaches of Inditex and Waterstones are similar in pushing decision making closer to the customer and setting up the rest of the organization to support that local flexibility. The difference is that Inditex has consciously evolved as an organization to be able to respond in the moment in a sustainable way, continually on the front foot responding to changing consumer preferences. Its operating model is responsive to fashion fads. Waterstones, on the other hand, had to rip up its operating model in response to a game-changing competitive threat. That it was able to is credit to its managers throughout the company, from the CEO to the store teams, who responded quickly and effectively. Interestingly, both organizations have a strong sense of purpose, which drives engagement and underpins their continued success in challenging markets.

In terms of the choices both organizations made, Waterstones' was the more reactive, and it turned out to be critical to its survival in the face of digital competition. The decisions at Inditex have evolved over time, creating a customer-driven approach to stock management and in-store experience, with the supporting infrastructure throughout the tightly controlled supply chain. The lesson is clear: if you can see the opportunity to build a dominant capability based on agile responsiveness to customers, you have a winner. If, on the other hand, you find yourself in the position of being undermined by a change in the rules created by an Uber moment, it's best to be able to react quickly and take the whole organization with you. If not, the consequences are unlikely to be positive.

Senior leadership commitment

In business and management, the word 'agility' is used in a variety of contexts to describe agile ways of working, agile culture and agile leadership. Our focus is on the last of these because this helps to create the type of culture where agile ways of working can flourish. If you do not start with the leaders of whatever organizational unit you are interested in changing, you will struggle to make changes stick. This is true at the team level, where I see month after month in our work with clients the disproportionate influence the team leader has on how their team operates. If the leader is open to feedback and learning, so is the team. If the leader is defensive and finds feedback difficult, the team will tend to avoid difficult conversations and conflict, leading to weaker decision making and performance. It is also true at the divisional and organizational levels, as the culture in the senior leadership team sets the tone for the rest of the organization.

It is particularly helpful in developing a more agile style of leadership if the senior leaders in an organization see the link between agility and the most important business results. At Three (UK), for example, Dave Dyson, ex-CEO, understood this link. He said in our research:

> As a business the outcomes we were looking to achieve were being most loved by our customers *and* our employees, and ultimately this enabled us to deliver our financial targets for the shareholder. I think being a more agile business helped us to achieve all these things.

Three developed leaders to be more agile through improving their ability to engage people emotionally as well as intellectually, and their ability to lead teams for shared outcomes. As a disruptor in its market, Three saw remarkable success in the late 2010s by creating a more customer-driven business, in tune with trends and able to provide new customer propositions quickly and effectively.

Our focus is on how to become a truly agile leader, able to be the role model for agility across the organization, whatever your context. One aspect of this is becoming aware of time and being able to manage it for yourself and the business by thinking slow to act fast. As we said earlier, once we *think* agile we can *be* agile. The best tennis players seem to have more time on each shot, even though the opposite is often true. The best leaders seem to have time to think, to choose and to adjust their movement and that of their teams, according to the situation. This is the responsive agility highlighted in elite sport earlier.

Agile leaders can accelerate action when needed, as they and their teams sense the opportunities and threats around them. This leads to entrepreneurial opportunism – making the right choices and understanding where to invest innovation efforts to meet current or future customer needs, quickly. They appreciate the need to experiment, to fail fast if that is the result of the experiment, and to learn to improve the odds the next time. They obsess about getting better, about continuous improvement, with an intolerance of waste and a desire to minimize time to serve the customer. In an era of big data, they practise the critical interpretation of data to see the patterns, to learn about what colleagues and customers want, and what motivates their behaviour. This focus on learning, getting better every day, and assimilating new ways of thinking, being and performing, is at the heart of the agile leader's mindset. Fundamentally this is within our grasp, if we are willing to make the difficult choices every day to stay disciplined and focused. Like an agile athlete, being an agile leader takes determination and a strong will. My first marathon was in New York in 2008 and the running top I got after the event said on the front: 'What does it take? It takes guts, determination and heart-thumping dedication.'

Agility is often focused on learning new skills, adapting to changing circumstances and finding new ways to create value for customers and colleagues. Being a disruptor is not about being negative: it is more about challenging the status quo, taking risks to find new ways of providing a service or making a product, and pushing for simplicity and speed in processes and systems. I will develop these themes during the book.

How connected leadership contributes to agile leadership

The factors in connected leadership support agility as a leader and as an organization. In this section, let's explore each factor in turn and define the ways that each helps to equip you with increased agility as a leader. The first is purpose and direction.

Purpose and direction

At Cirrus, our purpose is 'Better leaders. Better business. Better lives.' This is what we get out of bed in the morning to achieve. It gives us a shared sense of meaning and feeling that our efforts are contributing to the world of work, and to the people who are affected by our work. It also helps us decide on our strategic direction, priorities and daily choices. If we are not equipping our clients' leaders to be better at both leading their business and improving the lives of the people they lead, we are focused on the wrong thing. Our purpose in society and our strategic direction give us all a shared understanding of what is important and what is not. They define our noble endeavour.

Having clear purpose and strategic direction is a key factor in creating the focus and motivation necessary to achieve your long-term goals. Aston Martin, the iconic sports car manufacturer, for example, has 'Power. Beauty. Soul.' at its core, and this drives the product development as well as the customer experience behind the brand. If everyone in your organization knows why you exist, what your higher order mission is, and how you intend to deliver it, they can make the appropriate choices about what to work on. They can also choose what to stop doing. This is liberating for people, as they have clarity on what is at the top of their 'to do list'. I would also say that if your organization lacks a purpose relevant to all stakeholders, it makes it more difficult to change the culture from being risk averse to agile, as the guiding light which would steer risk taking for people is lacking.

Prioritization is at the heart of agility. It is about making difficult choices, about doing the few most important things better. In Chapter 3 I will explore the way agile product development approaches such as Scrum have influenced how we need to manage projects, and what we can learn about prioritization. At the heart of the issue is the need to focus on what is adding the most value to the customer, and which is most in line with your purpose as an organization.

Prioritization is also about ensuring that your people have clearly defined roles, so they know what is expected, which is particularly helpful when you need to make rapid changes in direction or focus. In the McKinsey research I mentioned earlier, the authors identified the top management practices that differentiated the most from the least agile companies. Top of the list was role clarity or what they described as 'organizational clarity, stability, and structure' (McKinsey, 2015). To achieve the strength and balance that we know we need to be agile, it is important for us to ensure our organizations are well defined and clearly structured. If each role has clear priorities and these are coherent across the processes we use to operate, we will have aligned priorities, which reduces complexity and internal conflict.

Another, more disruptive aspect of reducing complexity is to drive a robust agenda on simplicity. As organizations grow, they tend to introduce more processes and systems to coordinate the disparate parts of the body. As time goes by, this set of rules and procedures tends to become more complex, with more regulation and control adding extra layers to the labyrinth of bureaucracy. Eventually this becomes an industry in its own right, requiring an army to manage and report on the rules and procedures. This all slows down the organization, restricting pace and entrepreneurial flair. The need for simplification is clear, but the challenge is immense because the system is difficult to change. Therefore, you need to take a surgeon's view of your organization and get everyone to challenge every rule and process to see how it can be stripped back, pruned to within an inch of its life, so that you reduce the burden of bureaucracy and ensure process simplicity. We will explore this more in Chapter 7.

Authenticity

The second factor in connected leadership is authenticity, which is about our values and relationships. For us to be agile we need to have a values-led culture in our organizations. If we draw on the wealth of research into authentic leadership that has been conducted over the last 20 years, we find that there are four aspects of authenticity that stand out: 'self-awareness, a strong moral compass [based on clear values], balanced processing of information, and open [trusting] relationships' (Walumbwa *et al*, 2008).

The agile movement in software development is based on creating a culture of trust and mutual respect, which enables people to work in empowered teams that deliver improved output in short sprints of activity. Authentic leadership represents an inclusive style of leadership, less individualistic than much of the emphasis we see in descriptions of inspirational leadership. The danger of placing so much emphasis on the inspirational leader is that it encourages a sense that all leaders should be heroic figures who 'save the day'.

Authenticity is about building shared trust so that others feel comfortable in taking risks and making decisions. As leaders, we need to trust others to do a great job, working from the assumption that they are competent and well-motivated, rather than assuming they are not and therefore needing close supervision. The corollary of this for leaders is being trustworthy, inspiring confidence in others that they can trust you not to punish them if they make a mistake, trusting that your intentions are positive and that your behaviour will be fair. We will explore both sides of trust in Chapter 5.

The other aspect of authenticity that is particularly relevant to agility is emotional intelligence. If we are engaging others in change, or new ways of working, our ability to establish strong relationships with others is critical. This works on multiple levels, from the one-to-one conversations we have with our team members and peers, to creating a guiding coalition of leaders who can work with one accord, to building a movement across the business: a wider group of people committed to a cause. We will explore this more in Chapter 5.

One of the challenges of being an agile leader is that agility works best when the whole body is involved, committed, playing its part in the agile balance and motion. If we can only get part of the organization on board, we will struggle to achieve real agility because the rest of the organization will be working in a different way, at a different pace, with different assumptions about how to work together. If we have the emotional intelligence to gain the trust of others, to influence them in a helpful way to commit to changing how they operate, to adopting more agile ways of thinking and doing, we can build a company-wide adoption of agile ways of working. To do this we need to overcome resistance to loss, both in ourselves and others. We need to create a wave of enthusiasm for change and moving towards a strong vision of being an agile organization. This is not easy. In Chapter 9 we will delve deeper into how to engage the whole organization on the agile journey but suffice to say at this point that it will require you to be at your most engaging to succeed.

Devolved decision making

The third factor in connected leadership is devolved decision making, pushing decision rights as close to the customer as is appropriate, keeping central only the strategic decisions that need an organizational perspective. In agile terms, this describes empowerment, which is giving teams the autonomy to make the decisions about what they can do and how to organize themselves, given that the priorities from the customer perspective are clear. To empower teams effectively, as leaders we need to provide a clear framework to the team and have regular communications so that there is a healthy flow of feedback both to and from the team and you. We will explore this in Chapter 8.

In my experience, many leaders find it difficult to let go so that others can take responsibility and act with autonomy. Too often senior leadership teams bemoan the lack of capability at more junior levels of the organization, which means they cannot empower as much as they would like. I remind them that this is their responsibility, to develop leaders from within, to build capability, to coach their teams to step up, to nurture talent across the business to drive growth and performance improvement. I ask boards to identify the decisions only they can make, and to delegate the rest. If they say they cannot because of 'the capability gap beneath them', I challenge them to bridge the gap as quickly as possible to unleash the talents that are almost always in the management populations reporting into the board.

Collaborative achievement

At the heart of physical agility are coordination and balance, which allow free and rapid movement. If processes such as new product development or customer relationship management are to work smoothly and efficiently, and deliver value to the customer, they require integrated coordination across functions, with smooth hand-offs and communication between teams.

To get effective cross-functional working, we first need to ensure each team is working well in itself. In agile ways of working the team is the essential unit of work. Each team needs clarity of its purpose and roles, simple ways of working and high-quality relationships.

A key agile leadership responsibility is to create multi-skilled teams able to deliver robust outcomes in short bursts of effort, teams that are self-managing and dedicated to learning how to improve their speed and quality. We will consider this more in Chapter 3, where we explore agile ways of working in practice.

Once we have strong teams delivering effectively, we can broaden our approach to create wider collaboration across teams and functions, focused on process delivery and delivering an integrated customer experience (see Chapter 8). Ultimately, we need to extend this further to working effectively with partners outside the organization, such as in an integrated supply chain in car manufacturing, or in software ecosystems like app developers for smartphones (see Chapter 10). All of this is summarized in Figure 1.3, showing how each of the connected leadership factors helps you to be agile and develop more agility around you as a leader.

FIGURE 1.3 How other connected leadership factors contribute to agility

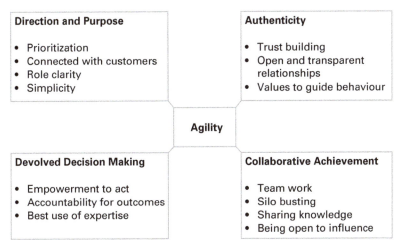

Direction and Purpose

- Prioritization
- Connected with customers
- Role clarity
- Simplicity

Authenticity

- Trust building
- Open and transparent relationships
- Values to guide behaviour

Agility

Devolved Decision Making

- Empowerment to act
- Accountability for outcomes
- Best use of expertise

Collaborative Achievement

- Team work
- Silo busting
- Sharing knowledge
- Being open to influence

Source: Hayward (2016)

Summary

In this post-Covid-19, digital age we need to be agile more than ever. Agile leaders are connected leaders. Connected leaders create organizations that can adapt and transform in the face of unprecedented levels of change and customer expectation, and the five factors of connected leadership help us to understand what this means in practice. But agile leaders are also disruptors, paradoxically, willing to challenge and reinvent themselves and their organization, sometimes out of kilter with their colleagues. They are both the enabler and the disruptor.

As you read the rest of this book it will be helpful to bear in mind where your innate preference lies: are you more of an enabler or more of a disruptor? The simple questionnaire in Table 1.1 can help you identify the answer – read each column and note which of the descriptors you would say are definitely like you. Add up the 'definites' for each column and see which has the higher score. Then, as you read, remember to value your stronger preference and to develop the weaker one, so that you can be a more balanced agile leader.

Agile leaders need both the enabler and the disruptor muscles working well if they are to continue to be effective over time.

TABLE 1.1   Diagnostic questionnaire: are you an enabler or a disruptor?

What enablers do	What disruptors do
1 I talk to people about our purpose, so that we share a strong sense of why what we do is important	**1** I read the evolving customer experience landscape
2 I provide clarity of direction to ensure aligned priorities across the organization	**2** I regularly challenge the status quo
3 I connect frequently with customers	**3** I cut through bureaucracy and re-imagine the operating model to drive efficiency
4 I consistently demonstrate an authentic character	**4** I bust silos and challenge tribal thinking
5 I have social adeptness to engage others with the need for change	**5** I think creatively
6 I consistently devolve decisions to empower others to step up	**6** I am bold and embrace radical possibilities
7 I coach my team to develop capability and take on more responsibility	**7** I am optimistic and confident about the future
8 I collaborate effectively to bring diverse people together to achieve shared goals	**8** I am determined to achieve breakthroughs in order to achieve the mission
9 I encourage people to learn from mistakes	**9** I adapt quickly in response to changes in the external environment
10 I nurture what's best in others	**10** I inspire others to push boundaries and find new ways to do things

Agility is both mental and physical. We need to read and respond to often rapidly changing circumstances with a mindset that is not locked in the present. Once we are thinking agile we can behave in an agile way, creating a connected organization and being able to disrupt how we operate as the circumstances dictate. The agile paradox is not always an easy place to be, sometimes existing on the edge of chaos, coping with the complexity of a discontinuous environment yet seeking to build a stable and effective organization. I will return to these themes throughout the book and explore how you can manage this challenge and lead others in a way that enables them to manage it too.

Please note that I refer repeatedly to 'customers' in this book and my intention is to use this as a generic term for all recipients of value-adding activities – whether they are, for example, consumers of products and services, businesses trading with other businesses, patients receiving medical care, citizens using public services, students receiving tuition, passengers using transportation, or teams inside an organization receiving services from other teams. The 'customer' is the user of your services and products.

References

Adweek (2016) Here's how Airbnb disrupted the travel industry, May

BBC (2020) Coronavirus: Primark sells nothing as retailers struggle, 21 April, www.bbc.co.uk/news/business-52365191 (archived at https://perma.cc/N3X7-QDXS)

Bosa, D (2020) Airbnb CEO Brian Chesky on the future of travel and outlook, CNBC, 22 June 2020, available at www.cnbc.com/video/2020/06/22/airbnb-ceo-brian-chesky-on-the-future-of-travel-and-outlook.html (archived at https://perma.cc/AR6S-Q77N)

Botelho, EL, Rosenkoetter Powell, K, Kincaid, S and Wang, D (2017) What sets successful CEOs apart, *Harvard Business Review*, May–June

Cirrus/Ipsos (2017) Leadership Connections 2017, research paper, Cirrus, London

Conley, C (2019) The three rules of innovation: how to stay ahead of the trends, Kasasa.com, www.kasasa.com/articles/strategy/three-rules-innovation (archived at https://perma.cc/RMC3-WJRW)

Cox, RH (2002) *Sport Psychology: Concepts and applications,* 5th edn, McGraw-Hill, London

Griffith, E (2020) Airbnb was like a family, until the layoffs started, *The New York Times*, 17 July 2020, available at www.nytimes.com/2020/07/17/technology/airbnb-coronavirus-layoffs-.html (archived at https://perma.cc/LC35-4J4M)

Hayward, S (2016) *Connected Leadership,* FT Publishing, Pearson, London

Hill, M, Cromartie, J and McGinnis, J (2017) *Managing for Variability: A neuroscientific approach for developing strategic agility in organizations,* John Wiley & Sons Ltd, London

International Data Corporation (2020) www.idc.com/getdoc.jsp?containerId=prAP46737220 (archived at https://perma.cc/YLT9-KZXF)

Lin, C-T, Chiu, H and Tseng, Y-H (2006) Agility evaluation using fuzzy logic, *International Journal of Production Economics*, 101, pp 353–68

McKinsey (2015) Why agility pays, *McKinsey Quarterly,* December

Oxford English Dictionary (2017) definition of 'agile'

Sheppard, J and Young, W (2006) Agility literature review: Classifications, training and testing, *Journal of Sports Sciences,* 24 (9)

Sheppard, J, Young, W, Doyle, T, Sheppard, T and Newton, R (2006) An evaluation of a new test of reactive agility and its relationship to sprint speed and change of direction speed, *Journal of Science and Medicine in Sport,* **9**

Stiehm, J and Townsend, N (2002) *The US Army War College: Military education in a democracy,* Temple University Press, Philadelphia, PA

The Economist (2017) A different breed of unicorn, May

Walumbwa, F, Avolio, B, Gardner, W, Wernsing, T and Peterson, S (2008) Authentic Leadership: Development and validation of a theory-based measure, Management Department Faculty Publications, Paper 24, University of Nebraska, Lincoln, NE

CHAPTER TWO

Being an agile leader

Existence precedes essence. SARTRE (1948)

Introduction

As a leader of others, you can play a key role as a catalyst in creating a more agile organization. In later chapters, we will explore changes to ways of working and the overall culture of the organization that will lead to your business being more agile, better able to flourish in the rapidly changing post-pandemic digital world in which we operate. We will build up a picture of what agile means for you, your team and the whole business, why it is important and how you can make it happen.

But we need to start with you. You are the key to whether the people you lead will embrace agile ways of working and play their part in building an intelligent learning culture. I would invite you to look at your mindset, how you think, your behaviour, your decision-making approach, how you respond to people in the moment – these all influence how others around you think and behave, what they prioritize and where they focus their time and energy. Your essence as a leader is at your discretion.

You are the catalyst that will make or break the move towards being more agile for the people you lead. Of course, you can tell them to adopt agile ways of working, and for as long as you keep this as a priority they will most likely comply. But to embed real agility needs people to embrace it, to value it, to expect it of themselves and of others, and of you.

QUESTIONS TO ASK YOURSELF

In this chapter you may find it helpful to consider the following questions as you read:

- Which of the eight attributes below would it be most helpful for you to focus on?
- How open to learning are you every moment of every day?
- What shadow do you cast at work and what does it cause others to do (or not do)?

Starting with you

So, let us concentrate on you. How can you develop agility as a leader, to be a role model for others to follow? In the first chapter we looked at the agile leader paradox and how you can embrace it, being both an enabler and a disruptor in your leadership role. In addition to this, there are eight characteristics of agile leaders that provide a clear framework for creating an environment where agile ways of working can flourish (see Figure 2.1).

FIGURE 2.1 The agile leader wheel

In this chapter I will summarize them and then explore each in turn in the following chapters.

The characteristics around the outside of the wheel are important whether you are seeking to introduce in-depth agile ways of working such as Scrum, or a wider agile culture change across your organization or business area. And they work in concert, so please consider them together rather than as a set of options from which to pick and choose. You may find it helpful to see the characteristics as muscles, and to consider which of these muscles is currently strong (to be used effectively to accelerate progress) and which would benefit from a sustained fitness programme. Having all the muscles strong and supple leads to a healthier and more agile body.

The characteristics fall into four quadrants which we will consider in turn in Chapters 5 to 8. At the centre of the wheel is Purpose and Direction, which we explored in Chapter 1, through which you provide the guiding light for your colleagues. This is the clear sense for those around you of what is really important, in terms of the organization's role and contribution to society, and how you intend to deliver it. Purpose and direction enable you to define clear goals and outcomes which can then cascade throughout your teams across the organization, enabling real alignment of objectives and key results. In this post-Covid-19 world the importance of the wider role organizations play in society with a clear sense of social responsibility has never been keener.

> There's a danger you become massively obsessed with your shareholders. In the order of life, the shareholder actually needs to come last. If you do all the right things, the value will follow. In our world we focus on our three Ps: pets, people and planet. It's the impact we have on all three that will really define whether we're a good company. Not what we do but how we do it. If the shareholder wants to see the share price go up, run a good business and the share price will follow.
>
> Peter Pritchard, Group CEO, Pets at Home

Feeling safe to take risks

Our first goal as agile leaders is to lay a foundation of psychological safety for our colleagues. We have the discretion as leaders to create a climate where people feel confident and supported to speak out and take intelligent risks. The more we build their confidence to do so the more agile ways of working can flourish. And further benefits are likely, including people's wellbeing and productivity, which is particularly important in the era of flexible and often remote working.

To do this we need to put aside ego and recognize that as leaders one of our primary responsibilities is to create an environment where others can flourish. If you are naturally empathetic, you will have a head start, as empathy is a key ingredient in creating a safe environment. Showing others that you can see the world from their point of view helps to build trust and confidence. There are downsides of empathy, which I will explore later in Chapter 5, but for now let us assume empathy helps us to relate well to those around us.

In contrast to the athlete, who is often acting in a solo capacity, as a leader you are normally acting in a collective role. You are in the leadership 'goldfish bowl', being watched and interpreted by others, sometimes from a positive perspective as they seek to be aligned with your priorities, sometimes from a more sceptical view as they judge you. You can increase their sense of safety by showing them respect by treating their views and ideas at least as important as your own.

In a team context the same attributes of mutual respect and empathy are essential ingredients for agile teamworking to flourish. Your role as leader is often to help team members to build deeper respect for each other, and for those in other teams. Where you can help them to recognize other people's perspectives and show empathy, you will be creating the foundations for team members to feel safe and therefore willing and able to take intelligent risks. Research suggests (Goran *et al*, 2017) that a climate of risk aversion is a significant barrier to agile teamworking in practice, and reducing it starts with individuals feeling safer together and with those in positions of authority (see Chapter 4).

Team members in effective agile teams tend to be open and trusting with each other. Agile working requires them to work together and support each other to overcome challenges, so trust is a helpful if not essential ingredient in the team.

Trust helps to create the safe environment we are looking for. But it is fragile, and easily damaged. Human sensitivity to interpersonal risk means small pieces of evidence from you that you might not trust your colleagues can nag away in their minds and cause them to avoid challenging you or creating difficult situations between you. In my own experience, I recall over-reacting in frustration a few years ago when a colleague said there was a problem with the build of our new website and that it would be delayed by two to three months. In that moment I could see shock in her eyes as her head moved back involuntarily. The damage was done, and she was more cautious for a long time as a result. My reaction had reduced her sense of psychological safety. The result was damaged trust and her caution meant we had less productive conversations about the website. A momentary reaction, months of consequence.

Encouraging learning

In *Humankind: A hopeful history* (2020), Rutger Bregman describes an optimistic interpretation of human nature, where people are naturally connected, social and keen to learn. This is consistent with McGregor's (1957) thesis that leaders tend to get the best from their people by assuming positive motivation and seeking to work together for shared outcomes. Leaders have a role to play, therefore, in having supportive and respectful conversations that reduce the emphasis on hierarchy and give people confidence to test, learn and improve. As a leader you influence others by the way you communicate, by the examples and stories you relate, and the language you choose to use. So, if you choose to encourage people to speak their minds, to tell the truth, and not to withhold information in case it 'upsets the boss', and you respond consistently over time in a way that demonstrates you believe this is right, you can draw people out of their caution and into a more constructive and agile way of working.

If we recall the agile athletes in Chapter 1, we know that their ability to move quickly and easily is based on both their cognitive and physical attributes – how they read and respond to situations, as well as their physical ability to move in an agile way. They are learning constantly, and this is the second characteristic of agile leaders on which we will focus.

Agile working works best when teams are focused on learning. In an agile team people are universally committed to learning through experimentation so they can perform better, in a diverse and multi-skilled environment. They are seeking feedback from colleagues and customers frequently and use that feedback to improve team performance and customer satisfaction.

In the same way, agile leaders are curious and create opportunities for learning for themselves and their teams. They instil a growth mindset (Dweck, 2017) in their teams, where people believe they can learn new skills through hard work and study. They promote diversity of thinking, to enable more creativity and deeper insight. And agile leaders consciously create the space for learning through, for example, regular team retrospectives, in which teams review their most recent sprint and identify how they can increase their performance in the next.

Learn through failure

One of the most important ways teams learn is through experimentation. James Dyson famously said that he and his research colleagues at Dyson failed 5,000 times before successfully launching their first cyclonic bagless vacuum cleaner in 1983. 'The cyclones for my vacuum cleaner took over 5,000 prototypes. That's 5,000 failures before I'd cracked it. So, the moral of the tale is, keep on failing. It works' (Dyson, 2010). The Dyson Dual Cyclone became the fastest-selling vacuum cleaner ever in the UK and achieved market success around the world.

A helpful mantra that has become popular in recent years is 'fail fast and learn' or 'test and learn'. It describes how teams try new things and experiment with different approaches to solve problems for customers. Teams learn from both successes and failures as they work towards enabling customers to do what they want to do, more easily, quickly or cheaply. Agile teams take intelligent risks, so that failures are manageable, and they do not 'bet the house' on a single success. This iterative approach that Dyson describes above is an important aspect of the learning process, as it means the team is regularly reviewing progress, learning, and putting that learning into practice. It is a virtual cycle of insight and progress.

Broad skill sets

Another aspect of encouraging learning that is important here is teams having a range of skills so that they can combine these skills to solve complex problems within the team. This has the dual benefit of accelerating output as the team is self-sufficient and increasing the shared skill base in the team which helps improve productivity.

Agile team members typically have broad, diverse and complementary skill sets. They do work that plays to their strengths and they recognize others' contribution to achieving successful outcomes. But this kind of multi-skilled working is not necessarily easy, as it requires a level of mutual respect and valuing of diversity among the team. As a leader you have a key role to engender this respect and appreciation of the skills of others between team members. One way to do this well is to include each team member explicitly in team discussions and decisions to maximize diversity of thought. The quality of dialogue is a good measure of a team's maturity, with high-quality dialogue helping teams to solve problems better and make better decisions based on a rich diversity of input and discussion. In teams I have facilitated it is typically clear within a short period of observation whether the team is able to sustain shared thinking, and shared decision making, based on divergent and then convergent thinking.

Quality debate

In the *New Statesman* magazine (July 2020), the editor, Jason Cowley, writing about 'cancel culture', describes the continuing need for quality debate and a respect for the free exchange of a diversity of views:

> *Enlightened thinking in dark times*
>
> In an open letter published by *Harper's Magazine* on 7 July, more than 150 authors and intellectuals warned that 'the free exchange of information and ideas, the lifeblood of a liberal society, is daily becoming more constricted'. But on both sides [of the political divide], reactions to this intervention reflected the hyper partisan atmosphere of the debate on social media, a medium that thrives on outrage and is corroding the space for scepticism and deeper reflection.
>
> In our efforts to make sense of the world, however, and to deepen our comprehension of what is at stake for people in it, [the *New Statesman*] will continue to champion pluralism and independent thought, embrace the spirit of criticism and the open exchange of ideas, and revel in what the Italian philosopher Norberto Bobbio called 'the complexity of things'.

This is the level of thoughtfulness that we need in our teams and organizations, making sense and thinking deeply together, listening to views that are different to our own and looking for insight rather than a reason to reject. As leaders we have, I believe, a responsibility to enable this. The example we set – either questioning and seeking to understand or asserting our view as the 'right' view – sets the tone for others. Either we are curious and encourage the same in others or we risk reducing the opportunities in our teams to discuss, to see things differently, to innovate and to improve. We need to build strong learning capability in our teams, or we risk cutting off learning, which is the lifeblood of agility.

Disruptive thinking

During the initial weeks of the Covid-19 pandemic, many organizations were forced to change working practices in a more radical way than they had expected to do in years. Within days of lockdown in countries around the world, most people that could were working from home, office buildings were empty, millions of people were furloughed, public transport was disrupted, and care workers were thrust into working in personal protective equipment and working long days and nights to cope with the influx of patients. The disruption was huge.

At the time of writing, the shift to virtual working for many has become semi-permanent. Large organizations around the world like Fujitsu, Siemens and Google have said their employees can continue to work from home for months or years if it suits them. We have seen a major disruption to ways of working which happened quickly, for many with little fuss, and is now becoming normal.

And yet only months earlier I was witness to organizations debating whether more flexible working was even a good idea. We saw retailers with limited or no online presence espousing the virtue of the bricks-and-mortar model. Even in March 2020 we saw some governments dismissing the risks associated with the pandemic and urging their populations to carry on as normal. Some politicians continued to shake hands, not to wear masks, and to suggest that everything would be 'back to normal' within a few weeks.

THE VEGAN SAUSAGE ROLL

Greggs is a nationwide operator of food outlets focused on providing affordable 'food on the go'. It is a bold company, it sometimes does the unexpected, and it is really focused on its colleagues and customers. One example is the vegan sausage roll, launched at the beginning of 2019, as the trend towards more plant-based diets was gaining momentum. The normal meat-filled sausage roll has been one of Gregg's signature products for years, and to create a plant-based version was brave and not a little risky. But it caught public attention, was a great success and helped re-position Greggs as a place for *healthy* food on the go. Some had seen it as a stunt, but in fact it was a powerful statement of intent to embrace plant-based diets. Customers responded to this calculated risk with enthusiasm.

One of the lessons of the Covid-19 experience is that leaders need to read the external signs of change. They need to embrace digital opportunities, look outwards to understand how their customer's world is changing and what opportunities and threats this creates, and enable innovation in their teams to achieve break-throughs in outcomes. In most sectors there were corporate winners and losers, and typically the winners were those organizations that were already delivering digitized and flexible services, already anticipating changes in the ways we work, travel and enjoy leisure time. They maintained services throughout or, where this was not possible, were the first to return to service delivery. Cirrus was an example of this. The leadership and talent consulting firm has throughout its history embraced digital and virtual ways of assessing and learning, and these came to the fore when clients stopped all face-to-face delivery within a two-week period in March 2020. Almost overnight all design and delivery flipped to virtual and clients which had not embraced this approach before were back up and running within days or weeks. Some competitors were less ready and had to lay off or let go significant numbers of their high-value employees.

Do you recall the agile leader paradox we explored in Chapter 1? There is a balance to be struck between enabling your people to work in a secure and predictable system – with confidence that goals are aligned, and surprises will be minimized – and encouraging people to disrupt the very stability they value. It is helpful to encourage people to explore externally for examples of innovation or different ways to approach work, for examples of how technology has transformed a product or process. It is also helpful to support those who are brave enough to break the rules, to challenge assumptions and to ask the difficult questions. As leaders we are at risk of taking such actions personally, to see them as a challenge to our capability or status, and to close them down. But if we respond with curiosity, we can avoid extinguishing the flame of improvement and innovation, and not pour cold water on our people's courage to be bold and hungry for change.

Customer vision

As Greggs demonstrates, at the heart of agile thinking is an obsession with the customer. What do they want to do, but cannot? What would help them be more effective? What would give them what they want faster, easier or to a higher quality of experience? When you are leading in an agile way, these questions are on your mind a great deal. And as you work with colleagues to articulate these innovative responses in practical examples, you are helping to build a shared understanding of and commitment to the vision of what your customers want, which guides your people's work and priorities in a practical way.

In setting your teams up for success it is helpful to focus on two related areas: customer value and customer engagement.

Customer value

Customer value is about team members being curious about their customer. They use insight and direct contact to understand what customers want and know what their needs look like in practice. Vitally, they share customer insight with other team members. They do this iteratively, as we know that customer needs change over time. In public services the focus is on what citizens need and value most from their service provider. In healthcare it is about what is in the best interests of patients.

When leaders in healthcare lose sight of the patient and turn their attention internally, there is a risk that the patient experience is undermined, and ultimately in the most extreme cases patients die – as happened in the UK at the Mid Staffordshire NHS Foundation Trust in the early 2000s. The Healthcare Commission's investigation into what appeared to be unusually high mortality rates at Stafford Hospital was published in 2009 and was highly critical of the Trust's leadership and of care standards in the hospital. Patients were reportedly left to sit in their own urine, for example. The subsequent public inquiry (Francis, 2013) made 290 recommendations for improvement and called for increased openness, and candour from Trust leaders. The combination of a culture of poor care caused by leaders who did not focus on the patient experience, and a lack of accountability for patient outcomes, was toxic and led to a public outcry.

Customer engagement

Customer engagement is about team members demonstrating to customers (or other stakeholders) their work early on to seek feedback. They do this through developing a minimum viable product, something that works, so the customer can experience it in practice. The customer is then more able to provide helpful practical feedback on what they value, what they don't, and what they would prioritize next. The team uses this customer feedback to review their focus for the next sprint, and to ensure their effort is focused on what the customer values most.

For some teams, their customers are internal to the organization, so they need to have a dual focus: on the internal customers and on their external customers. They work with their internal customers to meet their explicit needs and anticipate hidden needs that the internal customer may not yet have seen. They also need to understand the end consumer, so that they can be more intelligent in working with their internal customers. (It is helpful to remember that if we are not serving a customer, we are supporting someone who is.) To give you an example, in one financial investment organization with which I work, the software development teams are organized to support the front-desk teams that are working with the different groups of clients. The development teams partner with the front-desk teams to work out how they can, together, provide better services or a competitive advantage through developing applications and system enhancements that add most value to the client. The development teams are learning about the end clients, and this is helping them to be more innovative in the way they approach their work. They benefit from knowing they are making a difference, and the front-desk teams benefit as their lives are made easier and their clients are more loyal.

For all of this to work well in practice, you need your teams to be curious about the customer, to share knowledge and customer understanding and to be keen to refocus their efforts as a team on what matters to customers and stakeholders. A simple way to encourage this mindset it is to keep asking questions like 'do we really know what our customers think about this idea?' or 'have we tested this idea with our customers yet?'. Your curiosity will prompt others to think similarly. But it takes persistence, so stick with it and keep going – when you start hearing your colleagues asking similar questions you will know you are putting customers more at the heart of your teams' thinking. As your teams embrace this customer vision and prioritize it in how they approach their work, you are laying a keystone in becoming more agile.

Ruthless prioritization

This intense customer focus leads us to the next characteristic of agile leaders, and agile working in general; the focus on working on the few tasks that are most important for our customers at any one time. This requires a thoughtful approach to ruthless prioritization from you and all your teams, which in practice can prove to be easier said than done. The key component parts of such prioritization are focus and simplicity: focus on the few things that make the biggest difference, and simpler ways of working, reducing wasted time and resource.

Multi-tasking is inefficient, whether it is at a personal level, in teams or across a whole organization. Having too many things on the go at the same time clogs up the time available. We see this in IT departments with hundreds of projects on the go, or in department stores selling a myriad of categories and ranges outmanoeuvred by more focused retailers who are brilliant in their particular product category.

As an agile leader we want the direction and focus for our teams to be crystal clear and aligned with our vision of what our customers value most. Clearly, there is an overlay of business priorities here, so we are seeking to bring together the priorities of our business and our customers, leading to profitable and therefore sustainable sales of what customers value. These are the outcomes of the team's work. In the public sector this would equate to balancing what citizens need most with budgets and wider social responsibilities. In a hospital it is the balance between patient care and managing the sustainability of the institution.

Backlogs and sprints

So, what does this look like in practice? In agile teams we use a technique called the backlog. This involves the team creating a list of all the 'want to do' activities needed to achieve their customer vision, and then regularly reviewing the list and ranking the activities in order of priority. Prioritization is, in practice, based on a balance between adding most value to the team's customers and staying aligned with their organization's strategic priorities. The team selects from the top of the list the tasks they can complete in the next sprint – and leave the rest. If an activity is too big to complete, it is broken down into smaller tasks that can be completed inside two sprints.

At the end of the sprint the team demonstrates its outputs to the internal or external customer to get feedback and to understand how to adapt their next round of work to take the feedback on board. The team then reviews their backlog of tasks in light of the feedback, re-prioritizes where necessary, and then picks off the next set of top priorities to focus on in the next sprint. In this way, the full range of activities to be done is not lost, but only the top priorities are worked on at any one time. This helps to accelerate output and quickly move the team closer to the outcomes identified in the customer vision. The team is not switching between activities during a sprint, juggling conflicting workloads or priorities – they are just focused on getting the identified tasks done.

Getting out of the way

As leaders, our role is often to get out of the way. We do need to help teams get set up to work in this way, and we do need to protect them from interruption from other parts of our organization that want something else. This may need negotiation to work out how to balance the priorities of your teams with those of other parts of the organization, using the overall strategic priorities of the organization as a guide. Sometimes as a leader you will need to work with your teams to agree and review the backlog of activities as you will have a different perspective and it is helpful to share that insight directly. But your most important role as leader is to give the team space to operate as efficiently as they can, to protect them from outside interruption, and to support them to keep true to the customer vision.

This clarity of focus can, I have found, be a difficult shift for leaders in large, long-established, often conservative organizations. It takes guts to stay focused on a few deliverables, rather than accepting the multitude of tasks normally present in large organizations which have often been successful in the past as efficient bureaucracies. You may need to disappoint stakeholders who want something different or stop projects that they want to see completed. Your powers of influence will be called upon to maintain the focus – explaining your reasons and asking them whether they agree with the trade-off you have had to make will often help assuage the pressure from others to accept more tasks than your teams can complete. But you may also need to compromise 'for the greater good', so being open to influence by others is also important.

When organizations manage to embrace ruthless prioritization, the benefits can be significant. Greater simplicity, for example, comes from focusing on fewer priorities, and leads to simplified planning and reporting, having fewer and more efficient meetings, and improved use of management time. Delivering outputs faster is also a benefit of targeting resources on fewer priorities, based on reducing wasted time and effort.

But agile prioritization needs to be relentless. It is not sufficient to clear the decks, focus on the few things that will make the biggest difference, and then leave it at that. Like cleaning a house or staying fit, it is not a one-off event, it is an ongoing activity, one that needs regular attention and disciplined action. Otherwise, the house gets dirty again, and one's fitness gradually reduces. It is often easy to accept more tasks, to agree to do more things, whereas staying focused on the top priorities takes discipline.

Performance improvement

Once priorities are clear for a team, an agile leader will typically invest time to coach and support the team's continued performance improvement. Performance improvement in an agile world is a commitment shared between individual team members and the coach. The focus for everyone is enabling the team to accelerate outputs (get work done) and increase the team's cohesion and collaboration.

Ambition is contagious, so share yours for the team, in the context of the organization's purpose and direction. Discuss and agree goals with the team that will stretch them and encourage a desire to improve performance on an ongoing basis. The quicker you deliver valued benefits to customers, the quicker your organization will grow and flourish competitively. In this performance improvement stage of agile leadership, we are really focused on acceleration, following the thoughtfulness of the prioritization stage. Agile coaching is about short and regular conversations with individuals and the team to work out how to go faster, about moments of reflection to achieve higher velocity of outputs.

In agile teams, these regular reviews of performance are called retrospectives. The team reviews its overall performance at the end of a sprint against their goals, making sense of what helped or hindered progress, and identifying how to increase productivity and drive continuous improvement in the next sprint. Your role as coach in these discussions can help the team to identify key barriers to progress so that they can work out how to remove them.

Senior leadership teams

Coaching is not just about effective task completion. As leaders we are also responsible for coaching our teams to work well together, to communicate well, to support each other for the team's benefit, and to challenge each other where opportunities for improvement become apparent.

Linked to this is the importance of having a shared view on what culture you want as an organization. We will look at culture through different lenses as we go through this book, but from a performance improvement point of view, your senior leadership teams have a disproportionate influence on whether your people really seek constant improvement or not. The people you employ are likely to be tuned into what is really valued in your organization. In my experience people in organizations are pretty good at sensing whether senior leaders really believe in team performance, with its need for compromise and selflessness, or not.

Satya Nadella recognized this when he took over as CEO at Microsoft in 2014. He worked hard, he writes in *Hit Refresh* (2017), to bring senior leaders to embrace a shared view of the world, to move beyond fiefdoms and embrace the greater good of the whole enterprise. 'We needed a senior leadership team (SLT) that would lean into each other's problems, promote dialogue and be effective. We needed everyone to view the SLT as his or her first team, not just another meeting they attended. We needed to be aligned on mission, strategy and culture.'

This set the tone for a major review of how performance was managed across Microsoft, and the company did a U-turn from a highly structured performance and incentive system based on stacking (ranking people and focusing performance management and ultimate exit on the bottom performers) to a more agile approach. They moved to a system that encouraged innovation and professional growth. Fundamentally, the new approach focused on teamwork, collaboration and employee growth. Managers now had the flexibility to allocate rewards in a manner that would best reflect the performance of their teams and individuals, rather than listing them in order and replacing those at the bottom of the stack. Performance reviews were not just focused on how well the employees performed, but also on how they engaged with their peers. Employees now needed to demonstrate how they went about leveraging input and ideas from their teammates, and how their contributions enhanced the success of others.

This all started with the senior leaders spending time together, making sense of what culture they wanted, and how they wanted to lead the performance of their people in practice. Furthermore, Microsoft implemented a system called 'Connects', through which employees received real-time feedback that helped them learn, grow, and focus on their strengths and key learning areas. This flexibility allowed managers to discuss performance and development throughout the year. Microsoft's share price all-time high was recorded in August 2020, at the time of writing, capping a long period of sustained growth (in spite of Covid-19) based on this high-performance culture.

Agile decision making

Agile decision making involves making thoughtful decisions and devolving them as close to the customer interface as possible. Thoughtful decision making involves slowing the process down to think so you can make more informed decisions you can execute more quickly. Devolving them means enabling teams to make their own decisions within well-defined parameters.

A central tenet of agile working is that teams are self-managing when it comes to what they are able to achieve. Leaders articulate the customer vision with the team and work with the team to define the backlog of priorities, but they leave the team to decide what they can deliver in each sprint. This means that team members need to feel comfortable to make such decisions, which goes back to the importance of leaders creating an environment of psychological safety. As leaders, our behaviour will largely determine whether our teams feel empowered and able to take decisions or nervous about getting it wrong and the consequences of error. I see this play out in practice at the most senior levels in some organizations, where well-paid executives defer to the chief executive or the chair rather than taking the risk of deciding in their own teams. (We will explore the psychology of empowerment and thoughtful decision making further in Chapter 8.)

Resources

Devolving decisions closer to the customer also means that we as leaders have a responsibility to ensure our teams have access to the information, tools and skills needed to make good decisions, and that they know how to use them effectively. In Zara, the successful global fashion retailer, the store teams have frequent reviews of sales, what customers have chosen and what has not sold, and feed this data back to head office in Spain. The store teams also decide what to order, based on their interpretation of the data they have discussed, predicting what will sell in their own market. This closeness to the customer has helped make Zara one of the world's most disruptive and successful retailers in recent years. Zara's parent company, Inditex, saw net sales climb 7.5 per cent to €19.8 billion in 2019 and gross margin increase to 58 per cent of sales, with net profit increasing by 12 per cent.

In Zara, leaders empower their store teams to decide how to achieve their goals, and people are comfortable to take responsibility and are clear about what decisions they can make. They have the information they need to make decisions. The company is geared to deliver quickly to store from a wide range of items, and technology supports local decision making. People are empowered and encouraged to share responsibility for their store's success.

Role clarity is also important in this context, to avoid the chaos of ad hoc decision making in an uncoordinated manner. Team members at Zara are clear about their responsibilities. They know the decisions they can make and when to escalate. Likewise, in head office and in the supply chain, roles are clear and aligned with the customer-focused strategy. The resulting speed and efficacy of execution is difficult for more traditionally organized retailers to compete with.

Collaborative achievement

In an agile organization, teamwork is seen as a natural way of getting things done. People commit time and energy to working together in teams and to improving their team's performance. This requires people to subsume their ego and individual objectives to the team's identity and goals, which can be challenging for some. As leaders we also need to be great team players, thinking 'we' more than 'I', focusing our time and effort on team success rather than on our own. We often think of leadership as way of influencing others, and in many ways it is; but it is also about being open to influence, to being open to ideas, open to challenge, open to changing our minds.

Sports teams

Sir Alex Ferguson was, until 2013, the highly successful manager of Manchester United, a club which has had its share of great footballers over the years. He said on this topic: 'The work of a team should always embrace a great player, but the great player must always work' (Ferguson, 1999). He knew that the club and its team discipline had to be the priority, not any individual player. More recently in the 2020 European Champions League Quarter-final, Barcelona, one of the best teams in the world at that time, lost 8–2 to Bayern Munich. Many commentators described afterwards how

Barcelona had lost its way as a club, where some individual players had become bigger than the club. Team discipline had been undermined and the group of highly paid, highly skilled players went down in the most significant defeat in modern Champions League history. The irony is clear: focus on team and organizational success and this will often bring greater individual success as well. Focus on individual success in a team activity and neither form of success will result.

An interesting similarity between team sports and agile working is the short cycles of activity and output. In football, teams train hard and then play a competitive match. They review, learn, and then prepare for the next match. In agile working, teams also work on short cycles or sprints, delivering outputs, reviewing, and then cracking on with the next sprint. The opportunity to learn, implement improvement quickly, and demonstrate publicly the results of the hard work, are true of football and agile teams.

Agile teams are working on shared goals to achieve outcomes quickly and effectively, just like the sports team – the team's success is the reward. In 1999 Manchester United came from behind to beat Bayern Munich in the European Champions League Final, scoring two goals in extra time to win 2–1. The intensity of the competition brought out the best in the United players. Ferguson described one of them, Roy Keane (actually for his semifinal performance against Juventus) thus (Ferguson, 1999):

> It was the most emphatic display of selflessness I have ever seen on a football field. Pounding every blade of grass, competing as if he would rather die of exhaustion than lose, he inspired all around him. I felt such an honour to be associated with such a player.

At each stage of the competition Keane and the team played with discipline, passion, and an unwillingness to give up. It was a season in which United won the Treble, and I was fortunate to see them win the FA Cup Final at Wembley.

One more parallel springs to mind. Agile teams, like most sports teams, are made up of a mix of all the skills needed to win. Agile teams bring together colleagues from different functions and skill sets so that they can complete their tasks and deliver the end result. In a football team, the defenders are great at anticipating attacking plays, tackling, and regaining the ball. Strikers are quick, accurate and able to 'finish' a play with a goal. A team made up of the same skills would not do so well, as Meredith Belbin recognized many years ago (1981). A multi-skilled team which is good at playing to each person's strengths can outplay competitors and win. This is true for an agile team as much as it is for a sports team.

Collaboration across teams

The sporting analogy is less helpful however in illustrating another aspect of teamworking that is key to agile working at scale. Collaboration between teams is an essential ingredient of a connected and agile organization (Hayward, 2016). Many of the same principles described above apply: less ego, more mutual support; working in sprints with regular reviews to learn and adjust; playing to each other's strengths to accelerate output. But increasing collaboration across teams can be deeply challenging.

Breaking down the silos is one of the most effective ways to improve organizational performance (JDA, 2017) and the Zara example above demonstrates what a well-orchestrated approach to collaboration across the enterprise can achieve if done with discipline and clear roles and decision rights. But our tribal human nature means we too often look inwards, rather than instinctively reaching across boundaries to improve overall organizational effectiveness. Bregman writes: 'It seems we're born with a button for tribalism in our brains. All that's needed is for something to switch it on' (Bregman, 2020).

As leaders our job is often to switch the tribalism button off, to enable our people to embrace this cross-functional collaboration, to remove silos and accelerate processes. We need to encourage regular communications between teams, and repeatedly reinforce the shared purpose and accountability for outputs across teams. We will explore this further in Chapter 8.

And as leaders it is often our responsibility to make the first move, to encourage teams to reach over boundaries to seek out ways to make the overall customer experience better. We can be the catalysts for accelerating collaborative achievement.

Summary

In this chapter we have explored the eight characteristics of an agile leader. In Table 2.1 is a summary of what each characteristic means for the teams you lead.

TABLE 2.1 Agile leader characteristics

Agile leader characteristic	What this means for the team
Feeling safe	A climate of psychological safety where people feel confident and supported to take intelligent risks.
Encouraging learning	People are universally committed to learning through experimentation so they can perform better, in a diverse and multi-skilled environment.
Disruptive thinking	There is widespread openness to the opportunities created by technology to improve performance and customer value. Disruptive ideas and innovations from outside are welcomed and explored in a balanced way.
Customer vision	There is a shared understanding of and commitment to the vision of what customers want, which guides people's work and priorities in a practical way.
Ruthless prioritization	The direction and priorities are clear and aligned with customer vision. People review a backlog of activities and focus on delivering the top priorities with quality and pace.
Performance improvement	Performance improvement is a shared priority. Coaching is common for both individuals and teams to accelerate performance improvement in line with stretching goals.
Agile decision making	Decisions are made thoughtfully and executed with speed and determination. People feel comfortable to make shared decisions on how to achieve their goals. They have the information, tools and skills needed to do so.
Collaborative achievement	Teamwork is the norm. People commit time and energy to improve their team's performance. They embrace working across teams on shared goals to achieve outcomes quickly and effectively. Team processes are consistent and efficient.

At the end of Chapter 9 is a brief survey you can take to understand better your strengths and areas for development using this model of agile leadership.

References

Belbin, M (1981) *Management Teams*, Heinemann, London

Bregman, R (2020) *Humankind: A hopeful history*, Bloomsbury Publishing, London

Dweck, C (2017) *Mindset: Changing the way you think to fulfil your potential*, updated edition, Random House Publishing, New York

Dyson, J (2010) James Dyson on Failure, Official Dyson video, www.youtube.com/watch?v=P5eIyRVpwmc&feature=youtu.be (archived at https://perma.cc/S9DD-2N95)

Ferguson, A (1999) *Managing My Life: My autobiography*, with Hugh McIlvanney, Hodder and Stoughton, London

Francis, R, QC (2013) Report of the Mid Staffordshire NHS Foundation Trust Public Inquiry, House of Commons, London

Goran, J, LaBerge, L and Srinivasan, R (2017) Culture for a digital age, *McKinsey Quarterly*, July

Hayward, S (2016) *Connected Leadership*, Financial Times Publishing, London

JDA (2017) CEO Viewpoint 2017: The transformation of retail, JDA, now.jda.com/rs/366-TWM-779/images/PWC_Executive-Summary_Final_Digital.pdf (archived at https://perma.cc/L9JT-Q23T)

McGregor, D (1957) The human side of enterprise, *Management Review*, American Management Association, New York, pp 41–49

Nadella, S (2017) *Hit Refresh*, Harper Collins, London

New Statesman (2020) Enlightened thinking in dark times, New Statesman Limited, London, 22 July

Sartre, J-P (1948) *Existentialism Is a Humanism*, Methuen and Company, Paris

CHAPTER THREE

Agile ways of working

We don't need another hero. BADARACCO (2001)

Introduction

In this chapter, we explore the evolution of agile methodology and how it can be relevant to your whole organization. I draw on leading research into agile teams and ways of working to explore how they can work well in different types of organization. I will describe the way the Scrum approach has developed, how you can adapt this agile method on a broader basis across your organization, and how you can lead that adaptation to maximize its beneficial impact on innovation and performance. And I will describe how traditional leadership styles need to change to enable agile teams to work effectively – shifting from hero to enabler.

QUESTIONS TO ASK YOURSELF

In this chapter you may find it helpful to consider the following questions as you read:

- Are you ready to change how you think about work?
- Do you really want to let go of control of how things are done?
- Do you believe that teams can manage their work without interference?

Agile management

Agile management is a flexible and incremental approach to solve complex problems. Often it is used to manage the design and development of products and services (for internal as well as external customers) so that they are focused on what customers need most. I will use the widely adopted Scrum approach to agile working to explore how leaders can embrace agile working on a broader, enterprise-wide basis. Scrum working requires high levels of process discipline, but more importantly it requires very high levels of openness between people collaborating in teams, openness to regular customer feedback, and openness in the way managers manage. It recognizes that customers' needs will change, and that technical issues will be encountered that mean the best-prepared plans will often not be delivered as expected. This requires an agile response and freedom to adapt to changing and often complex circumstances without the encumbrance of strict hierarchy and management control.

Part of what makes agile companies special is their ability to balance fast action and rapid change on the one hand with organizational clarity, stability and structure on the other. Role clarity and operational discipline are highly valued among the most agile organizations, but not among the least agile ones (Aghina *et al*, 2015). Agile organizations are also typically powerful engines for innovation and learning. So, a balance is needed between agility and stability. It is helpful to explore in more detail the ways of working that lead to this agility, drawing on the incredible changes that have happened over the last 20 to 30 years in the software industry, which is where the methodology first took hold.

A key milestone in the development of agile management was the publication of the Agile Manifesto (Highsmith, 2001) by a group of software developers who had gathered in the Snowbird ski resort in Utah. They got together because they believed there was a better way to develop software than more traditional sequential approaches that involved long-term plans that were typically delayed and over budget. The methodology described in the Agile Manifesto is built on four values:

1 individuals and interactions over processes and tools
2 working software over comprehensive documentation
3 customer collaboration over contract negotiation
4 responding to change over following a plan.

Underneath these values was a belief among the 17 developers present that creating a culture based on collaboration, trust and respect was fundamental to great development happening.

Scrum

Prior to this in 1986, Hirotaka Takeuchi and Ikujiro Nonaka introduced the term 'scrum' in relation to commercial product development in their classic *Harvard Business Review* article, 'New new product development game' (Takeuchi and Nonaka, 1986). They outlined a fresh approach to product development that would increase speed and flexibility, drawing on lessons from the Toyota Production System, which still has relevance today. They called this the 'holistic' or 'rugby' approach, as the whole process is performed by one cross-functional team across multiple overlapping phases, where the team is working towards the try line as one unit, 'passing the ball back and forth'. The 'scrum' metaphor is suggestive of the interlocking teamwork in the rugby scrum, which is used to restart play and after which players interact flexibly to move the ball downfield to score a 'try' over their opponent's line. Rugby relies on high levels of teamwork, clarity of goals and fluid inter-operability between roles in the midst of battle for teams to win. It is not a sport where strong individual performances are typically highlighted or celebrated.

In the early 1990s Scrum ways of working were developed by leading figures in the United States, many of whom later attended the Snowbird ski resort meeting in 2001. They included Ken Schwaber, Jeff Sutherland, John Scumniotales and Jeff McKenna, with the emphasis on planning and managing product development that involved devolving decision-making authority to the level of operational working.

The Scrum Alliance, founded in 2001, is one of the largest membership organizations in the agile community. It states that (Scrum Alliance, 2001):

> Scrum is an agile framework for completing complex projects. Scrum originally was formalized for software development projects, but it works well for any complex, innovative scope of work. The possibilities are endless. The Scrum framework is deceptively simple.

Let us review what Scrum looks like in practice, so we can then explore how we take this philosophy and approach and relate it to leading in the wider organizational context. In his book *Scrum*, Sutherland (2015) lays out the process of Scrum working as follows:

1 *Product owner* – select someone to own the outputs; 'this person is the one with the vision of what you are going to do, make or accomplish' and who can set the overall priorities for action for the team.

2 *Team* – pick a small team of (three to nine) people with the cross-functional skills needed to turn the vision into a usable output.

3 *Scrum Master* – select someone who can coach the team and help them to remove barriers to team velocity during sprints.

4 *Backlog* – 'create and prioritize a product backlog – the list of everything that needs to be built or done to make the vision a reality'. It evolves during the lifetime of the programme. What is priority is based on value to the customer, as well as to the business.

5 *Scope* – the people doing the work estimate the relative effort required to deliver each 'increment' (a concrete usable output) in the backlog. It is important to have a definition of when an increment is 'done' that everyone agrees on.

6 *Sprint planning* – the team meet with the owner and the coach to plan the sprint. 'Sprints are always a fixed length of time that is less than a month.' The team agrees a sprint goal that cannot then be changed during the sprint. They calculate team velocity based on recent performance to say how many tasks can be completed in the next sprint. The team works autonomously during the sprint to achieve the goal.

7 *Visualize work* – typically using a 'Scrum board', with three columns (To Do, Doing, Done), and with real or virtual post-its to move items along as they progress. This allows the team and others to see progress easily.

8 *Daily stand-up* – 'this is the heartbeat of Scrum'. The team meets every day, at the same time, no more than 15 minutes, with a set of simple questions to review progress and agree the focus for the day.

9 *Sprint review* – a meeting to demonstrate what has been achieved during the sprint. It is open to all, and they only show what meets the definition of 'done'.

10 *Sprint retrospective* – following the review, the team sits down and discusses 'what went well, what could have gone better, and what can be made better in the next sprint'. This needs open discussion and honest feedback. They then agree one improvement to their process that they

will put into practice during the next sprint, which gets added to the backlog as a priority in the next sprint.

11 *Start again* – move straight into the next sprint.

This process flow was defined for use in software development but is now being used much more widely in agile ways of working across organizations. As a leader, one of our key challenges is to work out, often through experimentation, where it can be used to improve innovation or efficiency of output in line with customer priorities, and in what form. In the rest of this chapter I will provide some guidance on how to take agile working and use it in a practical way across many parts of your business. It can work well, for example, in functions such as marketing and human resources, and in business areas such as new product development and improving delivery. Wherever you need innovation it is particularly relevant. It can also work in varying degrees across the whole organization as a mindset and way of working, depending on the extent to which stability or speed is the priority. I will explore this further in subsequent chapters.

Leadership needs to change

Key to this style of working being successful in practice is the leadership approach of those 'in charge'. Through the Scrum process outlined above you can see the levels of discipline, focus and collaborative working that are required to achieve faster and higher quality outcomes. As leaders we need to create the environment where this can happen in practice, where the fear of failure is replaced by the productivity benefits of short bursts of focused energy.

Scrum thinking 'embraces uncertainty and creativity. It gives a structure to the learning process, enabling teams to assess what they've created and, just as important, how they've created it' (Sutherland, 2015). The team is focusing its effort on producing the product or service features that are the priority for the customer, and of greatest value therefore to the business. The Pareto Law applies, in that 80 per cent of the value of a product or service is typically in 20 per cent of its features, so Scrum forces teams to focus on the 20 per cent first. In a world of rapidly changing customer expectations, this helps avoid investment in features that are either no longer needed or are quickly obsolete.

Clearly, operating in this way, with short cycles, customer-driven priorities and team autonomy in the production process, requires a style of leadership that is neither controlling nor distrustful. In my experience, if senior managers do not fully get it, the rest of the organization will find it very difficult to make 'agile' work in practice. The leader's role is actively to support the approach, removing barriers to productivity gains and creating an environment where teams can be free to get on with doing a great job. Each team needs to have the authority to decide how many tasks they can get done during each sprint. Plans need to be flexible in the face of changing circumstances: 'Planning is useful. Blindly following plans is stupid' (Sutherland, 2015). Mistakes need to be seen by managers genuinely as opportunities to learn and make faster progress in the future: 'fail fast and learn' is the mantra.

The leader's role is to create an environment where people are free to make decisions, adapt to what is in front of them, and feel confident to make mistakes and learn from the experience. If you don't have faith in your team or people in your organization and trust them to do the right thing, if you don't feel able to give power to others to make decisions, if you feel the need to interfere and check on others frequently to ensure that things are on track, you will struggle with agile ways of working.

The transition to more agile working can also be challenging for the senior managers who are responsible for how the organization is performing. We know from complexity theory (Uhl-Bien *et al*, 2007) that complex adaptive systems emerge and become stable over time, and that during that time the chaos and flux can be disconcerting. As a leader, embracing more agile ways of working will often mean working through this sometimes challenging transition, keeping the faith that the outcomes will be worth the pain.

If you ensure the organization has a clear sense of purpose, with a clear strategic sense of direction and clear values to guide behaviour, you are providing the framework in which people can take responsibility, work together in teams, collaborate more effectively, and provide what the customer really values more quickly and more effectively than your competitors. This is agile: it is about having a lightly connected organization that can flex to change and act quickly to seize opportunities as they emerge. We saw many organizations act in this way during the early days of the pandemic in 2020, with thousands of people working from home with digital access set up in days, and companies shifting their product focus rapidly to meet the demand for personal protective equipment and pharmaceuticals needed by front-line health workers. Agility is about responding in this way, as well as on occasions being able to create Uber moments, to move with the confidence of a top athlete to change the rules and achieve breakthrough success.

It is also about you losing some control as a leader and having to trust the team around you to act together intelligently and effectively.

Teams are key

You will have realized by now that teams are at the heart of agile ways of working. The autonomous team in flow will always beat the talented individual, as Meredith Belbin's classic experiments in the 1970s and 1980s indicated repeatedly. Getting a broad balance of skills and styles led to stronger team performance over more individually oriented and imbalanced teams (Belbin, 1981). This was reinforced by Professors Takeuchi and Nonaka (1986) in their classic study. They described the characteristics of the teams they saw at the best companies in the world as being 'transcendent' (having a sense of higher purpose), 'autonomous' (self-organized and self-managing), and 'cross-functional' (all the skills needed to achieve the task). All three are important, they assert, and I would agree. I will explore this more in Chapter 8.

One of the five factors of connected leadership (which was itself the result of research into the transition to becoming more agile) is collaborative achievement, which is rooted in high-performing teamwork. Without a relentless emphasis on teamwork in your organization, in hiring decisions, rewards and bonuses, leadership development, succession planning and performance management, the holy grail of becoming a truly agile business will be very difficult to attain. Teamwork creates a positive cycle of personal fulfilment for team members, improved productivity, and more joined-up outcomes across each process. In my experience, teams with the autonomy to make decisions about their work, and the ability to improve regularly, become powerful forces for change in their organizations, which is why so many universities have set up innovation incubators to give life support to new teams as they pioneer new business ideas for future commercial value. Scrum Alliance (2001) describe it thus: 'An agile framework allows team members to collaborate to decide on the most effective and efficient ways to complete work while making sure that the end users receive what they want and need. The focus is on people and interactions, not processes and tools.'

One of the principles of Scrum is to know your team's velocity. If you and your team know how much work they can complete in each period, they can plan effectively for the next sprint and then work on how to accelerate in future sprints. One of the main tasks for leaders in teams is to remove the barriers that waste time and effort, thus slowing the team down. During sprint retrospectives the team is encouraged to identify barriers or impediments to greater velocity. It is the same in sports like rowing, where after each training session the crew review their performance and identify ways to make the boat go faster next time. This often involves direct feedback between crew members, which is helpful if the crew has the mutual respect and focus on their shared goals to take such feedback as insight rather than personal criticism. There is huge value in regular direct feedback as a source of insight to 'make the boat go faster'. Through this feedback it is important to articulate the problem or barrier specifically, so that it can be resolved effectively.

In a business context, it is often helpful to identify a senior person who can take responsibility for resolving the issue to free up faster work across the organization. In a client in telecommunications, for example, senior leaders identified through in-depth discussions with teams across the business that there was an issue with selling services from different divisions into large corporate clients. This was because there was not a culture of sharing client insight across the business. A board member took the lead to address this issue and developed a cross-functional team to work on it with her. The team identified several underlying causes of the problem. They agreed with colleagues from across the business that the top priority was changing the management mindset that gave higher priority to local success and internal competition than to the overall performance of the enterprise. So, the team put in place a management training programme focused on collaborative working, with a supporting online system to encourage sharing of knowledge and customer insight. The result was a significant shift in cross-selling opportunities being identified, and improved collaboration between teams working on those opportunities, to the benefit of both the clients and the business as a whole.

Agile team practices

I am involved in a longitudinal research project with academics from Alliance Manchester Business School (AMBS, 2020) into agile teams and how leadership and culture influence their performance. We are collecting data from several major international organizations which are on a journey to becoming agile, and the initial findings are helpful in defining what agile teams do and how to help them perform as effectively as possible. Results from the statistical analysis suggest that leaders who are empowering and who develop good work relationships with their teams will tend to enable higher levels of team agility.

Empowering leadership (Vecchio, 2010) is about devolving decision making to the team (see Chapter 8) and requires a high degree of psychological safety to work in practice. The empowered individual or team takes a risk when it accepts the responsibility (and consequences) of decision making. So, as leaders, we need to create a safe environment and support agile teams in practice to take decisions, even if the decisions are not always the best available. Our reaction to error determines whether the team will risk further error in future.

The quality of relationships between team leader and team is also significant in determining the performance of the team. We measured this in our survey using Leader Member Exchange (LMX) items in the research (Markham et al, 2010). The better the quality of relationship, the more productive the team. This illustrates for us the importance of building trust with our teams, based on open and transparent dialogue, and genuine attention to them as people. Higher relationship quality leads to increased confidence in the team, and a sense of being valued. Interestingly, interpersonal conflict negatively affects agile team performance – this refers to emotional conflict between people, rather than diversity of debate about the task which is healthy if focused on 'making the boat go faster'.

This research highlights how the success of agile teamworking in practice is fundamentally about teams feeling safe, supported and empowered. Interpersonal conflict has a detrimental impact on agile team performance, whereas effective leadership and a fair culture give teams confidence to experiment, take risks, be bold and deliver improved results to the business.

The research team has also developed a model of team agility, drawing from extensive research (Lin et al, 2006; Liu et al, 2015), which showed that agile teams are defined as multi-skilled, with the skills needed to complete the task within the team. They maintain a clear set of priorities for action and recognize that these may change through regular and in-depth iterative planning. They are customer-centric, involving the end user in regular reviews of output to gain feedback to steer future work. Agile teams enjoy high levels of team autonomy, deciding how they organize their work and achieve outputs. And they work with speed and can adapt quickly to changing customer requirements.

The research suggests that high levels of team agility are associated with the key outcomes of increased employee engagement (feeling energetic, dedicated, and absorbed in work), individual performance and team performance. It is helpful to have robust research supporting what we see day to day as agile teams perform well and are engaged in their work.

As leaders we create the climate where agile teamworking can flourish, or flounder. Tools, processes, rituals and training are all important elements of agile teamworking. But the bottom line is that without your active and genuine support that demonstrates the eight characteristics of agile leadership I described in Chapter 2, the agile transformation in your organization is less likely to achieve its goals.

Time: the sprint

The 100 metres is always one of the most popular and dramatic events at the Olympic Games. The athletes are some of the most famous, and the margins of victory the closest. The sprint is an intense spectacle, with athletes unleashing tremendous power for a short period of time as they race towards the finish line. An essential part of agile is thinking and acting in short bursts, with an intensity of focused effort in a predetermined 'sprint' or 'time box'. This creates the opportunity to create rapid outputs or prototypes that can be shown to customers or end users to get their feedback. Do they like it, do they value it enough to pay for it, and what would they want most to see in addition?

It is helpful to be planning with your teams several sprints ahead of the one you are about to start. When you start planning for a sprint in detail you realize there are unanswered questions that may require consultation or further thought before the exact scope of work can be defined. If that consultation is from within the team it is relatively easy to complete, but if the answers need to come from another party, this takes time and can slow things down, so that work may be pushed back into a later sprint to allow time for the consultation.

TIME

What Scrum does is alter the very way you think about time.

Sutherland (2015)

One of the most powerful parts of Scrum is the sprint review, or when a product is introduced to the customer or end user. It is very engaging for a team to be driving towards a demonstrable product on a frequent basis.

They can see what they are aiming for, and they can then see the fruit of their hard work in something that is useful. Returning to the rugby analogy, during a season a team will have a series of games, each of which is their absolute focus leading up to it. This punctuates their efforts, making their immediate goal specific and tangible – ie to beat the team in the next match. This is both motivating and practical, as it allows the team to learn through regular post-match reviews and adjust how they play together through training for the next match.

The sprint review, therefore, is a helpful short-term focus for the team, and allows feedback and learning about what the customer thinks that can be carried into the next sprint. The team is delivering the customer vision incrementally, so it can be tested and refined as they go. This increases productivity through improved collaboration and ensuring the team is focused on the highest value outputs for the customer. The quicker you demo something new to your customers, the quicker they can tell you if you are building something they need. Facebook, for example, effectively started life in 2004 as a demo. A group of Harvard students set it up for other students to share photographs of themselves to facilitate introductions, mimicking the 'face book' directories often given to US students. It worked, and through the feedback the group of originators developed the platform to extend it across other universities and then to the worldwide social media platform we know today.

Another aspect of agile working linked to time is the daily stand-up. Teams use it to stay aligned and to address immediate issues. Each day the team meets briefly to discuss three questions. In pure Scrum working, these are about yesterday, today and obstacles in our way. In a broader business context, the following is a helpful set of questions to maintain a daily rhythm of review and issue identification:

- How are we doing? (Update on what we did yesterday and key performance metrics.)
- What's coming up? (What are we doing today and key events or activities in the next 24 hours.)
- Where are we stuck? (What could prevent progress.)

It is important that the meeting is held at the same time every day, with everyone present. This helps the team develop a heartbeat that is important to thinking and acting in concert. Our regular leadership team check-ins at Cirrus, for example, help us to stay joined up and focused on our colleagues and customers. We often identify problems that we can then solve, removing barriers to progress across the business. For significant issues that come up it is better to take them offline, so they can be discussed afterwards in an appropriate level of detail. There are also teamwork benefits, as we knit closer together as a team, benefiting from the regularity of connection between us, even though some of us are not located in the same place most of the time.

This frequency of communication is important. Sutherland is clear on this: 'The greater the communication saturation – the more everyone knows everything – the faster the team.' This requires a high level of transparency from you as a leader, and throughout the management population in your organization. Giving teams and local managers access to all the information they need to make great decisions is a prerequisite to effective devolution of decision making, as I will explore in Chapter 8. Giving teams as much information as possible provides them with more opportunities to adapt to changing priorities, and to work intelligently on their part of the picture. Withholding information persistently in my experience is a sign of an insecure manager who does not trust his or her people sufficiently to deserve the title 'leader'.

The increase in working from home that followed the 2020 pandemic response has changed the nature of time for many people. Less time for many on crowded commuter trains, less time in the car, less time waiting for a connection. More time at home or local, more time with family, more time to work. There is a risk of 'living at work' becoming the norm for many, so it is incumbent on leaders to cause a rethink of time as new ways of working emerge. Clear boundaries between work and non-work time are clearly important, especially to protect the mental wellbeing of our people. But how we use working time also needs to be redefined. When working at home we could have more time to think, as well as being productive in our day-to-day role. When in the office we could be using the time together to socialize and bond, to collaborate, to create new ideas and plans, and to review and learn. The possibilities are exciting.

Do one thing at a time

I have been a manager for over 30 years, and for many of those years I cherished my ability to juggle several tasks at the same time. For me it was a sign of being a good general manager, able to take on responsibilities across a wide range of functions and customer requirements. However, I have come to realize that multitasking causes significant inefficiency.

As we touched on in Chapter 2, the impact of doing one thing at a time on productivity can be dramatic. Each time we focus on a different task we need to tune into the context and refresh our understanding of what we were doing. If we reduce the amount of context switching we do, staying focused on one activity until it is finished, we will achieve more output in the time available. Sutherland quotes Pashler's 1990s research which identified 'dual task interference', which means that we cannot switch seamlessly between activities in our brain; it slows us down as the brain is trying to hold them as active at the same time. 'Just by doing one thing exclusively before moving on, the work takes a little more than half as much time. *Half*' (Sutherland, 2015). There is huge inefficiency in mixing up tasks rather than focusing on one at a time due to this dual task interference, which causes a waste of time in context switching and which becomes worse as you introduce more projects to work on, so that if you have five activities running in parallel the loss is 75 per cent of the time. This is true for you as a leader and for your teams working on specific projects. Staying with one activity until it is finished, through ruthless prioritization, will increase agility as well as improving satisfaction levels from the sense of having achieved something concrete or 'done'.

If you are like me and enjoy the challenge of multitasking, you need to make a conscious and sustained effort to switch to single-activity working. It can be helpful to change environment to somewhere relevant and conducive to the task you are focused on. This cuts out distractions and reduces the temptation to multitask. I was working recently with a colleague from a different office on a piece of design for a key client. Normally I would have worked from my desk and connected via video with my colleague. Instead I went into a different meeting room, where we worked together over video for two hours, enough time to do the complete design, and I was not distracted by my emails or preparing for the next meeting. A simple change of context helped us complete the task so that it was 'done', and we took a lot less time in doing so than if we had continued over several calls and email exchanges. We were disciplined, highly productive and concentrated on the single task in hand. It felt good, like an athlete achieving a personal best.

Visualizing the story

A helpful aspect of agile working for wider use by leaders is using stories to describe objectives in a way that makes them more real for the team working on them. We want teams to be clear about the customer experience that will result from their work, whether the team is working in software development, research and development or a support function in head office. It is therefore helpful to create a story about the outcome of a piece of work in terms of what the customer will be able to do differently as a result. Who are the customers? What do they like or value in particular? Why do they want this output? How will we know when the output is 'done'? What benefit will they experience as a result? Sprint planning involves looking at these stories and making sense of the next priority. If you can make the story tangible, you are helping make it come alive so that others can visualize the outcome in practice.

This approach works at the micro level of activity planning in individual teams and at the macro level across the organization. The principle is the same – telling a vivid story about the customer experience helps your colleagues to relate to the outcome and make more intelligent judgements about how they go about their work as a result. At the ultimate level this can be seen in the way some organizations have created a story to describe their purpose, so that colleagues identify with it and understand better what it means in practice. Walmart, for example, says that, 'we save people money so they can live better'. We can see the family in their kitchen, unpacking the grocery bags, filling the fridge, enjoying the little luxuries that their cost-effective shopping allowed them to buy. In 1992, shortly before his death, Walmart's founder, Sam Walton received the US Presidential Medal of Freedom. In accepting the award, he said: 'If we work together, we'll lower the cost of living for everyone... we'll give the world an opportunity to see what it's like to save and have a better life.'

A key way to make the story of a team's performance more powerful is to make it visible, using techniques such as the Scrum or Kanban board. By making everything visible you create more opportunity for discussion about the work, about progress and about improving velocity. The Kanban board summarizes the team's current workload, with post-its used to move items across the board as they progress, so that the status of the team's sprint is immediately visible and clear. Table 3.1 is an example of such a board, with several user stories describing the features that each task will deliver. The physical board is used widely where teams are co-located, but there are some great software equivalents that are more helpful when teams are spread across locations.

TABLE 3.1 The Kanban board

PROJECT/TEAM NAME					
	Backlog	To do	Doing	In review/QA	Done!
User story 1	▦	▦	▦	▦ ▦	
User story 2	▦	▦	▦	▦	▦
User story 3		▦	▦ ▦	▦	
User story 4	▦				

A popular children's television programme in the UK when I was growing up was *Blue Peter*. It first aired on the BBC in 1958 and is the longest-running children's TV show in the world, still popular at the time of writing. Each year I recall the show had an appeal for a charity at Christmas time. The producers knew the power of visualizing progress. Each year, the presenters would do a weekly update on progress towards the fund-raising target using a large visual measure such as a traditional thermometer, with a red level moving slowly up the calibrated tube as more funds were raised by children all over the country. We all became part of the team, sharing the excitement when the red 'mercury' moved up, and the frustration when it hardly moved. Eventually, we would hit the target – children all over the UK felt they had shared the experience and played their part in supporting the charity challenge. To this day I can see the thermometer clearly in my mind. It united a generation!

Where you have project teams working the Kanban board is likely to be highly useful in managing prioritization and progress. In other areas of work, other techniques for visualizing work may be more relevant. However, the principle of visualizing priorities, and managing work in teams within tight timescales, is widely applicable.

I would encourage you to experiment, to use the board and all the associated ways of working we have looked at in this chapter in a way that brings the discipline and focus we see working so well in agile development. Take, for example, the business planning process. If you are like me you will tend to include too many priorities in the plan, as they are all important. The agile approach is to see this list as a backlog, and to prioritize it in the plan so that you can focus the resources of the business on the few things that will make the biggest difference to the business over the coming period. Visualize these priority activities and exert maximum effort to get them done as soon as possible. In a retail context, these might include giving the consumer a seamless returns experience across all channels or reducing waste by 1 per cent. Define the user experience and set up cross-functional teams to deliver them. Then get out of the way and support the teams with resource and organizational commitment.

THE BENEFITS OF AGILE

Quality has improved. We are more flexible. When organizations like ours start to embrace devolved responsibility and ownership, the insurance systems our teams build naturally become more resilient and quality is in the architecture from the start. Feedback of failures is not short circuited by other organization groups but is felt directly by the team so it's in their interests to build it right. By encouraging that sense of ownership across the full life cycle, and having more dynamic teams, we are constantly delivering benefits to our clients.

Michael Lambert, former head of development, CDL

Summary

Get started by defining a vision, creating a backlog, and pulling together a multidisciplinary team to work on it. Deliver something of value regularly and keep learning. CDL is a successful software company that has dramatically changed its approach to working with customers based on agile ways of working. It is a brave business, and it is seeing great results.

I will end with the principles that the 17 developers agreed on when they defined the Agile Manifesto back in 2001 at the Snowbird ski resort in Utah (Beck *et al*, 2001). Please read them through and see how many describe your organization or team right now. Ignoring the references to software per se, which of these is the most challenging for you to respond, 'Yes, that's how we work'?

These principles still give us key insights into the culture and mindset we need to create if we are to build truly agile organizations. So many years later, these principles summarize a mindset which is truly connected and yet disruptive at the same time.

PRINCIPLES BEHIND THE AGILE MANIFESTO Which are most relevant to your agile journey?

1 Our highest priority is to satisfy the customer through early and continuous delivery of valuable software.

2 Welcome changing requirements, even late in development. Agile processes harness change for the customer's competitive advantage.

3 Deliver working software frequently, from a couple of weeks to a couple of months, with a preference to the shorter timescale.

4 Business people and developers must work together daily throughout the project.

5 Build projects around motivated individuals.

6 Give them the environment and support they need and trust them to get the job done.

7 The most efficient and effective method of conveying information to and within a development team is face-to-face conversation.

8 Working software is the primary measure of progress.

9 Agile processes promote sustainable development.

10 The sponsors, developers and users should be able to maintain a constant pace indefinitely.

11 Continuous attention to technical excellence and good design enhances agility.

12 Simplicity – the art of maximizing the amount of work not done – is essential.

13 The best architectures, requirements and designs emerge from self-organizing teams.

14 At regular intervals, the team reflects on how to become more effective, then tunes and adjusts its behaviour accordingly.

References

Aghina, W, De Smet, A and Weerda, K (2015) Agility: It rhymes with stability, *McKinsey Quarterly*, December

AMBS (2020) *Agile Team Research*, Alliance Manchester Business School and Cirrus, UK

Badaracco, J (2001) We don't need another hero, *Harvard Business Review*, **79** (8)

Beck, K, Grenning, J, Martin, R, Beedle, M, Highsmith, J, Mellor, S, van Bennekum, A, Hunt, A, Schwaber, K, Cockburn, A, Jeffries, R, Sutherland, J, Cunningham, W, Kern, J, Thomas, D, Fowler, M and Marick, B (2001) *Principles behind the Agile Manifesto*, available at agilemanifesto.org/principles.html (archived at https://perma.cc/Z537-A5YQ)

Belbin, M (1981) *Management Teams*, Heinemann, London

Highsmith, J (2001) *History: The Agile Manifesto*, available at agilemanifesto.org/history.html (archived at https://perma.cc/6REJ-W9FB)

Lin, C, Chiu, H and Chu, P (2006) Agility index in the supply chain, *International Journal Production Economics*, **100**, Elsevier

Liu, M, Liu, N, Ding, C and Lin, C (2015) Exploring team performance in high-tech industries: Future trends of building up teamwork, *Technological Forecasting & Social Change*, **91**, Elsevier

Markham, S, Yammarino, F, Murry, W and Palanski, M (2010) Leader-member exchange: Shared values and performance, *The Leadership Quarterly*, **21** (3), pp 469–80

Scrum Alliance (2001) www.scrumalliance.org/why-scrum (archived at https://perma.cc/4UV8-5B3X)

Sutherland, J (2015) *Scrum*, Random House Books, London

Takeuchi, H and Nonaka, I (1986) New new product development game, *Harvard Business Review*, January

Uhl-Bien, M, Marion, R and McKelvey, B (2007) Complexity leadership theory: Shifting leadership from the industrial age to the knowledge era, *The Leadership Quarterly*, **18** (4)

Vecchio, R, Justin, J and Pearce, C (2010) Empowering leadership: An examination of mediating mechanisms within a hierarchical structure, *The Leadership Quarterly*, **21** (3), pp 530–42

CHAPTER FOUR

Barriers to agility

No speed limits. Agility rules. RIDDERSTRALE AND NORDSTROM (2000)

Introduction

In this chapter, we will look at the main barriers to building a more agile business and explore strategies to overcome them. We will draw on the eight characteristics of agile leaders described in Chapter 2, as well as insights from the Agile Manifesto and the agile leadership paradox from Chapter 1.

QUESTIONS TO ASK YOURSELF

In this chapter you may find it helpful to consider the following questions as you read:

- Does the culture in your organization encourage risk taking or risk aversion?
- Could your colleagues consistently define the few priorities you are focused on together right now?
- How tuned in are you to how your customers experience working with you every day?

A transformation

My own doctoral research (Hayward, 2015) was into the leadership factors that help or hinder successful transition to greater agility. I focused on large organizations, where typically there is a significant legacy of bureaucracy, ageing systems and silo-working that are not agile-friendly. Yet the post-Covid digital world in which we operate requires us to be able to pivot the organization rapidly into new markets and to respond quickly to fresh 'Uber moment' threats. What my research and that of many other respected sources suggest is that we need to create a more connected environment, where our people can adapt and learn within a stable framework of purpose and direction. We need to maintain a balance between adaptability and stability if we are to stay strong and yet be able to change quickly.

This may sound like a relatively modest adjustment in how your organization works, but it is a transformation for most. The legacy of the past in many large organizations I visit is huge and slows the organization down. Imagine a middle-aged person who has not done much exercise for 20 years thinking he wants to 'get fit'. He needs to change his diet to eat well and avoid many of his favourite foods and drinks and start an exercise regime that will take extraordinary dedication to see through. He needs to revise his priorities and break old habits to form new ones, which requires incredible persistence and a deep-seated commitment to the outcome he has in mind. Many people find it helpful to visualize this outcome and to articulate why it is so important to them and to their friends and family. Often, they will benefit from the advice of a coach to establish a fitness regime. The coach can then hold them to account as they build fitness over the coming months and years. Above all, it requires a new mindset if the good intention is to become a reality.

I went through this experience in 2004 when I started running. It was painful. I had to find the self-discipline to get up early to go running when the children were still asleep. I needed a set of short-term goals such as signing up for public events and organized runs, as well as a long-term sense that this would change my life for the better. Also, I had to learn to resist my penchant for chocolate and red wine. I am still on that journey, creating new habits and making decisions every day about what to eat, whether to go out for a run in the rain (or stay in my warm bed), and making sure I have a goal to train for, to make these decisions a little easier. I don't always make the right decision, but I do so enough of the time to make the journey fruitful. Being 'fit' is indeed a mindset but it is also a set of physical attributes that need dedicated work to build and maintain. Becoming an agile organization is similar.

Barriers to building an agile business

There are four main barriers to building an agile organization, summarizing much recent research (Goran *et al*, 2017):

1 *Culture* – having an organizational culture that creates a fear of risk and failure.
2 *Clarity* – having a lack of clarity about priorities, from individuals to the whole organization.
3 *Closeness to customers* – not being sufficiently close to the customer, so customer needs do not drive day-to-day priorities.
4 *Collaboration* – weak collaboration across strong silos.

The most fundamental is the organizational culture, which we will explore in some detail; the other three reflect the prevailing culture. We will look at each in turn and explore how to reduce and ultimately remove each barrier so that you can move more rapidly towards becoming truly agile.

> Shortcomings in organizational culture are one of the main barriers to company success in the digital age. That is a central finding from McKinsey's recent survey of global executives, which highlighted three digital-culture deficiencies: functional and departmental silos, a fear of taking risks, and difficulty forming and acting on a single view of the customer.
>
> Goran *et al* (2017)

1 Culture

A hockey player who is on top of their game plays with a confidence and sense of freedom to express their talent that adds extra pace to their stride. They see opportunities other players might not see, and act with a pace and determination to succeed. They are 'in flow' and enjoying the game. When you get a team of players who share this self-belief and desire to express their abilities together, it can be an unstoppable force. If you look behind the scenes, you are likely to see a team coach who has nurtured a culture of shared confidence and a dedication to teamwork based on discipline. The results on the field can be beautiful to watch. The same can be said of an orchestra that is able to combine the individual talents of the musicians into a harmonious blend of beautiful music. The conductor is enabling the musicians to use their individual skills as part of a shared effort, and to do so at the peak of their ability.

Number 6 in the list of 14 agile principles from the Agile Manifesto we looked at in the previous chapter is, 'Give them the environment and support they need, and trust them to get the job done.' This hints at the type of culture we need if we are to achieve agile performance. As a leader you need to create a supportive environment based on discipline, trust and confidence, just as the coach or the conductor does, to give the people in your organization the opportunity to express their talents with confidence.

Culture is defined as 'the way of life, especially the general customs and beliefs, of a particular group of people at a particular time' (*Cambridge English Dictionary*, 2020). It describes the prevalent behaviours and norms of a social group, and the symbols of meaning that are important to that group in defining their identity. In other words, it is 'how we do things around here'. In the hockey team the culture may be based on customs such as everyone turning up for training on time, players helping each other in technical sessions, daily team reviews of performance to identify ways to improve tomorrow, and so on. The coach asks the team to describe their best moment after every game and insists that no player is above the team. The team's way of life is focused on a shared belief in playing with style, playing to win, and playing for each other.

CULTURE IS KEY

The bull's-eye is a culture that embraces new concepts and new capabilities and doesn't choke them out.

Satya Nadella (2017)

So, what is the way of life in your organization like? What are the customs and beliefs that shape how people behave day by day? What are the constraints on people's behaviour that stop them from being truly agile? In one large international travel organization I visited a while ago, after I had met a few senior people across the business it became clear that there was a strong culture of fear, which led to people avoiding risks, making slow decisions and always seeking higher approval to cover their backs. This slowed everything down and left talented people frustrated at the lack of progress and trust. The CEO was also frustrated with the lack of pace, the slow decision making and the endless meetings. He pushed for more speed and was met by a wall of subtle resistance from people, who feared the consequences if they acted more quickly but got something wrong.

The irony was obvious to everyone except the CEO, who did not appreciate that he and his senior leadership colleagues were creating the debilitating fear in the business through their reactions to failure and their willingness to blame people for mistakes. The way of life in the organization was overshadowed by their attitude and approach. What they needed was a major change in culture as a basis for developing more agile ways of working. This had, in my view, to start with the senior team – they needed to recognize that they were a central part of the problem. Only then could they begin to reverse their approach in a sustained way to rebuild confidence among their people based on giving trust rather than waiting for it to be earned. This is not easy, but in the post-pandemic digital world, where competition is both fierce and often from unpredictable sources, it is not optional. Without an agile culture, you cannot build an agile organization.

Catriona Marshall used to be CEO of Hobbycraft, the successful UK hobby retailer. Catriona became CEO after a fast-track career to senior leadership roles at Asda and Pets at Home. When asked what kind of behaviour from senior leadership is most helpful to foster real agility, she replied simply:

> Trust. You've got to have trust in your people and really see it through. So, you've got to get that right balance between agreeing the goal, agreeing whatever parameters you think are important, whether it's time, skills, budget, and then trusting them to get on with it and giving them support and advice when they need it.

Catriona highlights that as the leader it is in your gift to trust others and to see it through even when things go wrong. I meet many managers who believe that people need to earn their trust, and that it can be given and then withdrawn at their personal discretion. This is not trust, it is conditional support, and it is a corrosive approach that undermines a healthy, agile culture.

What is an agile culture? It is a connected culture, one where there is balance, strength, speed, coordination and endurance, as we learned in Chapter 1. The research into connected leadership (Hayward, 2016) described in that chapter shows the six main factors of an agile culture:

1 *Leadership commitment:* people really feel they have the support of senior leaders in working in agile ways.
2 *A shared sense of purpose and clarity of direction:* the mission is clear, the priorities are agreed, and this frees people to act quickly, safe in the knowledge that their actions are aligned with the organization's intended outcomes.
3 *Authentic leadership:* leaders are truly role models of the organization's values and instil trust around them. When we trust our leaders and in turn feel trusted by them, we have greater psychological safety and are more likely to take risks and act boldly.
4 *Devolved decision making:* decisions are consistently made as close to the customer as possible. While there are strategic decisions that should be made centrally, most decisions are better made by experts and by people closer to the customers. All decisions are made thoughtfully.
5 *Collaboration across teams, functions and specialisms:* there is clear commitment that teamwork and working cross-functionally are part of company culture – that's the way things get done around here.
6 *Experimentation and constant feedback:* there is persistent learning from customers and testing new prototypes which helps to differentiate the offer for customers.

When these factors are combined, they create a culture that encourages people to move quickly and with confidence, like the winning hockey team and the inspiring orchestra. In our increasingly complex digital world, however, building and maintaining a strong connected culture is ever more difficult. It is helpful therefore to explore how complexity theory relates to leadership, so you can understand how to combine strength and flexibility in your organization's culture to succeed in a complex environment.

Complexity leadership

Complexity leadership theory (CLT) is one of the key areas of leadership research that has informed the six factors above. In our VUCA post-pandemic world, we are living in an increasingly complex and potentially chaotic environment, where the tendency for structural change to happen quickly is increasing. The agile leadership paradox, being both an enabler and a disruptor, is about existing on the edge of this chaos, navigating through uncertainty yet seeking to build a stable and effective organization. McKinsey research confirms this view: 'In our experience, truly agile organizations, paradoxically, learn to be both stable (resilient, reliable and efficient) and dynamic (fast, nimble and adaptive)' (Aghina *et al*, 2015).

CLT has evolved from complex systems theory, which states that adaptive systems perform better than static ones in fluid situations (Coveney, 2003). We need to adapt to survive, and in the digital world of accelerating change, we need to be constantly learning and making sense of what is going on around us. Stacey (1995) talks about organizations operating in 'far from equilibrium states' in which negative and positive feedback drives changes in behaviour and increased innovation and creativity. Rather than seeking to minimize uncertainty, Stacey saw its benefit in being a catalyst for change in organizations. As we saw in how some organizations responded to Covid-19 in 2020, if we are disruptive and embrace the uncertainty around us, and ride the wave of change, we can survive and flourish in the new unstable environment. AstraZeneca, for example, seized the initiative by establishing a partnership with Oxford University to distribute 2 billion Covid-19 vaccines. Their share price rose by 50 per cent between a March low and a July 2020 high. For others, the rapid switch to online retail, remote teamworking, and localization of supply has left many organizations in a stronger relative position than before. Amazon, for example, saw its share price more than double between March and August 2020.

To embrace uncertainty, we need teams which will act with confidence, knowing that senior leaders have their back. They need to be clear about where the organization is going, and why it is important, so that they can align their efforts to these goals and purpose. They need to feel trusted and empowered to act appropriately to their changing circumstances and know the parameters within which they are free to make decisions. They also need to be able to experiment and learn what works (and what does not) and be able to share this with other teams to drive innovation and improvement. The alternative is eventually to become a casualty of the changes happening around us all.

As we know, balance is critical for any person or organization to be agile in practice. The balance between enabling and disrupting is one example. Another is the balance between stability and dynamism mentioned above. CLT echoes this need for balance in the organization if it is to be able to operate in a consistent manner as well as responding to, and evolving with, its changing external environment. In CLT there are three functions of leadership (Uhl-Bien *et al*, 2007): administrative, adaptive and enabling. In combination, these create balance in the organization so that it can succeed in unpredictable and constantly changing environments.

The *administrative* function is 'associated with the bureaucratic elements of organizations. It occurs in formal, managerial roles and reflects traditional management processes and functions aimed at driving business results' (Uhl-Bien and Marion, 2001). According to Uhl-Bien, this function 'recognizes that although organizations are bureaucracies, they do not have to be bureaucratic'. It is the spine of the organization, the structure that connects the parts and aligns objectives into a coherent force, like the efficient operating model and supply chain of McDonald's, which delivers consistently around the world.

To balance this strong administrative core you also need a strong *adaptive* function to help the organization respond to rapid changes in its environment. The adaptive leadership role creates an environment, often on the edge of the organization, where people can interact with and learn from customers, competitors and other influences, creating new ways of surviving in a rapidly changing environment like we saw with Covid-19. It is the dynamic skin of the organization, sensing and adapting, in touch with the outside, like the retail outlets of Zara, where store teams learn about local customer demand through careful analysis of their daily shopping habits. In the military context, this is a result of what von Clausewitz called *Friktion* (Bungay, 2011), in which human interaction in war is messy, unpredictable and specific to the context. Officers in the field need the freedom to act with initiative, responding to what they see in front of them, within a framework set by the generals in advance, based on clarity of mission and the acceptable parameters of flexibility. It is called 'mission command'.

The administrative and adaptive leadership functions work in dynamic tension with one another. To manage this, a third function is needed: the *enabling* function operates at the interface between the administrative and adaptive functions. The enabling function works to 'loosen up the organization – stimulating innovation, creativity and responsiveness and learning to manage continuous adaptation to change – without losing strategic focus' or spinning out of control (Uhl-Bien and Marion, 2011). It is the balancing force, the nerves and muscles that coordinate action and control the body so that it can be agile.

FIGURE 4.1 Complexity leadership theory

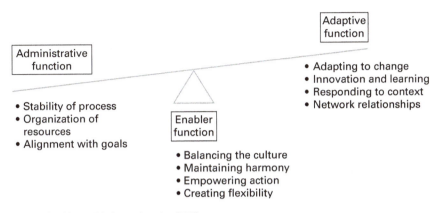

Source: Derived from Uhl-Bien and Marion (2011)

Our leadership role is to create a coherent culture in which we are balancing speed and operational stability, and empowering teams to act flexibly within a well-understood framework. In Figure 4.1 we see how the enabling function balances control and adaptation, alignment and learning.

The implication for us, as leaders, is that it is helpful to define how well the three functions are working in mutual harmony. Do you have robust values, systems, and processes to maintain cohesion, *and* innovative teams creating new value and ways to compete, *and* an empowered culture that enables them to act with confidence in line with your organization's direction and purpose? Balance is a recurring theme: balance of central and decentralized organizational leadership, and balance at a personal level between structure and flexibility. CLT gives us a cultural framework that provides the environment for agility to flourish.

2 Clarity

After culture, the second barrier to creating an agile organization is the lack of clarity about your goals, roles and expectations. This relates to the administrative function in CLT, as it is part of effective governance. I see many large organizations that are burdened by the legacy of complex bureaucracy, often driven by their desire to manage risk (and often in a regulated environment). That bureaucracy is slowing down decision making and action, which is making these organizations slow and uncompetitive when compared with their newer digital rivals. Stripping away the bureaucracy is a real challenge, often because the people in the middle of it quite like it – it acts like a comfort blanket, reassuring in its warmth and security.

When you give people the freedom to adapt and to experiment, you need to ensure that you also provide real clarity about where you are going, what role you want each person and team to take, and what your expectations are in terms of outputs and standards of behaviour. To quote Angela Spindler, ex-CEO of N Brown, the online clothing retailer, where agile working has helped transform results:

> The onus is on the leadership of the organization to set a really clear framework. If you don't have that and you move to agile ways of working, you are basically inciting anarchy, because you're empowering groups but you're not being clear enough about what the parameters are, and what you are expecting them to achieve through applying these agile working processes. But if you're confident that that framework is in place, then empowering these groups, the product owners particularly, to go ahead and make it happen is terrific and it does accelerate outputs in the business.

Another example of the need for clarity I experienced at first hand was at a leading property company, where we held a metaphorical bonfire for initiatives, where the whole senior leadership group discussed and compared the multitude of current projects and work streams. They selected a few to keep, the ones they all agreed were going to add most value to the business and its customers. The rest went up in rhetorical flames, in a ceremony that left them all in no doubt as to what they had all agreed. They had developed a clear vision of what they wanted to achieve together, so it quickly became clear which initiatives were really driving them towards that vision most effectively. We will explore the importance of ruthless prioritization in Chapter 7.

Clarity of roles and expectations is particularly important in a matrix organization structure. Once again, we need to see balance between functional and operational priorities. Functions focus on functional coherence, clear policy and technical parameters, and standardization. Operations focus on quality of output and meeting customer expectations. Leaders at all levels need to demonstrate commitment to the matrix and manage this balance in the best interests of customers and the whole organization. They also need to facilitate joint resolution when tensions arise, with emphasis on collaboration and joint decisions. Leaders need to exploit opportunities for synergy and business improvement and be intolerant of bad behaviour such as sabotage, unilateralism and unhealthy competition.

3 Closeness to customers

A fundamental principle of agile working is to stay close to customers, to test products with them as soon as they are demonstrable, and to get regular feedback from them, wherever they are located. This enables you to deliver what they value more quickly and economically and removes much of the risk of innovation in a vacuum that may or may not meet customer needs. Agile product and service development, using an iterative approach to customer involvement, reduces risk and accelerates product release velocity in industries as diverse as software development, aerospace and clothing retail.

In the world of service delivery, working closely with your customers is also helpful. If, for example, you train your front-line colleagues to work with customers to resolve issues quickly and intelligently, customer loyalty increases and cost-to-serve decreases. Giving contact centre workers accurate information about customer buying patterns, preferences and profitability, and empowering them to make decisions within agreed parameters, enables them to resolve customer issues more quickly or increase average order value in each transaction. A UK telecoms provider, for example, has seen its customer net promoter scores improve dramatically in the last two years, from 0 to 20, based on this approach, with a continued upward trend. At a challenger bank, sales conversion rates for insurance products improved from 40 to 48 per cent by adopting this approach. The customer is getting an improved experience, and the company is reducing costs or making more money.

If you have a connected culture, and clarity on what is important for people in their role, you can create competitive advantage through every interaction between customers and your digitally empowered front-line people. For many large organizations with heavy legacies and dispersed international workforces, this can be a challenge. One technique that can work effectively to disrupt the internal focus and bureaucratic tendencies of these organizations is to introduce a customer-centric catalyst. This can be done either through creating an internal 'start-up' incubator, where new ideas are given the time, space and resource to blossom, or through acquiring a customer-centric organization and protecting its culture so that it can influence the host through osmosis.

I have seen an excellent example of the incubator route at a global services company that has created a hub for innovation and agility. The hub brings together employees from different countries within a specially designed space next to its European head office location. The aim of the hub is to revisit and enhance the overall customer experience, with a focus on digitalization. It was deliberately set up as a separate working environment to co-create the customer experiences of the future and is culturally quite different from the rest of the business. There is close collaboration with customers who are involved in ideas generation and testing.

This company attributes much of the success of the design hub to the use of fixed timeframes, which accelerate innovation. Employees join for an intense eight-week period where a concept can go from idea to prototype. People then return to their permanent role in the organization, share what they have learned with colleagues and spread more agile ways of working.

An example of the acquisition route is from 2016 when BT Group acquired EE, the largest UK mobile company. Instead of rapidly absorbing EE into its structure, BT kept it separate, and through a series of coordinated swaps moved people between the two companies to encourage learning and the transfer of the more entrepreneurial culture at EE. The result so far has been senior managers who moved into BT accelerating decision making and a company-wide drive to connect more with the customer. The key was that senior leaders at BT recognized what they could learn from EE, and then took concrete steps to encourage that learning to happen in a sustainable way.

But the best route to agile transformation is to change the way your organization thinks about and works with customers. At one multinational bank, leaders have seen the benefits of combining agile working with a 'client obsession'. After 18 months of intensive development in one large area of the bank's operations they have seen a 60 per cent reduction in turnaround time for application processing, a 43 per cent reduction in cases that require rework and a 123 per cent increase in new accounts being opened each month. In other areas, they are now seeing the performance of the entire business portfolio being reviewed monthly, based on a 90-day backlog. At this forum, decisions are made to start, stop or continue work, based on empirical performance data. This is effectively a combined showcase (review) and retrospective, but at the most senior levels of the business, including all functions, breaking down the traditional silos. They have moved away from 'managing progress against annual plans' (often obscuring not delivering to plan) towards short iterations, complete transparency of progress and issues, and the ability to change direction based on what has been learned. Through this new approach, leaders can now set clear priorities and deliver faster.

CASE STUDY Learning from successful start-ups

Successful start-ups are often admired for their agile ways of working. They are unencumbered by the bureaucracy of big corporates, which often look to them to see what they can learn. One organization that helps to bring big corporates and start-ups together is Collider, founded by Rose Lewis. Collider is an accelerator that brings start-ups and investors together, helps start-ups to bring innovation to corporates, and ultimately delivers investor returns.

'Most large organizations want to be more agile and have traditionally relied on internal innovation', says Rose. 'Working with start-ups is a way of bringing that agile mindset into the organization and tapping into innovative new ideas that might help power innovation internally. If you look at big tech companies like Google, they are constantly bringing the outside in. More big corporates are now coming around to that way of thinking.'

Rose observes that the big corporates that succeed most from working with start-ups have senior leadership buy-in. Leaders constantly reinforce the value of bringing the outside in and give people 'permission' to be agile, to learn new things, do things differently, and make mistakes along the way. Otherwise, organizations often revert to doing what they have always done.

---

4 Collaboration

Working collaboratively between teams, functions and organizations is becoming the new norm for those who are driving innovation in our digital world. Open banking is transforming how banks operate, for example, pushed along by FinTech innovation and customer demand. Research by PwC (2017) confirms this trend:

> More inclusive operating models, such as open innovation, design thinking, and co-creation with partners, customers, and suppliers, are now all embraced ahead of traditional R&D, and by a wide margin – almost twice as many companies favour these models.

Yet one of the most common issues I hear from both large and mid-size organizations is of silos getting in the way of innovation and agile working. A sector where this is affecting business performance is in retail, where the customer experience is now across several different points of contact. The JDA/PwC survey of retail CEOs (2017) found that most CEOs are focusing their investment on digital transformation, and that their priority in terms of making this investment work is removing the silos that get in the way of a seamless customer experience. 'Stripping down of silos is the key to profitability' stated the global survey of more than 300 retail and consumer goods chief executives. Yet the survey also found that 'only 18 per cent have eliminated operational silos to deliver seamless omnichannel shopping experiences'. This has a material impact on their expected growth in both revenue and profitability, so it is affecting the organizations' financial performance. Collaboration is not a nice-to-have any longer.

In the digital world the way teams interact has become a business-critical issue. As a leader, you can be the role model for this, both by ensuring your team is highly collaborative and by creating opportunities for collaboration with other teams and organizations where your skills are complementary or where you can create more value by working together. Sally Hopson, CEO at Sofology, calls out the importance of creating diverse teams in driving rapid success: 'Diversity is important in an agile world. You need diverse teams who can share different perspectives. Leaders who have worked across a range of functions also have a diverse understanding, which helps encourage deeper collaboration.' We will look more at how collaboration is at the heart of agile working in Chapter 8.

You can also increase levels of collaboration by introducing more agile working practices to support flexible working patterns. We have a changing demography in the workforce, with five generations present, changing retirement practices and an increasing need for 24/7 working to satisfy global working (Cannon, 2017). Research by the Agile Future Forum in the UK has identified that more agile working practices, for example, are already delivering value equivalent to between 3 and 13 per cent of workforce costs in employers adopting them effectively (Cannon, 2017).

The Covid-19 pandemic only accelerated this trend. Examples include sharing pools of labour to encourage more flexible project working to meet changing demand, and multi-skilling to enable people to move between teams in a more seamless way. We will explore more of these examples in Chapter 9. The rapid shift to virtual working when the Covid pandemic struck in early 2020 changed the way many organizations view flexible working for ever, but the challenge is now to see increasing levels of collaboration between virtual teams, with deliberate investment in inter-teamworking required to support this shift.

CASE STUDY   Agile transformation at Three (UK), 2013–2019

Launched in 2003 as the UK's first 3G-only network, Three's goal was to be the customer champion. Ten years on it was losing money and losing customer confidence. It needed to reset, to change course. Its leaders and colleagues agreed on an ambitious goal: to become the best-loved brand in the communications industry by both colleagues and customers.

Leaders at Three developed a core 'Being Three' philosophy of working in a collaborative, agile and customer-driven way. Connection was what Three was all about. It describes what it does as: 'Connecting people to people, people to things and things to things.' Underpinning the 'Being Three' philosophy were three core behaviours that the organization sought to embed in all aspects of work: collaboration, ruthless prioritization and empathy.

To drive collaboration, Three drew on agile methodology to establish shared ways of working. The concept of 'circles' was introduced – small agile teams made up of cross-functional capabilities, each with a circle coach. Team members signed up to shared goals and agreed how individual contributions could combine to achieve these goals.

Three invested in developing the leadership skills to support effective collaboration. Psychometric profiling helped leaders to understand their collaborative preferences, highlighting the factors that sometimes held them back (such as a desire for control) as well as areas of strength (such as a preference for inclusivity). Leaders were then coached to 'let go' and develop an increasingly collaborative style of leadership across the business. This investment in leadership development helped to create a significant behavioural shift, which Three leaders saw as fundamental in driving more collaborative teamworking.

Three saw ruthless prioritization, the second core behaviour, as fundamental to freeing up time to focus on the few things that could have the greatest impact. Leaders were encouraged to be bold and to stop or postpone non-essential activities, keeping people focused on top priorities.

The third core behaviour, empathy, helped leaders to create an environment of psychological safety where people were more likely to take risks, experiment, learn and improve. Through developing their emotional intelligence, leaders built higher quality relationships. They were encouraged to really listen to colleagues, to provide positive feedback and reassurance, and to involve others wherever possible. This helped to build trust and increase colleagues' confidence to try new things. The adoption of retrospective meetings, which focused more on learning rather than a pass/fail review of work, encouraged shared learning and helped to develop more of a learning culture.

Leaders at Three highlight some particular changes which helped the organization to become more agile. One was a shift away from individual functional plans to one overall view of activities across the business. Another was the introduction of a decision-making tool to clarify whose opinion and input was needed and, most importantly, who had overall accountability for each decision made. This clarity streamlined the decision-making process.

Being customer-driven was ultimately about Three's external customers. However, the organization's goal was to be the best-loved brand in the UK not only by external customers but also by internal colleagues. There was a fundamental belief that if colleagues loved Three, they would deliver amazing experiences to Three's customers.

There was an emphasis on doing the right thing for all employees through a focus on mental health and wellbeing, supported by benefits such as personal days and enhanced compassionate leave. Many shared stories of the positive difference these things made to their lives.

Three's eNPS (employee Net Promoter Score) grew from +14 to +30 during a period of significant transformation when the workforce was downsized by one third. Customer NPS improved persistently to +17 in 2019, among the highest of all UK mobile network operators (Three UK, 2019).

By working in a collaborative, agile and customer-driven way, Three saw some impressive results. Evaluation showed that colleagues felt more trusted and more able to try new things, make mistakes and move on – a fundamental shift in company culture.

Summary

Agile organizations are more able to adapt to the rapidly changing world around us, so it is helpful to reflect on what barriers are stopping you optimizing the agility in your own organization. There are four barriers that research suggests you should pay attention to: culture, clarity, customer closeness and collaboration. If you create a balance between having an appropriate administrative structure, a healthy adaptive approach to innovation, and an enabling culture that brings a united sense of purpose to the organization, you will be well on the way to building an agile business.

You may find it helpful to stop for a moment and assess where your own organization is currently relative to these barriers. If we rephrase them, we see how they enable an environment where agile working can flourish:

1 *Cultural* safety gives people confidence to act.
2 *Clarity* of vision, roles and expectations frees people to focus and deliver.
3 *Closeness* to the customer accelerates relevant innovation.
4 *Collaboration* and teamwork drive output and performance improvement.

Which is the biggest challenge for you? Where should you focus your attention first, to reduce the barrier and accelerate progress towards agility? Rank the barriers from 1 to 4, with 1 being the biggest challenge, and 4 the smallest. For number 1, think back through the content of this chapter related to this challenge and select one key insight you can implement in practice. In the next section we will explore more ways to remove these barriers and build agility in practice.

References

Aghina, W, De Smet, A and Weerda, K (2015) Agility: It rhymes with stability, *McKinsey Quarterly*, December

Bungay, S (2011) *The Art of Action*, Nicholas Brealey Publishing, Boston, MA

Cambridge English Dictionary (2020) Cambridge University Press, Cambridge

Cannon, F (2017) *The Agility Mindset*, Palgrave Macmillan, Basingstoke

Coveney, P (2003) Self-organization and complexity: A new age for theory, computation and experiment, paper presented at the Nobel symposium on self-organization: The quest for the origin and evolution of structure, Karolinska Institutet, Stockholm

Goran, J, LaBerge, L and Srinivasan, R (2017) Culture for a digital age, *McKinsey Quarterly*, July

Hayward, S (2015) Successful factors in the transition towards distributed leadership in large organisations, University of Manchester, Manchester

Hayward, S (2016) *Connected Leadership*, Financial Times Publishing, Pearson, London

JDA/PwC (2017) CEO Viewpoint 2017: The transformation of retail, JDA, now.jda.com/rs/366-TWM-779/images/PWC_Executive_Summary_Final_Digital.pdf (archived at https://perma.cc/BEB8-8X34)

Nadella, S (2017) *Hit Refresh*, William Collins, London

PwC (2017) *Innovation Benchmark Report*, PwC's Innovation Benchmark Report 2017, PwC

Ridderstrale, J and Nordstrom, K (2000) *Funky Business*, Pearson, London

Stacey, RD (1995) The science of complexity: An alternative perspective for strategic change processes, *Strategic Management Journal*, **16** (6)

Three UK (2019) www.threemediacentre.co.uk/content/three-uk-reports-h119-results/ (archived at https://perma.cc/99G3-FHNS)

Uhl-Bien, M and Marion, R (2001) Leadership in complex organizations, *The Leadership Quarterly*, **12** (4)

Uhl-Bien, M and Marion, R (2011) Complexity leadership theory, in *The Sage Handbook of Leadership*, eds A Bryman, D Collinson, K Grint, B Jackson and M Uhl-Bien, Sage, London

Uhl-Bien, M, Marion, R and McKelvey, B (2007) Complexity leadership theory: Shifting leadership from the industrial age to the knowledge era, *The Leadership Quarterly*, **18** (4)

PART TWO

Becoming an agile leader

CHAPTER FIVE

Safe to explore

Dialogue is about shared inquiry, a way of thinking and reflecting together. ISAACS (1999)

Introduction

The first quadrant of the Agile Leader wheel is entitled Explore (Figure 5.1). It is about looking in. Exploring and learning are at the heart of agile innovation and accelerated outputs. They are the source of the constant improvement, of breakthrough ideas, of diverse insight, that characterize agile when it is working well. When we explore we create new possibilities. And we learn best when we feel safe – secure to explore, not fearing consequences if we do not get it right first time. This chapter looks at how as leaders we can create a safe environment through empathy and dialogue and enable ourselves and others to maximize learning and consequent improvement.

Feeling safe and encouraging learning are both about being an enabler. If we recall the agile athletes in Chapter 1, we know that their ability to move quickly and easily is based on both their cognitive and physical attributes, how they read and respond to situations, as well as their physical ability to move in an agile way. They are learning constantly, managing themselves and their interactions with others in an effective way, building trust and being open to feedback.

FIGURE 5.1 The agile leader wheel

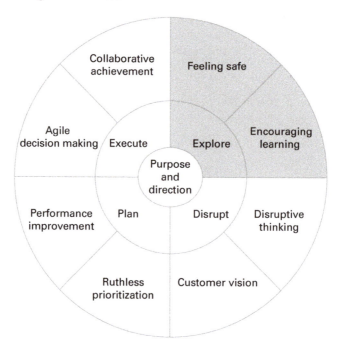

Some athletes operate solo, some in a team. As a leader you are almost always working in a team context. As I described in Chapter 2, you are in the leadership 'goldfish bowl', under constant scrutiny from others who interpret your behaviour as a set of cues about what you believe to be important. Their learning agility is underpinned by your empathy and your ability to create a safe environment. How you behave and how you react to stimuli like other people's mistakes will have a significant effect on how those around you feel, and therefore how willing they are to experiment, take risks and learn.

QUESTIONS TO ASK YOURSELF

In this chapter you may find it helpful to consider the following questions as you read:

- How do you react when challenged? Do you always make others feel safe?
- How do you react when people make mistakes?
- Do you create enough time to reflect and learn?

Feeling safe

Two Boeing 737 MAX planes crashed, killing 346 people within a year (*Newsweek*, 2019). In October 2018, Lion Air flight 610 crashed 12 minutes after take-off from Jakarta airport. Barely six months later Ethiopian Airlines flight 302 crashed in March 2019, six minutes after take-off from Addis Ababa airport (Associated Press, 2019). Both flights were at the time of impact configured to dive to restore air speed. The planes' automatic MCAS system thought the aircraft had stalled, and therefore placed them in a dive. The system was installed by Boeing only on MAX planes to compensate for the tendency of the plane to pitch upwards after Boeing installed larger engines to increase fuel efficiency (BBC, 2019). Unfortunately, Boeing had to move the engines further forward on the wing which altered the flight dynamics intended in the original design. To make matters worse, the FAA (the US regulator) allowed pilots to fly the MAX without additional training as it was deemed essentially the same aircraft. This helped to save retraining costs for airlines and therefore increase sales of the planes, but it did not prepare pilots for the altered flight dynamics.

As Amy Edmondson has commented in an article on the Boeing case (2019a), it sometimes takes a disaster to change a culture. She cites this as a 'textbook case of how the absence of psychological safety – the assurance that one can speak up, offer ideas, point out problems, or deliver bad news without fear of retribution – can lead to disastrous results.' The risks associated with the MCAS system were not addressed effectively within Boeing, which is perhaps unusual in an industry renowned for its obsession with safety. Edmondson describes how our human attention to interpersonal risk can cause us to prioritize immediate personal security (such as keeping my job) over vaguer 'probably-won't-even-happen' risks in the future.

The Boeing story is a sad reminder of how culture influences behaviour. If an organization's culture, which Rigby describes as 'behaviour at scale' (2020), supports speaking the truth to power, employees can feel safe in challenging managers to improve quality and passenger safety. If, however, the culture supports compliance and managers react badly when challenged, people will quickly learn to keep quiet, and to go with the flow. The perceived risk to personal security is too high.

Agile working is based on people working in teams with high degrees of autonomy, and on people experimenting and learning what customers really value. Neither will work if people are scared to speak out or ask awkward questions. As a leader you have a disproportionate influence on the culture of the organization in which you work. It is interesting to reflect on how you respond when asked a challenging question, or when your judgements are called into question. What behaviour do your colleagues see at that moment? Are you defensive and critical or do you welcome the challenge? The aggregation of these behaviours across all leaders in your organization on a day-by-day basis will influence the extent to which people feel safe to speak the truth, safe to fail, safe to learn.

In *The Fearless Organization* (2019b), Edmondson suggests three successful practices:

- **Time** – establish specific times and locations for team members to speak their minds together with you.
- **Frequency** – ensure these happen frequently, 'so the "ouch" is diluted' and people become used to a straightforward discussion.
- **Norms** – agree 'rules of engagement' with people and write them down so they become part of everyone's normal language.

These practices will help to build an environment where people feel safer to speak out, which is vital for agile working in practice. Additionally, as we read in Chapter 1, being authentic also helps to build trust in you as a leader, and to create an environment where people are drawn to trust each other more. This leads to a quality of dialogue that supports shared thinking, innovation and psychological wellbeing. There are four aspects of authenticity it is helpful to focus on (Walumbwa *et al*, 2008):

- Developing your self-awareness is a key starting point, as it increases your ability to manage your own responses to situations and avoid the moment of frustration or blame that makes others recoil and withdraw into a self-protective bubble.
- Secondly, having a 'strong moral compass' based on values such as honesty, caring and respect for others, means that other people can predict where you will be coming from in any given situation, and whether you can be relied upon to act in the best interests of the team, the customer and the organization, rather than in your own.
- Thirdly, how you process information will give others clues about whether you are able to take a dispassionate view, whether you value alternative perspectives, and therefore whether you will make balanced and well-informed decisions they can trust.

- And finally, how good are you at developing open and straightforward relationships with colleagues? The better you are at building such relationships with others the more they are likely to identify with you and feel they matter to you as a person. Recent research (AMBS, 2020) has highlighted the link between quality relationships between manager and team members and their performance in agile teams. We will explore this further in Chapter 8.

These four aspects of Authentic Leadership are a helpful checklist to reflect on. As a human being, how authentic would your colleagues say you are, and how might this affect how much they believe they can trust you and feel safe to learn and make mistakes under your leadership? If you recognize any of these aspects as being less strong within your leadership practice than the others, it is worth seeking feedback from colleagues. This will enable you to understand better how you come across in practice and how you need to change your beliefs and your behaviour to develop this aspect further. In my experience working with leaders across a range of sectors and levels, small changes can have disproportionately positive effects in terms of how others respond to you and trust you.

ENABLING OTHERS TO FEEL SAFE: LARRY PAGE, CO-FOUNDER, GOOGLE

In 2012, Google's Project Aristotle researched the behaviours of hundreds of teams across the organization to understand which factors most influenced performance. The results indicated that psychological safety – the ability to share ideas and challenge others in a safe environment – was critical to making a team work (Duhigg, 2016). Google co-founder and former CEO Larry Page encouraged employees to come up with new ideas whether or not they relate to Google's core business. In 2010 he set up Google X (now simply known as 'X') to encourage moon-shot thinking – an 'anything is possible' approach to creating innovative solutions. He also held weekly 'TGIF' open meetings where employees were encouraged to talk freely. Page has summed up his philosophy as, 'If you're not doing some things that are crazy, then you're doing the wrong things' (Levy, 2017).

Empathy

Empathy is your capacity to understand or feel what another person is experiencing from his or her point of view. As a leader, you must be able to place yourself in another's position and to act or respond in a way that demonstrates you care about them. This is relevant to agile leadership in two ways. First, it helps you to deeply understand your customers or end users and what problems you might be able to solve for them (which we will explore further in Chapter 6). The second is that it helps you to develop trust among your colleagues and team members, as other people can then have confidence that you will take their views and feelings into account in your decision making and behaviour towards them.

On the face of it, therefore, empathy is a good thing. It helps create an environment around you where people feel understood, safe to speak up and know that you have got their back. And this is right as far as your own teams are concerned. When your teams know you care and understand, they are likely to have more confidence in your support. Difficulties, however, emerge when you look beyond your teams.

Rutger Bregman, the Dutch historian, describes in *Humankind* (2020) how in 1978 a Russian psychologist, Dmitri Belyaev, published his research into silver foxes in Siberia. The foxes are bred for their pelts – they are aggressive and never tamed. He selected those that were the friendliest, the least aggressive, and bred them separately. Their hormones meant that they soon bred more friendly and docile fox cubs, which resisted the urge to become ferocious as they became adults. They had fewer stress hormones and more serotonin (the 'happy hormone') and oxytocin (the 'love hormone'). His theory was:

> that people are domesticated apes. That for thousands of years, the nicest humans had the most kids. That the evolution of our species, in short, was predicated on 'survival of the friendliest'.

The friendliest foxes turned out to be the brightest. Social learning is what separates us from the other primates. 'Human beings, it turns out, are ultra-social learning machines. We're born to learn, to bond and to play.' Our empathy fuels our learning, and our learning drives our success as a species.

But empathy, as Bregman describes, is a double-edged sword:

> We humans also have a dark side… [we] can also be shockingly cruel. Why?…
> The mechanism that makes us the kindest species also makes us the cruellest
> species on the planet…. People are social animals, but we have a fatal flaw: we
> feel more affinity for those who are most like us.

The hormone oxytocin was more prevalent in the Siberian foxes that became domesticated. It caused the foxes, like humans, to nurture relationships and love others. But in 2010 researchers at the University of Amsterdam found that 'the effects of oxytocin seem limited to one's own group'. Bergman notes that the hormone not only increases affection for friends, but it can also intensify aversion to strangers. 'It turns out oxytocin doesn't fuel universal fraternity. It powers feelings of "my people first".'

Showing a lot of empathy can be a powerful way to create a safer environment for teams to work in, an environment that encourages experimentation and learning from mistakes. However, the very safety and affinity that empathy fosters within the group can also turn into less cooperative behaviour towards those outside the group, whatever the group is. The impact of oxytocin can be to create barriers rather than to remove them, driven by the 'my people first' mindset, which will ultimately make organizations less productive. Empathy, as it turns out, creates silos as much as it creates unity.

It helps us as leaders to be aware of this effect of oxytocin on ourselves and our teams. We are drawn to be warm and loyal to our own, and therefore less warm and loyal to those outside our group, whether they are in other organizations or simply in other parts of our own organization. We need to encourage our people to go beyond this instinctive view and to intentionally reach out to people outside our group. (I will discuss collaboration further in Chapter 8.) Bregman describes humans as collections of chemicals, and as leaders we can therefore influence behaviour by activating the right hormones. A team is a collection of humans with personalities and feelings; it is also, in some ways, a chemistry set. If we evoke the more helpful hormones in our colleagues, we can influence behaviour to create a happier and more emotionally positive team climate.

One way to do this as leaders is through careful use of language. Social constructionism is the belief that we create the future at least in part through how we describe things, and the narrative we create as a society. I believe strongly in the power of words to change what we believe and therefore how we behave, and as leaders, parents, citizens, colleagues, we have the choice every day of what words we use, whether we are conscious or not of the effect they have on those around us. If a colleague makes a mistake, we can either criticize them or ask them to reflect on what they can learn from the experience so they can improve in the future. If our team needs to learn a new skill such as feedback in the moment, we can introduce this by saying 'we don't give each other enough feedback' or we can say 'how can we increase the level of feedback we give each other?' We can replace 'we can't...' with 'we can't yet...' when faced with significant challenges. We can follow Rousseau and liberate people's energy, commitment and compassion for others. Or we can follow Hobbes and reinforce hierarchy, deference and cynicism (Bregman, 2020). By choosing to create a liberating environment through using language consistent with this, we encourage psychological safety in others to learn, to challenge and to disrupt the status quo. Without such an environment, empowerment is difficult and collaboration (which is built on trust and mutual respect) will be more challenging to embed as the norm.

Quality relationships

If you have developed high levels of empathy with your team and in the wider organization, you are likely to have some high-quality relationships with those around you. These relationships are the lifeblood of being an agile leader, as they enable you to create a connected organization that can adapt and move in a coherent way depending on the changing environment. The agile organization is like an organism that can move and change direction easily, in line with significant changes in the surrounding ecosystem. These changes are likely to be driven by disruptive technology or events like pandemics or trade wars. Without robust relationships, cracks are likely when rapid and joined-up movement is needed. So, how do you build these relationships that bond the organization together in this flexible, intelligent way?

Much research over the last 25 years (Goleman, 1995; Newman and Purse, 2011) has shown how emotional intelligence is a key indicator of a leader's ability to develop and maintain high-quality relationships. You may have explored your emotional intelligence in assessments or development programmes, or you may be new to the topic. Either way, it is helpful to consider how confident you feel in answering the following questions, honestly, to yourself:

- Do you understand your emotions and how you react to various stimuli?
- Can you manage your emotions when they are strong? Can you remain calm when emotionally charged inside?
- Do you understand how you interact with others, how you come across to them?
- Can you manage how you interact with others to the benefit of the relationship between you?
- Are you optimistic, seeking to find the positive in others and to resolve issues effectively?

It is worth reflecting on which questions you are more able to answer with a resounding 'yes', and which perhaps make you feel a little less certain of yourself.

There are several well-researched profiling tools you can use to measure your emotional intelligence, available typically through an occupational psychologist. One that is particularly relevant when we are looking at leadership in an organizational context is the Emotional Capital Report (Newman and Purse, 2011). There is a range of capabilities in emotional intelligence, and typically managers are stronger on some than others. I should note that there is an ongoing debate about the psychological validity of emotional intelligence as a discrete construct, versus personality, which is better established via academic research. Whether we think of our ability to understand our own emotions and relate well to others as driven by emotional intelligence or by our personality, there are three lessons you can take from this area of discussion:

1 Play to your strengths, building on where you have already developed good self-awareness or relationship skills. It is important, however, not to overdo strengths as these can derail performance, such as when drive becomes ruthless ambition, or attention to detail becomes micro-management.
2 Develop skills in areas of relative weakness, as these may be holding you back in creating high-quality relationships. You may, for example, be low on empathy, so you sometimes come across as aloof and fail to recognize that other people's emotions are important. If this were the case, it would be worth seeking out how others feel about particular decisions so you can appreciate better their perspective.
3 Build a team around you with a mix of capabilities. It is helpful if you explicitly welcome the differences and recognize how you are complementary to each other. For example, having colleagues on your team who are highly optimistic (if this is not one of your strengths) will help keep you looking forward as a team, seeking solutions rather than slowing down when problems arise.

With one board team with which I have worked, the chair was high on self-confidence and self-reliance but low on empathy and relationship skills. He drove organizational performance and tended to lead from the front. He was not, however, good at taking everyone with him. Fortunately, on the board were two colleagues who were strong on empathy and were often the people

I would ask to describe for their colleagues what impact the decisions the team took might have on other people in the business. Once the CEO realized how asking this question was helping rather than hindering progress, he was more receptive to it being discussed by the whole team. The empathetic colleagues felt more valued, the team's performance improved, and they engaged the wider business on a major transformation programme more effectively. As the CEO used this insight in his discussions with other people in the business, checking in with others about how they felt about things, his credibility and reputation grew significantly.

Understanding our emotional intelligence can therefore enable us to build stronger relationships and deeper trust, both with our immediate teams and with the wider organization. This in turn creates a climate of safety in which team members feel able to take risks and learn.

Encouraging learning

Research at Columbia University suggests that 'learning agility is a mindset and corresponding collection of practices that allow leaders to continually develop, grow, and utilize new strategies that will equip them for the increasingly complex problems they face in their organizations' (Burke *et al*, 2016). The quicker and more effectively we learn from experiences, the more agile we can be as the circumstances around us change. So, we need to create time and space to reflect, to make sense of what is happening to us and what we are experiencing, and to gain insight so we can improve our performance going forward. Encouraging learning is a key leader responsibility.

Learning agility was described by Lombardo and Eichinger (2000) as 'the ability and willingness to learn from experience and subsequently apply those lessons to perform successfully in new or first-time situations'. Their research focused on leaders who experienced sustained success and found that they tended to have more diverse experience than those leaders who derailed. The most successful executives were often those that demonstrated the most determined approach to learning from their experiences and putting it into practice thereafter.

In further research into the role of learning in executive career success, there is a growing recognition that 'today's organizational leaders must develop learning agility as a core capability, so they can respond effectively to the uncertainty and ambiguity of the modern marketplace' (Yukl and

Mahsud, 2010). The researchers define learning agility as 'the ability and willingness to learn from experience and subsequently apply those lessons to perform successfully in new or first-time situations' (Dai *et al*, 2013). If we as leaders can embrace learning agility, it is not only helpful in creating a more agile climate, but also good for our careers.

Homo sapiens is by nature wired to learn socially, according to Bregman (2020). Our capacity to learn is why we survived the last Ice Age (115,000 to 15,000 years ago) and the Neanderthals died out. We copied, we learned, we communicated with each other, whereas the Neanderthals were brighter but less social. 'We were slower, but better connected' and survived better the adverse weather because of our deeply engrained social learning capacity. 'Hunter gatherers the world over... believed that everything is connected' continues Bregman. 'Human beings crave togetherness and interaction. Our distant ancestors knew the importance of the collective and rarely idolized individuals.'

Our relationships fuel our learning which in turn fuels our agility. Being agile is most useful as a leader and for organizations in conditions where the old ways will not work, where the rules have changed and where survival and success depend on adapting quickly. This could not be more relevant in this post-Covid-19 world. Learning agility encompasses not only our curiosity and our ability to make sense of our experience, but also to convert that insight into helpful actions that increase our performance. As leaders we need to enable our teams to put learning into action with conviction. I will explore this further in Chapter 8.

So, how can you increase your learning? One way is to seek more opportunities for learning from experience, so that you are exposed to ideas and ways of working beyond what is normal in your current role. Taking non-executive roles is a common way to do this, especially in organizations that operate in different sectors, or with different customers. But you can also find new experiences in areas of your own organization where you have not previously worked. And reading about what is happening in other sectors or geographies to your own can give you helpful insight.

Another way is to create space and time for making sense of this learning, so you can relate it to your own and your organization's performance. Seeing new parallels, for example, between external events and internal challenges is a key aspect of learning agility. This can be through reflection, with time to make notes or create a presentation to share with others. It can be through discussion with colleagues or a partner or a coach, as talking through an experience helps make sense of it in your own mind. You can also seek more feedback, getting others to describe to you what you are doing and what effect it has on them. I will explore feedback further in Chapter 7.

One thing that is clear from my experience of working with senior executives for many years is that the failure to learn from experience can be the cause of sometimes rapid falls from grace. The chief executive of a UK government agency, for example, was suspended and then dismissed from his role after he had failed to respond effectively to a new chair of the board, whose approach was unconventional and led to accusations of malpractice. Rumours grew but the chief executive believed that the checks and balances that had served him and the agency well for several years could continue to act as a suitable governance structure, when in fact they were found to be woefully inadequate. The chair was finally forced to resign, which should have allowed the chief executive to re-establish his position of authority, but his personal reputation had been too badly damaged. He had not adapted quickly enough to the chair's overbearing style, and as a result he lost his job. Although the primary cause of the problems lay elsewhere, his inability to learn quickly and adapt on behalf of the agency was seen as unacceptable by key stakeholders.

ENCOURAGING LEARNING: MARY BARRA, CHAIRMAN AND CEO, GENERAL MOTORS

Mary Barra became chairman and CEO of General Motors (GM) in 2014. During her first year in the role, GM issued safety recalls involving over 30 million cars. The majority related to faulty ignition switches which had been linked to at least 97 deaths. It emerged that GM had known about the ignition problem for more than a decade (France-Presse, 2015). Barra apologized publicly, openly and frequently. Not only did she survive the crisis, she used it as an opportunity to free GM from its famously bureaucratic and siloed ways of working. She encouraged everyone across the business to learn from previous mistakes and to voice their concerns at any time. She pledged to keep the incident at the forefront of operational thinking, simplifying the company's complex systems and processes to promote shared responsibility and accountability. By learning from the crisis and placing it at the heart of GM's consciousness, Barra dismantled the decades-old culture that stifled employee voices and built a culture of openness.

Mental agility

A key aspect of learning is mental agility. People with high mental agility are described as 'attracted to newness and complexity and as mentally quick. They like to delve deeply into problems and search for meaning… they are also good at simplifying.' They tend to be good at presenting their views to others and can explain their thinking and that of others. People with low mental agility are described as 'not being comfortable with ambiguity, complexity or being mentally quick. They may rely on conventional wisdom. They may have trouble explaining how they arrived at a position' (Lombardo and Eichinger, 2000). We cannot change our IQ, but we can learn new habits that help us develop these attributes of delving deeper into problems, making sense of what is going on around us, and simplifying things. In the VUCA world in which we operate in this digital age, we can build stronger mental agility through using techniques such as practising mindfulness, which helps us create mental space and time.

Delving deeper needs time, and the CEO study above highlighted that the most successful tend to spend significantly more time (up to 50 per cent) on long-term thinking than those that are less successful (less than 30 per cent). They think more and seek to make sense of what the future holds for their organization. They consult advisers and experts more. They pause when challenges are serious, giving themselves time to respond better. Like top athletes, they seem to have more time under pressure. They are learning in the moment. You can do the same, if you are willing to commit time to this, and reject the tyranny of the diary that seems to afflict many senior managers I meet.

Building trust

What is trust? It is about confidence. If we trust someone, we are likely to have confidence in their competence (that they can do what they say), their conduct (that they do what they say they will do) and their communications (that they can be relied on to protect your reputation and keep confidences) (Covey, 2006; Reina and Reina, 2010). Trust is a belief in someone's integrity, that they will act fairly and warmly, with a balanced view of the situation they are in – essentially, that you are safe in their hands. This leads to confidence in others to act, to jump off a cliff believing that the person holding the rope can and will hold on.

Why is this so important? Because agility needs people to experiment, to learn, to move quickly without caution, and to change when it is required.

Building high levels of trust helps people to feel included and safe to experiment and take risks. It does not appear by chance. It takes effort and time to give people the confidence to trust that even when the results of their actions are seriously problematic, you will act fairly and with confidence in their motivation to do the right thing.

Throughout 2020, the Covid-19 crisis meant we were often working with people virtually that we may never have met in person. Building trust and a sense of inclusion in a virtual world can be particularly challenging and yet even more important. Research during the crisis in 2020 suggested 'that 77 per cent of leaders strongly agree that an agile mindset is very important right now, while 71 per cent recognize the criticality of an inclusive mindset' (GP Strategies, 2020).

A helpful starting point if you sense that you need to increase trust levels in you as a leader, or in your leadership team, is to adopt an agile and inclusive mindset, and to give more trust. You can start by ensuring you have a diverse team around you, in which you and your colleagues will benefit from a wide range of views and diverse insight. Listening to the different voices will help you to learn, to think differently, to gain a fresh perspective on old problems.

In some of the larger organizations I see in my work, the levels of trust in the organization's leadership are much lower than needed. Their engagement survey results indicate that people may be engaged with their colleagues and their jobs, but they do not trust the senior leaders to be fair or even competent. This is a difficult place from which to build a more agile organization. You can start by trusting others more, creating a positive cycle of trust improvement, increasing other people's confidence to act boldly, to risk failure, to experiment and to learn. As they learn they become more capable, and their ability to act boldly and effectively improves. How often have we heard people who have achieved unexpected success describing the person who gave them a break, who had confidence in them and gave them the opportunity to have a go? That is a great reputation to have, to be the leader who gave someone the chance to succeed, so let us create these opportunities as often as we can to give others the opportunity to shine.

Being trustworthy is the flip side of this coin, as the more people trust you, the more likely they are to take a risk and rely on your support. For them to trust you, you need to be competent, behave consistently and communicate with integrity always. You need to be authentic. For me to trust you I need to be confident that you will react to situations in a predictable and fair way. If I cannot predict your reaction, I will not take the risk. Like the person jumping off the cliff, if I am not sure whether you can hold me, whether you will bother, and whether you can be relied on to describe the event afterwards in a way that respects me, then I won't jump. I become static, not agile.

Another key aspect of being trustworthy is having a consistent story, which helps others to understand where you are coming from, where you want to go, why it's a good thing and what you think is important in moving in that direction. Professor Dame Nancy Rothwell, President and Vice Chancellor of the University of Manchester, is described by colleagues as being effective at building trust through having a consistent story. 'We're facing unprecedented external changes', she says, 'so agility is largely about our ability to respond to these changes, but it's also about the ability to respond to what we believe needs to change, irrespective of those external factors.' The university, which dates back to 1824, with 25 Nobel Prize winners among its current and former staff and students, is the largest single-site university in the UK, with the biggest student community at nearly 40,000 students from around the world, and 12,000 employees. This historic institution is going through a transformation of IT systems, a £1 billion estate upgrade, a shift in ambition and a redevelopment of the student experience. Covid disruption has increased the strains in the university as it seeks to provide a high-quality education to students from around the world. Nancy recognizes that what is needed through this period of major change and external challenge is 'very strong leadership in terms of a very good narrative about delivering what could be the benefits, what are the opportunities, what can we achieve through this'. It is the narrative that holds people's confidence that there is a clear direction and purpose to the change and reinforces their confidence and trust in the future.

Experimentation

If you want to drive innovation and improvement across the whole customer experience, you need to create the climate where learning is valued more than avoiding mistakes. To become more agile you need to increase the level of experimentation that is going on across the organization. The quantum is more important than the absolute quality at this stage, as you want people to be seeking new ways to add value and taking small risks to find out if they work. It is helpful to remember the four values of agile in the original Manifesto: 'people over processes and tools, prototypes over documentation, responding to change over following a plan, and customer collaboration over rigid contracts' (Highsmith, 2001). This summarizes the need to let people explore, experiment, be flexible and work with customers to find out what works and what does not.

LEARNING FAST

I think the world's getting faster, not slower. Things that previously would have taken years and months, we do in weeks and days. I think the real success of a business is actually making decisions quickly. It doesn't matter if those decisions are sometimes wrong if you can learn really fast. To be agile you need to have a learning culture. Make a decision, learn, adapt. You learn as much from your mistakes as you do from your successes. We've got to get beyond organizations thinking they've got to get it all right. What's more important is that you learn and you learn fast.

Peter Pritchard, Group CEO, Pets at Home

Digital technologies now make prototyping cheaper and often easier. This creates opportunities for you to test and innovate more frequently in line with what customers need and what they value (which is changing increasingly rapidly). You can develop ideas quickly into working products or services, test them with users, refine or redevelop through rapid iteration, and release minimum viable products (MVPs) quickly so that you can find out what customers will buy and what they will not, and adjust accordingly. Technology is also making changes to the customer experience quicker to prototype and refine, allowing you to test and learn without investing heavily in untested technology or processes.

Key to all of this is having a culture that supports people in taking intelligent risks, learning, and applying that learning in the next iteration. Teams of mixed capabilities are well placed to drive innovation based on their diverse experience and training, helping to refine the outcomes through open dialogue and shared decision making. A key concept in agile working is 'test and learn', where people feeling safe is a prerequisite if they are to take the risk of failing, which is implicit in the idea of experimenting. In *Bounce Back*, Susan Kahn states 'there can be a lot of pressure to perform well at work and keep up appearances. Therefore, it can be risky to admit that you made a mistake' (Kahn, 2019). Exploring failures is important for professional and personal development. The concept of 'failing fast' is 'used in system design and has been adopted by entrepreneurs but it's time to bring the practice into all types and areas of work'. As we saw in Chapter 2, Sir James Dyson famously said that it took '5,000 failures before I invented the cyclone' that led to the vacuum cleaner that launched his innovative business (Dyson, 2010). He personifies how resilience and acceptance of failure are necessary parts of innovation and progress.

Toyota has for decades been an exemplar of experimentation and continuous improvement. Its people test hypotheses and learn what happens – whether each one is a success or a failure. By encouraging people to experiment, Toyota 'moves out of its comfort zone and into uncharted territory' (Takeuchi *et al*, 2008). People at Toyota 'think deeply but take small steps – and never give up'. In developing the Prius hybrid car in the 1990s, for example, the G21 team were set what seemed to be deeply unreasonable targets to deliver a 100 per cent improvement in fuel efficiency. They had little choice but to experiment with a hybrid technology that one of the company's laboratories was developing. Progress was difficult, with engine and battery failures along the way, but the team persevered and Toyota was able to launch the hybrid concept car at the 1995 Tokyo Motor Show. One of the most interesting aspects of Toyota's success is its emphasis on open communication as a core value and how it has led to a culture that is remarkably tolerant of failure. Takeuchi *et al* (2008) highlight how Toyota encourages people to be 'forthcoming about the mistakes they make or the problems they face'.

Business functions have a big role to play in increasing the level of experimentation across the organization. Finance, for example, can see its role as one of risk control or risk encouragement. In the former case they are there to minimize spend to drive short-term profitability. In the latter case, they are there to invest in experiments that may secure the future success of the enterprise. It is a completely different mindset. Clearly, there is a need for financial controls to be in place to safeguard funds and manage cash flow. However, if you have a CFO who seeks control more than anything else, you will struggle to develop a culture in which experimentation and therefore innovation flourishes.

The same principle applies to Human Resources – if they prioritize whether people fit and the perpetuation of existing ways of working in hiring and promotion decisions, they are likely not to shortlist the entrepreneurial person who looks for a better way to do things. They will exclude the maverick who might look at the customer journey differently or see new market opportunities for the business. This is an important conversation for the C-suite team to have on a regular basis, so they can enable their teams to align with the drive towards greater agility, innovation, and step changes in performance across the organization.

CASE STUDY   Learning agility at DLA Piper

DLA Piper is a multinational law firm with offices in more than 40 countries. Many factors are driving change in the global legal sector. The market has been disrupted by innovative start-ups as well as by established professional firms moving into the legal sector.

'For DLA Piper, this has highlighted the need to be agile, scanning the environment constantly and actually adapting our service and offerings, and doing things that are fairly non-traditional for a law firm', says Drew Moss, head of leadership development at the firm.

One of DLA Piper's strategic pillars is radical change. 'It is a mindset we are trying to instil into people, that radical change is important. We also have a focus on design thinking,' says Drew. This focus on design thinking involves DLA Piper people challenging assumptions, finding new ways to address challenges, and focusing on the changing needs of clients.

This is quite different for a law firm. The design thinking process involves a change council that comprises people from different levels and locations across the firm, and with regular client input. It comes together frequently using design thinking principles to identify new ideas and opportunities, and there have been some real successes including new products and services for clients.

Cultural change and leadership development

'Part of the change in culture is an emphasis on leadership and leadership development. We're thinking about what leadership means now and in the future, so we designed a leadership framework that brings that kind of thinking to life and are developing leaders at all levels, from CEO and executive through to people just starting their journey at DLA Piper.'

The focus of the development is around the shift in mindset required to lead in a rapidly changing global context, focused more on innovation, growth and change. Drew goes on: 'DLA has created an environment where people can feel safe to experiment and learn. Ideas and experimentation are encouraged. There is a recognition that we need to be more agile and open to innovation.'

Record results speak for themselves

In mid-2020 DLA Piper announced it had pulled off a fifth consecutive year of profit growth for its International LLP while breaking the £2 billion barrier for global turnover and exceeding £1 million in profit per equity partner. The investment in leadership and a culture of safety to learn supports growth based on increasing levels of client satisfaction.

Summary

Our first responsibility as agile leaders is to create a safe environment where our people can feel confident to experiment and learn. We do this by showing empathy, building trust, and encouraging intelligent risk, so our teams can fail if necessary on their road to breakthrough success without fearing the consequences. This culture of safety underpins the other characteristics of agile leadership, and without it, agile working is unlikely to succeed.

References

AMBS (2020) Agile Team Research, Alliance Manchester Business School and Cirrus, Manchester

Associated Press (2019) www.worldpressphoto.org/collection/photo/2020/39610/1/Mulugeta-Ayene-SOY-nominee (archived at https://perma.cc/MWR4-AV8G)

BBC (2019) www.bbc.com/news/business-50177788 (archived at https://perma.cc/D7G3-VGGP)

Bregman, R (2020) *Humankind: A hopeful history*, Bloomsbury Publishing, London

Burke, W, Roloff, K and Mitchinson, A (2016) *Learning Agility: A new model and measure*, Teachers College, Columbia University, New York

Covey, S (2006) *The Speed of Trust*, Simon & Schuster, New York

Dai, G, De Meuse, K and Tang, K (2013) The role of learning agility in executive career success: The results of two field studies, *Journal of Managerial Issues*, Summer 2013, 25 (2), Pittsburg State University

Duhigg, C (2016) What Google learned from its quest to build the perfect team, *The New York Times*, 25 February 2016

Dyson, J (2010) James Dyson on Failure, Official Dyson video, www.youtube.com/watch?v=P5eIyRVpwmc&feature=youtu.be (archived at https://perma.cc/K7QF-GVQB)

Edmondson, A (2019a) Boeing and the importance of encouraging employees to speak up, *Harvard Business Review*, 1 May

Edmondson, A (2019b) *The Fearless Organization: Creating psychological safety in the workplace for learning, innovation and growth*, John Wiley, New Jersey

France-Presse, A (2015) Death toll in GM's faulty ignition-switch hits 97, *Industry Week,* www.industryweek.com/operations/safety/article/21965106/death-toll-in-gms-faulty-ignitionswitch-hits-97 (archived at https://perma.cc/8QDC-3EQP)

Goleman, D (1995) *Emotional Intelligence*, Bantam Books, New York

GP Strategies (2020) Business as usual: rewriting the rules of leadership, Columbia, MD, www.gpstrategics.com/wp-content/uploads/2020/09/GP-Strategics-Business-as-Unusual-Report2.pdf (archived at https://perma.cc/F2JB-USRR)

Highsmith, J (2001) *History: The Agile Manifesto*, agilemanifesto.org/history.html (archived at https://perma.cc/JT6Y-4PEU)

Isaacs, W (1999) *Dialogue and the Art of Thinking Together*, Random House, New York

Kahn, S (2019) *Bounce Back: How to fail fast and be resilient at work*, Kogan Page, London

Levy, S (2017) Google's Larry Page on why moon shots matter, *Wired,* www.wired.com/2013/01/ff-qa-larry-page/ (archived at https://perma.cc/X33C-JCH9)

Lombardo, M and Eichinger, R (2000) High potentials as high learners, *Human Resource Management,* **39**

Newman, M and Purse, J (2011) *Emotional Capital Report,* RocheMartin, Melbourne

Newsweek (2019) www.newsweek.com/southwest-pilots-sue-boeing-deliberately-misleading-airline-about-737-max-1463721 (archived at https://perma.cc/VGN6-3DD3)

Reina, D and Reina, M (2010) *Rebuilding Trust in the Workplace*, Berrett-Koehler, San Francisco, CA

Rigby, D, Elk, S and Berez, S (2020) *Doing Agile Right: Transformation without chaos*, Bain & Company, Inc, MA

Takeuchi, H, Osono, E and Shimizu, N (2008) The contradictions that drive Toyota's success, *Harvard Business Review*, June

Walumbwa, F, Avolio, B, Gardner, W, Wernsing, T and Peterson, S (2008) Authentic leadership: Development and validation of a theory-based measure, Management Department Faculty Publications, Paper 24, University of Nebraska, Lincoln, NE

Yukl, G and Mahsud, R (2010) Why flexible and adaptive leadership is essential, *Consulting Psychology Journal: Practice and Research,* **62**

CHAPTER SIX

Disrupt and innovate

Life's too short to build something nobody wants. MAURYA (2012)

Introduction

In this chapter we look at the Disruptive Thinking and Customer Vision characteristics of agile leaders. They form the second quadrant of the Agile Leader wheel – Disrupt – and are essentially about looking out (Figure 6.1). They also go together because they are two aspects of agile leadership that are particularly focused on innovation – innovation that represents a breakthrough in thinking and design, which adds tangible value to customers in ways they had often not anticipated.

They also go together because they can be particularly hard to achieve in large well-established organizations which have deep legacies of culture, systems, contracts and ways of working. The risk-averse culture we discussed in Chapter 4 is often reinforced by these legacies, so shifting large organizations to be more disruptive and focused on customer value can be more difficult. It typically requires more energy, persistence, and a wider coalition of support across the organization than in smaller or more digitally native ones.

The Covid-19 pandemic accelerated digital change across all aspects of life, forcing citizens, organizations and governments to adopt technology at a speed it was difficult to anticipate before it happened. This level of digital

FIGURE 6.1 The agile leader wheel

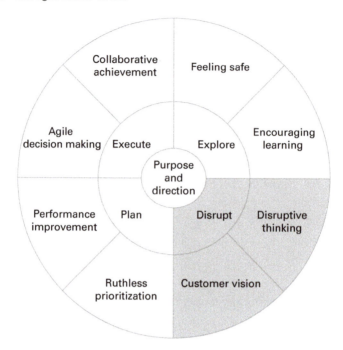

disruption has changed the rules in many sectors such as banking, retail and health. Our response as leaders will determine our future success.

QUESTIONS TO ASK YOURSELF

In this chapter you may find it helpful to consider the following questions as you read:

- How open are you to ideas that do not fit with your current views?
- How much is your customer in the forefront of your thinking day to day?
- What has been your most innovative achievement during the last few years?

Disruptive thinking

During the pandemic outbreak we saw both the most agile responses to disruption and the most conservative denials of change. Hospitals created

Covid-19 wards almost overnight and companies switched online while some politicians hesitated or even denied the potential threat of the virus. Underlying this contradiction are two human traits: our flexibility and willingness to adapt to changing circumstances on the one hand and our innate conservatism and desire to maintain the status quo on the other.

As leaders we are likely to experience both traits. Our job, however, is often to embrace our willingness to adapt, to think the unthinkable, and to supress our human desire to keep things as they are. We need to create an environment in which our teams welcome disruptive changes from outside and explore how to use them to achieve better innovation inside. We want teams which are open to the opportunities created by technology and other megatrends (such as pandemics, climate change and political instability) to improve performance and customer value. We need our teams to ask 'why?' or 'why not?' and to challenge the assumptions on which we operate.

This requires leaders to be both role models and supporters, asking the difficult questions and responding enthusiastically when others do the same. It is easy to write, more challenging in practice, in my experience. As agile leaders we need to keep an open mind, seeking the insight that will make the new product work, or the idea that reduces the time to process a customer interaction by a factor of 10. Or 100. We also need to be the cheerleaders for others who do the same.

Your efforts to accelerate change by disrupting 'group think' are likely to be more effective within your organization if you work closely with others. Challenging the status quo and questioning accepted wisdom can be seen by others as a threat, especially in large organizations. Individual action is rarely optimal, and I will discuss this more in Chapter 8. You can accelerate disruption and change more effectively if you create a community of people across the organization who share your intention and work together to drive fresh thinking and embrace the need for intelligent risk as a part of that.

Many organizations create an 'agile transformation' to help focus on changing old ways of working, and this can be helpful in the areas where the transformation effort and digital investment is focused. The opposite can be true, however, elsewhere in the organization, where the status quo is still accepted and the transformation agenda risks creating an 'over there' perception for those not involved. I see many organizations where there are islands of agile and the rest of the organization is watching on – the risk is a two-speed organization, with different ways of working and expectations of speed and iterative adjustment to plans between 'the agile' and 'the rest'. I would encourage a much wider adoption of agile leadership and ways of working across the whole organization, so that the expectations of speed and change are the same, but in some areas the extent of change is deeper.

DISRUPTIVE THINKING: JEFF BEZOS, FOUNDER AND EXECUTIVE CHAIR, AMAZON

Jeff Bezos is frequently cited as one of the world's most disruptive leaders. He believes that one of Amazon's greatest cultural strengths is accepting the fact that 'if you're going to invent, you're going to disrupt' (Levy, 2013). As Amazon's founder and Executive Chair, he has driven disruption across many industries including bricks-and-mortar retailing, grocery delivery, streaming services and logistics. Crucially, Bezos also believes in disrupting his own business. Amazon is focused on simplifying things for customers and eliminating operational defects. Bezos encourages employees to question everything and is renowned for sending emails to executives that simply read '?' (Bort, 2018).

Disruptive thinking is about being curious and asking your teams to be radical, to take a fresh perspective (not closing down ideas that challenge the status quo). It is radical by definition, because we are seeking to 'cause disruption' and to encourage 'innovative or groundbreaking' changes to how we do things (*Oxford English Dictionary*, 2012). In a global survey by Fujitsu in 2018 two employee types were identified as key to future success: Innovators (53.8 per cent) and Collaborators (49.0 per cent). As leaders we need to enable our people to be more 'creative, finding new ways of working and developing new products and services' and to 'work well with others in a team environment' (Fujitsu, 2018).

This does not mean that agile leaders are seeking change for its own sake. In operational environments, stability and scale are important to the economics of the organization and to ensure customers get quality products and services at a competitive price. Yet even in these parts of the organization, there is a constant opportunity to improve, to reduce time, to improve quality, to eradicate waste. Disruption may need to be within carefully considered parameters to enable the organization to function efficiently, but to assume stability means stasis is a key mistake, and the lean movement over many years has demonstrated the value of continuous improvement in such environments. In an article entitled 'Lean management or agile?', Raedemaecker *et al* (2020) suggest that:

both systems have been successful across a range of environments, and both share a similar set of foundational objectives: to deliver value efficiently for a customer; discover better ways of working to continuously learn and improve; transparently connect strategy and goals to give teams meaningful purpose; and enable people to contribute and lead to their fullest potential.

Both lean management and agile emphasize teams looking for disruptive opportunities in their work, so that innovation and improvement can be channelled effectively in practice.

Pace: from slow to fast

Disruption to demand during the Covid-19 pandemic caused widespread difficulties for many organizations where customers had either disappeared or changed their buying patterns significantly. Disruption to supply also caused major challenges, with factories closing and distribution channels ceasing to operate smoothly. Both types of disruption often forced organizations and their leaders to change gear from slow to fast, sometimes in a matter of days or even hours. Adapt quickly or die was the only choice for many organizations around the world.

Those that responded faster to the disruption tended to be ahead when the initial crisis passed, and opportunities emerged. A study of organizations emerging from the initial pandemic in September 2020 revealed 'the need to react more quickly to market changes as the reason that organizations have made changes during the pandemic' (De Smet *et al*, 2020). Responding more quickly than competitors to the disruption, according to the research, drove stronger subsequent performance in terms of growth, profitability and operational resilience.

Working from home had a dramatic impact on people's working lives during the Covid-19 pandemic. The switch to virtual working happened almost overnight for those organizations that had the infrastructure set up or those that had no choice, and it was a powerful example of the way organizations were able to achieve amazing feats of agility in a remarkably short time (Hayward, 2020). But for many leaders the shift to virtual working created issues of trust, connection and team coordination. Social contact suffered as many people became isolated, only connected by technology, which led, I believe, to a more transactional style of interaction between people. Tasks continued to get done through Zoom or Teams, but the quality of social interaction between people was reduced as there was less opportunity for informal chat and personal exchange.

How widespread did working from home become? In June 2020 research from Stanford University indicated 42 per cent of the US labour force was working from home full-time. Before Covid-19 this was about 7 per cent (World Economic Forum, 2020). 'Almost twice as many employees are working from home as at work', and this working from home group 'now accounts for more than two-thirds of US economic activity' (Bloom, 2020). The second wave of infection later in 2020 pushed people in many countries back into home working after a brief respite in the middle months of the year. The psychological damage of this return to isolation will take years to repair.

The switch to working from home demonstrates the incredible speed with which changes of seismic economic importance happened, as long-held beliefs and assumptions in many organizations were swept away. The bureaucratic, cautious, risk-averse approach to flexible working, which had been typical in many companies I have spoken to in recent years, disappeared for most. The hierarchical resistance from many managers to changing working patterns, with less in-person monitoring and control, had been overwhelmed by the Covid-19 reality. This has created a new set of demands on many leaders and managers in organizations, where the stability of office routines, reporting and review has been replaced by the more democratic Zoom or Teams screen where each individual is just one more video box, working under their own control.

The challenge therefore is for leaders at all levels in organizations to embrace this new pace, to shift gear in the way they make decisions, to enable their teams and businesses to make the most of the change in beliefs and to continue to accelerate rather than trying to slow down. This requires a new mindset, an agile leader mindset, which embraces disruption, and which seeks ways to accelerate the velocity of team effectiveness (Hayward, 2018). It needs leaders to challenge slow decision making, and to encourage intelligent risk taking in their teams, asking 'how quickly can we do it well?', rather than focusing on the risks and taking the safe route while competitors speed past.

Challenge and ideation

One of the skills of an agile leader is to create an environment where challenge is welcomed, and ideas are developed through dialogue. The more leaders encourage people to challenge everything, the more likely they are to enable real innovation and breakthroughs in customer value. This doesn't happen by accident – it needs leaders to give others the confidence to think the unthinkable, to create in meetings a feeling of security and involvement, so people are encouraged to ask awkward questions and think differently. Clearly this needs people to feel really safe, as we discussed in the previous chapter. It also needs leaders who are comfortable with less control of the agenda, willing to risk their own ideas being challenged.

One of the best leadership teams at this type of discussion that I have come across was the executive team of a major telecoms company. I worked with them for a few years, and during that time they developed a high level of honesty and receptiveness with each other. They discussed problems and opportunities with an energy and commitment to developing great ideas which led to some breakthrough concepts for their service areas. They also welcomed different ideas from others, whether it was from other colleagues within the business or from outsiders invited to share alternative ways of thinking or doing. They didn't take challenge personally; they were focused on getting the best possible decision for the business. They were focused on their team goals, and when they saw success it was shared, like an orchestra taking the applause at the end of a perfectly delivered concert. They derived real excitement from sharing brilliantly. Ideas were challenged without defence; one idea led to another. More junior colleagues looked forward to being invited into the executive team meeting to share ideas and proposals for action (not that common an experience in many organizations, I am afraid). Over time the quality of ideation spread around the business, and led to some breakthrough innovations in service delivery, marketing and contracting. The impact hit the bottom line. All from not killing the seed of an idea.

In an agile organization, this quality of dialogue needs to be germinated across teams at all levels, through the example we set, through coaching others to speak up, through responding to challenge with curiosity. This is first and foremost the responsibility of leaders across the business, and it is helpful if it starts at the top, as it creates a climate across the organization where agile thinking and ways of working can flourish.

External outlook

As we can see in the example of the telecoms team above, leaders who look outside their immediate environment, and outside their organization, are more likely to be tuned into the opportunities to learn from others such as competitors, or leaders in different sectors. Fresh perspectives can drive innovation and improvement in our own organizations. Looking outside also helps such leaders to enable their employees to do the same, as role models for seeking new ways of looking at things, and alternative ways of solving known problems.

At Cirrus, we like to take leaders on immersive experiences into other organizations which operate in very different worlds, such as start-ups, charities and technology leaders. This gives them the opportunity to see their own world from a different perspective, and to learn from what other leaders are doing. It can be a significant moment for leaders to step out of their bubble, to see their teams and their business in the cold light of day, to reflect on how another organization achieves outputs often without the luxury of the resources, systems and infrastructure many larger organizations can take for granted.

It is like going for a walk outside after a long morning in meetings or on video calls. The change of outlook helps us reset our understanding of how things fit together and regain a sense of perspective. Another example is travel. Some of my best thinking is done on long-haul flights where I am separated from the clutter of my daily life and left to my own thoughts. Travelling is an opportunity to see innovation and ingenuity in different cultures and environments, and to get new ideas which might apply back at work. It is an opportunity to step out in order better to see in.

Uber Eats is an example of a business that thought disruptively. It took its taxi booking app and looked across into other markets. It turned the booking logic into a food delivery opportunity, a bold flip into a new sector. And in so doing it helped to transform the food delivery market across the world.

Uber Eats has continued to innovate with different charging structures (based on order value in the UK or distance in the United States), experimenting with drone delivery and introducing virtual restaurants (or cloud kitchens) which are restaurant kitchens staffed to prepare and deliver food, either for existing bricks-and-mortar restaurants wishing to move their delivery operations offsite, or for delivery-only restaurants with no walk-in or dining-room service. The Covid-19 experience in 2020 accelerated this trend dramatically across the sector.

The trick for Uber was to look at its taxi booking app through a different lens, to see it not as a taxi app but as a booking app. What was being booked could vary, just as Amazon in its early years flipped from being an online bookstore to an online retailer with a much wider product range. Looking up and looking out opened new vistas of disruptive opportunity for both companies.

One of my favourite quotations on this topic pre-dates both Uber and Amazon. Ferry Porsche designed the famous 911 sports car which was launched in 1962, the same year I was born. Speaking about what inspired him to do so, he said: 'In the beginning, I looked around and could not find quite the car I dreamed of, so I decided to build it myself. Independence has always been the attitude of Porsche. To do, not what is expected, but what feels right' (Porsche, 1962). This independence of thought is at the heart of disruptive thinking – it is not constrained by previous assumptions, by history or tradition. The agile leader who can think, and enable others to think, in an independent way is creating the space and time for new insights, fresh ideas that might help us rethink what our customers can do. Such thinking led to the iPhone, the Uber app and the Toyota Prius.

One of the programmes at Cirrus of which I am most proud is a collaboration with the Academy of Medical Sciences in London which brings together highfliers from the National Health Service, universities, pharmaceutical and medtech companies and other health providers, to learn how to accelerate collaborative research and medical advance across the wider health ecosystem. Participants learn about other parts of this ecosystem and how to lead collaboration between partners which typically have not understood each other historically. It is building the ability to think independently and to work interdependently, to break down silos in service of the health of the nation.

I often see a striking contrast between leaders in large established organizations and successful entrepreneurs. The latter are typically more aware of and keen to learn from the outside. They enjoy meeting other entrepreneurs, speakers, authors and academics, and always seem to be seeking to learn something they can use in their own business. Many are hungry to learn, and you can almost see them linking someone else's experience or insights to their own business, seeing how it can help them be more successful. I am not saying that this is not true of senior people in large organizations, as I meet many who are equally hungry to learn from the outside, but it is particularly pronounced in the entrepreneurial world. Looking outside helps us to disrupt our own thinking and to tune into what customers are experiencing in the here and now. We can bring this insight into our own organizations on a day-to-day basis.

It is often the unexpected juxtaposition of stories that creates fresh insight that can drive real innovation and improvement. I remember one leader of a £2 billion private fashion company swapping stories with another highly successful entrepreneur. He was describing how they had improved product innovation across clothing brands by linking research activities in areas such as stretch fabrics. The other leader was listening and thinking at the same time, trying to use this insight to spot an opportunity for improvement in her own high-growth technology business. Later in the conversation she smiled and held up her hand in delight, and then proceeded to describe how she could see process improvements and efficiency gains from bringing her finance and procurement teams together. The link was tangential, but she would not have had that idea if she had not been talking with the man from fashion.

Customer vision

Agile working is about being focused on what matters most to your customers. So, as leaders, we need to be able to articulate a customer-driven vision based on a thorough understanding of what our customers want to do. Sometimes customers can articulate what they want, sometimes not. Our job as agile leaders is to work with our teams to understand customer insight, explore their human needs, understand their changing context, discover how technology could add new ways of doing things, and integrate this into a vision for customer value. This takes genuine empathy.

BEING AMBITIOUS FOR OUR CUSTOMER

We're giving people ownership of a certain product as part of a self-organized team. So, if you are the accounts squad, you're going to own that code base, and your job is to make accounts awesome. That's your purpose.

Michael Lambert, former head of development, CDL

Agile leaders regularly articulate this vision of what their customers want, telling stories that help others to understand what this looks like in practice, so they can translate this into priorities and outputs. They also encourage the same in others, as customer insight is not the sole domain of the leader – in fact ideally the team is involved in articulating the vision, describing the customers' needs in clear and simple stories. In our organizations, we need to build the leadership habit of articulating this customer vision on a regular basis, enabling teams to recognize its importance and to make sense of it in terms of their roles. Bringing customer data, insights and stories into day-to-day conversations helps to make it practical and relevant to people's jobs. As described earlier, developing outside-in thinking is key, and you can achieve this through targeted development programmes, storytelling and building networks outside your own organization. It is worth checking that your organization's learning and development programmes include sufficient emphasis on your customers and their worlds.

One of the consequences of the Covid-19 pandemic and the Black Lives Matter movement was an even greater emphasis on the societal impact our organizations have – particularly on all aspects of mental and physical health, on sustainability and on equality. It is helpful if we can actively support our people to bring their social awareness into work, to share social concerns, and to relate to the issues in society, such as saving the planet and equality and inclusion. This has the benefit of enabling our people to bring the consumer's context into day-to-day decision making. Consumers' desire to see greater fairness in healthcare and employment will increasingly be reflected in their buying decisions, and it is up to us to make business decisions in line with this vision.

As our teams convert customer vision into practice, building products and services that move towards it, they need to test these ideas with customers on a regular basis. Whether this is creating a new report by the finance team or a new version of an iPhone at Apple, engaging with customers and gaining feedback on prototypes (or minimum viable products) enables us to measure customer value. By repeating this engagement on an ongoing basis, we create a dialogue with customers where they can help us shape innovation based on what they value most.

CUSTOMER VISION: OPRAH WINFREY, CEO, HARPO PRODUCTIONS AND OPRAH WINFREY NETWORK

Although Winfrey is primarily known as a media personality, she is also one of the world's most successful media moguls, who has built on her experience as a journalist and broadcaster to grow a successful empire which encompasses publishing, radio, film and TV production. Renowned as an authentic communicator who makes a strong connection with her audience, Winfrey has astutely tuned into that audience's desires with initiatives such as 'Oprah's Book Club' which pioneered the use of television and the internet to encourage many non-readers to pick up novels, sending book sales soaring. A regular on lists such as the *Time* 100 Most Influential people and *Forbes* Most Powerful Women, she is also one of the United States' most prominent philanthropists.

Customer-driven innovation

Innovations come in many forms, from changing the business model (like Uber's taxi-ordering system) to creating new categories (like smartphones and mobile shopping) to creating novel experiences (like Amazon Prime delivery and automated boarding at airports). Rigby defines innovation as the 'profitable application of creativity' (Rigby and Sutherland, 2016): it is both creative and commercial. In an agile context, the priority for innovation is in making it customer-driven. As Sutherland, one of the original Agile Manifesto authors, said (Rigby and Sutherland, 2016):

> The word agile came from a book about 100 lean hardware companies who said that they were firstly lean, but they had become agile by involving the customer directly in product creation. So that would be my definition of agile. Lean plus getting the customer directly in the middle of innovation.

Agile innovation is all about being focused on what your customers need most, and prioritizing activity to concentrate your team's resources on the activities that will meet that need as fully as possible, as quickly as possible. In terms of innovation, it is essential that this focus is clear, and it needs to be on both your products or services and on how you deliver these to the customer. 'Leading companies understand that they are in the customer-experience business, and they understand that how an organization delivers for customers is beginning to be as important as what it delivers' (McKinsey, 2016a). Agile innovation is about starting without necessarily knowing the outcome, focusing on the highest priority customer problems or needs to solve, and working intelligently to solve these together. As Satya Nadella wrote: 'Innovation is about meeting the unmet and unarticulated needs of customers', and it requires 'real empathy to be close enough to the customer's experience to see what has as yet not been articulated' (Nadella, 2017).

Customer experience

A helpful way to introduce a more agile customer experience through innovation is to review the journey your customers take in dealing with your organization. Customers have multiple touch points, and these create opportunities for innovation and improvement, either by re-engineering the process to reduce time or friction, increasing customer enjoyment, or by reordering the touch points to create a more positive experience. Customers now expect from all suppliers the same kind of speed, personalization and convenience that they receive from leading online providers such as Google and Amazon. 'Customers want an efficient and enjoyable experience with positive surprises – and they will return if we can provide that' (Dodge, 2017). This applies in the business-to-business world as well as the consumer world. For example, David Wilson, Head of Organization Development at Standard Chartered, describes the impact of remodelling the customer journeys: 'We're bringing people together to work in agile ways. We have a strong sense of purpose and we work together on shared challenges and get results pretty quickly. Things that used to take a couple of months now take a couple of weeks.' The beneficiary is the customer.

EMPATHY DRIVES INNOVATION

In order to get to new solutions, you need to get to know different people, different scenarios, different places.

Emi Kolawole (2011), Editor-in-Residence, Stanford University d.school

---

Leading innovation

In the 2014 book, *Collective Genius: The art and practice of leading innovation*, researchers explored how some organizations can continuously innovate, while others cannot (Hill *et al*, 2014). The authors researched innovative organizations such as Pixar, Google, eBay and Pfizer and found that they 'organized for innovation'. They identified 'three capabilities of innovation':

1 *Creative abrasion* – the ability to generate ideas through discourse and debate, which is like the disruptive thinking described earlier.
2 *Creative agility* – the ability to test and experiment through quick pursuit, reflection and adjustment.
3 *Creative resolution* – the ability to make integrative decisions that combine disparate or even opposing ideas.

The authors recognize that 'creative abrasion' and 'creative agility' are not always compatible as many of us crave the clarity of assured decision making. They suggest that to create a truly innovative culture, leaders need the courage to explore multiple opportunities and a willingness to experiment. In innovative organizations, solutions are reached through collaboration and constant iteration, as we can read about in the Bayer case later. Leaders encourage others to test many ideas before choosing one. The need for speed, however, is also important; this was especially the case as we reacted to the radical changes wrought by the Covid-19 pandemic. These conditions for sustainable innovation are highly consistent with the agile leadership characteristics described in the wheel.

Research from Bain & Company (O'Keeffe, 2020) confirms that 'turbulent times favour companies that prepare well and that take bold steps despite uncertainty.' Their emphasis on boldness – both in decision making and execution – chimes with my own observation that those organizations that acted boldly managed to build far more depth of capability to operate in the new virtual world brought on by the pandemic than those which hesitated, clinging to the hope that 'normal' business would return soon. It did not.

Pixar has a culture that encourages experimentation, where nobody is blamed for trying something that did not work. Experimentation, feeling safe to fail and celebrating the learning from failing are key to building a risk-agreeable culture. Often, we hear that executives should simply encourage experimentation and not punish failure: everything will take care of itself, whereas in reality risk and failure profoundly challenge us as human beings. Ed Catmull of Pixar highlights how we tend to see failure in the past as 'it made me what I am', but looking into the future we tend to think, 'I don't know what is going to happen and I don't want to fail.' Catmull goes on to say that 'the difficulty is that when you're running an experiment, it's forward looking. We have to try extra hard to make it safe to fail' (McKinsey, 2016b). This spirit of learning sums up the mindset we are seeking in an agile organization.

CASE STUDY   Agile innovation: Bayer

Bayer, the multinational life sciences company, has always had a strong reputation for innovation. However, when start-ups began to disrupt its market and the pace of innovation increased, Bayer realized that it needed to embrace more agile ways of working. Traditionally, the business had been very product-driven. There had always been a lot of investment in research and development, but Bayer realized that to be truly innovative in a digital age, innovation had to extend beyond R&D.

Creating an innovation network

'We realized that it's not going to be about products alone any more, so we really needed to activate the whole organization to change its mindset', said Julia Hitzbleck, who founded the Innovation Network at Bayer. 'Our board member for innovation said that we needed to understand that innovation is everything, from research to sales, and everybody should contribute to this culture.' It was important to have board approval, but the team realized that they also needed to take the organization with them in a bottom-up movement.

A crowd-sourcing platform was launched in 2014 to ask employees to contribute solutions to specific technical or commercial problems. It focused on existing challenges and built a network of coaches, people across the company who were excited by the initiative and prepared to devote some discretionary time to the project.

To build on this movement, Innovation Ambassadors were onboarded and virtually met bi-monthly, to inspire and drive culture change further. They worked across the organization to understand where innovations typically got stuck, to define the key areas for focus. Together with their growing number of innovation coaches the network emerged across different countries, combining central goal setting with local roadmaps matching the local business priorities. This spawned over 1,000 talented volunteers who had developed an agile mindset and were curious to combine shared problems with local solutions.

They organized a series of innovation days to explore what agile really meant for them – 'it's not just about the IT guys doing a different type of development but also about our mindset and how we develop new things,' says Julia. Agile innovation coaches ran small idea creation and problem-solving sessions, saying, 'Okay, let's get five people together, let's dismantle the process and come up with a proposal which will work in practice.'

The Catalyst programme

Bayer launched the Catalyst entrepreneurship programme in 2017. It draws on Lean Start-up principles to drive innovation, encouraging colleagues across the business to come up with innovative solutions that can create real impact. 'We encourage people to think like start-ups', Julia recalls. 'We don't want ideas that would be hard to implement, we seek solutions to real business challenges that can be scaled globally. If your idea doesn't resonate with local business leads, it won't work. You need to have a business sponsor. To really get the buy-in, to ensure successful projects are implemented later, you need to involve the local business leaders very early on.'

They introduced Venture Boards for the different divisions, which approved projects aligned to Bayer's strategic needs. The teams went through a 12-week programme, with mentoring support, where they learned to work with business model and lean start-up experimentation, using a prototyping fund and needing to show progress every week. Julia says the teams 'were deeply engaged, and also open-minded, and embraced the need to think differently.'

A cross-functional emphasis

Bayer projects are often cross-functional, and through emphasizing the cross-functional nature of agile innovation people came to realize that 'it's the team's effort that makes the project fly and not just everybody looking at their small piece of the pie or area of responsibility.' Innovation is essentially a social activity, it happens in teams, in cross-functional workshops and through many people's involvement.

This was also a big lesson for senior leaders, whose responsibilities and identity were often primarily functional. The programme helped to accelerate the buy-in to cross-functional teamworking, in pursuit of innovation, through leaders seeing the benefits for themselves.

Expanding horizons

As the world of life sciences continues to change ever more rapidly in this post-pandemic world, Bayer is embracing innovation not just for new technologies and new products, but also for new services, new business models and entirely new ways of working. In response to significant market disruption both from competitors and big tech, Bayer is re-imagining how to problem-solve across all areas, enabling teams to create new ideas and to drive them forward to implementation. Agile innovation is leading to new products, new market strategies and digital learning solutions.

Summary

If agile ways of working are to deliver transformational benefits for your organization, there is a need to create new ways of thinking, as well as organizing work differently. The breakthroughs agile ways of working can deliver are based on radical experimentation and innovation, not just increasing productivity. Disrupting normal patterns of thought and behaviour is therefore essential. As a leader, you have more chance of causing such disruption than many of those who work in your teams because you have the organizational authority to make change happen. So, create space for your people to think, encourage them to look outside and connect more deeply with your customers, and help them to form the insights they derive from these experiences into new ways to deliver customer value. And be a role model for such thinking, as this will give others confidence that you are serious.

In the flux and ambiguity of the post-Covid-19 world, such thinking and customer-focused innovation is at a premium. We are at an inflexion point in many sectors, with digitization having moved faster in 2020 than perhaps in the previous 5 to 10 years, with working patterns turned on their head for the majority, and with supply chains and consumer-facing industries challenged beyond breaking point in many cases. Such ambiguity creates opportunities for growth, and clear strategy and bold execution will create competitive advantage for some organizations with which it will be difficult for others to catch up.

References

Bloom, N (2020) Stanford research provides a snapshot of a new working-from-home economy, Stanford University news.stanford.edu/2020/06/29/snapshot-new-working-home-economy/ (archived at https://perma.cc/TKM7-3C3N)

Bort, J (2018) Amazon founder Jeff Bezos explains why he sends single character '?' emails, *Business Insider*, April 2019, www.inc.com/business-insider/amazon-founder-ceo-jeff-bezos-customer-emails-forward-managers-fix-issues.html (archived at https://perma.cc/45DQ-KMYA)

De Smet, A, Mygatt, E, Sheikh, I and Weddle, B (2020) *The need for speed in the post-COVID-19 era – and how to achieve it*, McKinsey Global Publishing, MA

Dodge, T (2017) from research interview conducted in June 2017

Fujitsu (2018) *Co-creation for Success: Unlocking creativity, knowledge and innovation*, Fujitsu Corporation, Japan

Hayward, S (2018) Do employees have the right to make mistakes?, *People Management*, CIPD, London, www.peoplemanagement.co.uk/voices/comment/employees-right-make-mistakes (archived at https://perma.cc/FU22-RSXY)

Hayward, S (2020) Can the shift to remote working help us to become more agile and inclusive leaders?, Changeboard, www.changeboard.com/article-details/17225/perspective-can-the-shift-to-remote-working-help-us-to-become-more-agile-and-inclusive-leaders-/ (archived at https://perma.cc/FU22-RSXY)

Hill, L, Brandeau, G, Truelove, E and Lineback, K (2014) *Collective Genius: The art and practice of leading innovation*, Harvard Business Review Press, Boston, MA

Kolawole, E (2011) *The Field Guide to Human-Centered Design*, IDEO.org, San Francisco, CA

Levy, S (2013) Jeff Bezos owns the web in more ways than you think, *Wired*, November

Maurya, A (2012) *Running Lean: Iterate from Plan A to a plan that works*, O'Reilly Media

McKinsey (2016a) The CEO guide to customer experience, *McKinsey Quarterly*, August

McKinsey (2016b) Staying one step ahead at Pixar: an interview with Ed Catmull, *McKinsey Quarterly*, March

Nadella, S (2017) *Hit Refresh*, Harper Collins Publishers, London

O'Keeffe, D (2020) *Retooling Strategy for a Post-Pandemic World: Covid-19 has shown us the cost of short-changing adaptability, prediction and resilience*, Bain & Company, Boston, MA

Oxford English Dictionary (2012) Oxford University Press, Oxford

Porsche, F (1962) downloaded from www.quotewise.com (archived at https://perma. cc/5Z9T-SLV7) 22nd November 2020 and cited in Porsche marketing collateral (2020)

Raedemaecker, S, Handscomb, C, Jautelat, C, Rodriguez, M and Wienke, L (2020) Lean management or agile? The right answer may be both, McKinsey & Company, www.mckinsey.com/business-functions/operations/our-insights/lean-management-or-agile-the-right-answer-may-be-both (archived at https://perma.cc/2FYA-47BE)

Rigby, D and Sutherland, J (2016) Understanding agile management, *Harvard Business Review*, April

World Economic Forum (2020) www.weforum.org/agenda/2020/03/working-from-home-coronavirus-workers-future-of-work/ (archived at https://perma.cc/KHY3-W7FY)

CHAPTER SEVEN

Prioritization and performance

At the core, strategy is about focus. RUMELT (2011)

Introduction

Agile working accelerates performance partly because agile teams focus only on the top priorities and partly because they are regularly working on how to go faster. They are ruthless in their prioritization and they obsess about performance improvement. As agile leaders, your task is to support your teams with clarity of vision and as a proactive coach, who stretches, enables and recognizes achievements.

Ruthless prioritization is particularly challenging for many large organizations, so in this chapter we will explore how to make and keep things simple. We will also explore performance improvement and the power of retrospectives to identify the next marginal gain for the team to achieve. Together these two characteristics form the third quadrant of the Agile Leader Wheel – Plan – and are essentially about looking forward (Figure 7.1).

FIGURE 7.1   The agile leader wheel

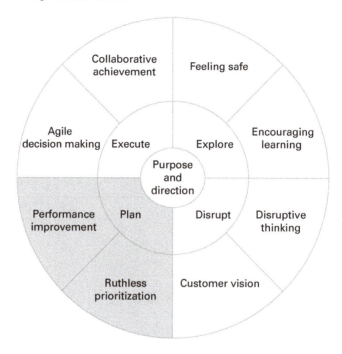

Ruthless prioritization

A key aspect of agile working is ruthless prioritization. Making difficult decisions is at the heart of creating a more agile organization, and this means identifying the right priorities based on your purpose and direction, and then acting on them with determination. By making the choice about the priority items to work on, you free yourself up to not work on the rest. Just as the elite athlete gets up early every day in all weathers to train, so the agile leader makes the difficult decisions every day about what to focus resources on. Top athletes tend to be very single-minded, dedicated to being the best they can be, and intolerant of any outside influence or distraction that will interrupt this focused approach. Hence 'ruthless', which is a word that suggests an unwavering determination to achieve an outcome. Priorities bring clarity.

In this chapter we will explore helpful techniques you can use as a leader to make this approach work in your own organization. If you focus on the few things that matter most to your customers and your organization, you can maximize benefits and minimize costs. This will accelerate your ability to create or seize opportunities quickly and effectively, in the way that a start-up business might. Without ongoing ruthless prioritization, the rest of this book will be very difficult to implement.

RUTHLESS PRIORITIZATION: SHERYL SANDBERG, COO, FACEBOOK

Sandberg is a huge advocate of ruthless prioritization – focusing on the few things that will make the biggest difference to your organization and your customers, rather than spreading your effort across a wide range of areas. At Facebook, colleagues are constantly encouraged to innovate and come up with new ideas, but the organization carefully chooses which ones to focus on. Sandberg has spoken clearly about how Facebook has learned to make hard choices to prioritize what's really important, and how that helps drive their continued success.

> I think the most important thing we've learned as we've grown is that we have to prioritize. We talk about it as ruthless prioritization. And by that what we mean is only do the very best of the ideas. Lots of times you have very good ideas. But they're not as good as the most important thing you could be doing. And you have to make the hard choices.

Source: Bariso (2017)

You are the ultimate product owner

If we go back to the Scrum approach we explored in Chapter 3 in the wider context of your organization rather than a single development team, it is helpful to think about your role as a leader and how it relates to the process. If you are the chief executive you are in effect the 'product owner' for the business, accountable for the customer outputs of the whole enterprise. The chief executive is ultimately responsible for setting the overall priorities for the business, in line with your customers' evolving needs and expectations, and this cascades through leadership roles throughout your organization. Wherever you sit, it is your vision of what you want to accomplish that needs to be clear and well communicated to the people who will do the work. It is your role to identify the strategic priorities at the top of the backlog, so that organizational resources can be focused on achieving them. If you are unclear, you risk causing confusion. If you are clear and really in tune with your customers, you can provide the prioritization that enables others to act quickly, effectively and collaboratively.

As we know from connected leadership, devolved decision making is very helpful in creating greater agility, and at its heart is a coherent approach to the conscious delegation of responsibility for outcomes across the organization. This empowers people closer to the customer to make the right decisions in a way that is aligned with the overall vision and purpose of the whole enterprise. It is each manager's responsibility to ensure this coherence is maintained, and that their priorities and actions are serving the overall priorities of the organization.

Purpose-driven prioritization

When the Covid-19 lockdown in many parts of the world began in early 2020, we saw leaders across many sectors forced to stop and re-prioritize on behalf of the whole organization. Hospitals had to switch to Covid-19 preparation. Many businesses had to react to a slump in demand. Universities had to stop in-person teaching and research. Charities saw funding streams dry up. The crisis forced a level of rapid decision making that would have taken months if not years to achieve previously. Many leaders had to close their operations and rely on governmental support. Some had to pivot their organization to operate virtually. Some had to stop major projects to focus resources on the ones that were critical for survival. The common theme was leaders making bold choices and focusing resources where they had most impact.

For some it became a moment of opportunity, an inflexion point in their market which opened fresh routes to growth and success. For others it forced priority decisions that had less positive knock-on consequences, such as hospital wards not being available for elective surgery and other emergency services. Agile prioritization in a crisis needs regular review of short-term decisions to negate long-term impact. A big concern for health service managers later in the Covid pandemic was how to ameliorate the public health impact of having to switch off cancer screening and other critical services. Hospitals had to rebalance services and resources as soon as they were able to do so.

Stepping back, the irony in all of this decision making was that most leaders I know understand the value of prioritization, of making difficult choices and following through by stopping projects that do not align with the few priorities that make the biggest difference to their purpose (Hayward, 2020). They knew, but pre-2020 most had found it very difficult in practice to make those decisions and stick to them. Our challenge going forward is to retain that laser precision of critical and timely decision making.

Nieto-Rodriguez (2016) describes a useful framework to use in making prioritization easier based on what he calls 'the hierarchy of purpose' (Figure 7.2). You can use it with your teams to make choices together and in line with the business's overall purpose and direction. The framework suggests a sequence of analysis to help make prioritization work. Be clear on your *purpose* and direction, and from that define the *priorities* for the organization over the next two to five years. Based on the answers to the first two points, which *projects* are 'the most strategic and should be resourced to the hilt, and which should be stopped or scrapped?' Then decide on who are the best *people* to execute on those projects. And finally, track *performance* 'based on the precise outcome-related targets that will measure real performance and value creation.' He suggests focusing on the most significant 20 projects in the organization, to keep it material and manageable.

This is a helpful approach, and where leadership teams apply it with discipline it can lead to the type of radical refocusing of the organization on

FIGURE 7.2 The hierarchy of purpose

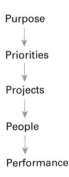

Source: Nieto-Rodriguez (2016)

what matters most that we saw in the early stages of the pandemic. It requires strong will and bold decision making, however, if it is to lead to the level of focus that will really lead to breakthrough improvements in performance.

This purpose-driven approach also helps to change budget planning from a controlling activity into a performance improvement activity, which has '30 times greater impact on shareholder returns' than planning simply to predict and control outcomes, according to Bain & Company analysis (Rigby *et al*, 2020).

As you plan together it is important to be very clear about your vision and purpose. What is your big goal, what Jim Collins called your 'Big Hairy Audacious Goal' (Collins, 2001)? It is essential to have a sense of what you are aiming for, and to make it an exciting vision for others; but it is also important to be able to express clearly *why* it is important. Without a sense of purpose, your people are less likely to follow you towards the vision. As mentioned in Chapter 1, in research we conducted with Ipsos into what engages people in today's digital world, one of the main factors was that 'people would rather work for a cause than a company' (Cirrus/Ipsos, 2017). The power of purpose is in giving people a reason to believe, a reason to be proud. It gets them out of bed with a spring rather than a sigh.

The main thing

If you have a clear vision of what you as an organization or a team need to achieve each week, each month, each year, you can empower others to deliver it with zeal. As Stephen Covey famously wrote: 'The main thing is to keep the main thing the main thing' (Covey, 1988). Your key role in setting up the organization to be more agile is to be clear on the 'main thing' and to keep everyone focused on its achievement. Clarity is key to unlocking agility. I would encourage you to be clear on the main thing in both the short and longer term. What is the main thing tomorrow? Focus on doing that and do not move to other tasks until you have completed it. What is the main thing for the longer term for your organization? Focus your resources and efforts on achieving it and cut out as much activity as you can on anything else. In the case study below, we will see how Haymarket has transformed itself from being a print-based publisher to a digitally enabled global content house through disruptive thinking and ruthless prioritization.

CASE STUDY   Haymarket Media Group: adapting to a changing environment with clear priorities

Haymarket Media Group was founded in the UK in 1957. In the decades that followed, the media company built an international reputation based on market-leading business and consumer publications including *Management Today*, *Campaign* and *What Car?*

Haymarket is a radically different business today. The company operates more than 50 brands in Europe, Asia and the United States. In the past decade, the business has become increasingly data-led, creating specialist content and services that resonate with – and are relevant to – valuable, engaged and discerning audiences. Print remains an important part of the mix, where there is audience demand for it. By putting audiences first, Haymarket has evolved rapidly, creating new digital and live platforms, reinventing legacy brands and launching new products. Although the organization serves different audiences in different markets in different ways, every business has the same modus operandi. CEO Kevin Costello believes that, 'You have to know the audience and truly understand their needs if you are to create the innovative products and services that will engage, stimulate and inspire them.'

Digital disruption

Kevin joined Haymarket in 1994, when the company was a traditional, predominantly British print-publishing business, driven largely by advertising revenue.

In 1999 the group began to diversify internationally and invest significantly in digital media. 'We were intrigued by the imminent shift to online,' says Kevin, 'and, over the next few years, we began to understand the opportunities this could present for us as a business.'

At that time, Kevin was managing Haymarket's consumer electronics brands (*Stuff* and *What Hi-Fi?*). He remembers being inspired by a Bill Gates speech at CES, the international annual gathering for the consumer technology industries:

The message was clear: the internet was a tidal wave that would rewrite all the rules. It was an enormous opportunity and an enormous challenge. It was already, in Gates's view, becoming so ubiquitous that it was changing the way people and businesses communicated with each other. His message struck home, reminding us that the potential rewards of change were much greater than the risks involved in not changing.

We could see that technological innovation was already disrupting the media industry, changing consumer behaviour and, therefore, our proposition to our advertisers and sponsors. We had a clear choice – we could see change as a threat or an opportunity. We lobbied hard for Haymarket to disrupt our own traditional models, to explore emerging technologies and see what opportunities we could create. To be honest, at that stage, it was more curiosity than strategy but, for a traditional print-based company like ours, these initiatives broke new ground and gave us the courage to persevere.

Clear direction

Fast forward to 2010, when Kevin became CEO and, as he admits:

> We had begun to grasp the international opportunity, but we didn't really have a strategy as such. Most of our revenues were still in print.
>
> We were an emerging hybrid business – delivering content across digital and non-digital platforms, serving B2B, B2C and experiential audiences – but we could not stand still. We needed to foster collaboration and cohesion, diversify our revenue streams and invest our resources on fewer bigger, smarter bets.
>
> As a leadership team, we took a step back to make a realistic appraisal of our strengths and weaknesses. Wherever we looked in the business, the same message came through. Our competitive advantage came in our deep understanding of our audiences, whether they were in marcomms, medical or motoring. Their trust in – and passionate engagement with – our brands, gave us permission to offer them new targeted products and services.
>
> We developed a group growth strategy which we imaginatively entitled our Group Growth Plan.

Their aim was clear: to become the best international specialist media and information company, in their chosen markets. Because the strategy was led by key audiences and clients, they could not just force existing solutions on the customer. The clear plan gave the divisions and brand leaders the chance to be agile and use the business models most appropriate for their audiences. 'In most businesses today – especially in the media – attention is the scarcest commodity. We needed to deploy it where we were confident we would get the best return.'

'Our previous plans had become too much a function of finance', says Kevin. 'In this case, alongside new, agile business processes, we focused on culture, behaviour and ways of working. We had a clear strategy, but we needed to bring people with us – and that was a challenge. You can't force that.'

Creating an agile culture

Haymarket's new strategy was founded on five core values: integrity, creativity, expertise, dynamism and independence. 'These values are an authentic expression of our business', says Kevin. 'They don't just define our heritage; they define our future – and they explicitly underpin everything we do.'

According to Kevin, restructuring any business is, by definition, disruptive. 'Change can be very unsettling. It creates a considerable degree of uncertainty.

Maintaining motivation and morale, while remaining determined to achieve your goals, is one of the greatest challenges any leader can face.'

One of the difficult balancing acts leaders face in times of transition is to be firm yet flexible. Kevin says:

> You have to be clear about your goals, but not be dogmatic about how you achieve them. To be truly agile, you need to recognize fundamental shifts in the marketplace and react accordingly. That is particularly true in the media industry where things change so fast businesses like ours are under constant pressure to develop new ideas.

To bring people with them, Haymarket's leaders encouraged all colleagues to help change the business, harnessing their collective wisdom and empowering teams to make their own decisions, based on the group's mission and values. 'We needed to focus on our common goals, but our people needed to feel they had our blessing to challenge the status quo where necessary; disrupt existing models and become more entrepreneurial and innovative.'

Haymarket's leadership team has worked hard to develop collective responsibility, become more transparent and communicate more effectively. 'We encourage our leaders to model this behaviour. Business culture isn't a set of rules: it's a set of value-driven behaviours that empower your people and drive customer experience,' says Kevin.

Today Haymarket is a globally successful media, data, information and analytics business. Since the launch of their Group Growth Plan in 2012, the proportion of revenues generated from the UK has gone from 80 per cent to less than 50 per cent. Digital revenues have grown from 25 per cent, to today representing 64 per cent of total revenues. In its chosen markets, the company meets the needs of its audiences with data-led advertising, business intelligence, e-commerce and e-learning, paid-content and live events.

Culture in a crisis

When Covid-19 struck in 2020, Haymarket's drive to create a more collaborative, agile and responsive leadership culture helped protect the business. The business had the technology, the capability and the agility to adapt to remote working. 'I'm not saying it was easy – we had to re-engineer the business in a very short space of time – but we were adaptable and resilient,' says Kevin. After an aggressive programme of debt reduction in the preceding years, Haymarket was financially sound and, once it had adjusted to the new reality, was able to focus on delivering its strategic objectives.

'When we were in that classic first phase of crisis management, we set very clear direction and purpose from the centre,' says Kevin. 'Our chief financial officer, our human resources director and I worked very closely together. We had a clearly defined mission which we reduced to a simple mantra: contain costs, preserve cash, save jobs. We were rigorous about its implementation.'

In times of such intense uncertainty, with employees worrying about their health as well as their livelihoods, a clear direction from the centre was essential. 'We all know that losing your head in a crisis is a good way to become the crisis,' says Kevin. 'Even though we changed our ways of working radically and rapidly, as leaders we could sense the anxiety. In such circumstances, our messaging needed to be simple, clear and consistent and we needed to acknowledge fear and uncertainty. We shared what we knew and were open about what we didn't.'

'Agility comes from people – technology only enhances it,' says Kevin. 'That's why we are very clear about our purpose and values in an ever-changing world. The things that were important to Haymarket when we were founded in 1957 – investing in strategically important areas, building strong partnerships, helping our colleagues well and behaving with integrity – are still important to us today.'

Kevin Costello: lessons I've learned

- Provide clear direction from the centre.
- Think global, act local. A 'one size fits all' approach is limited.
- Strategy is not a straitjacket – we were willing to realign our expectations.
- Create a mission and values that people believe in.
- Play to your strengths and be clear on your priorities.

Planning together

In agile working, the way the 'main thing' is defined is by creating and prioritizing a backlog of tasks. You start by listing out all the tasks needed to achieve your goal or vision. Best to do this with your team members, to create a shared list that draws on everyone's insight into what needs to be done. In the Haymarket example, Costello emphasized the need to take people with you, and this starts at the planning stage. You need a healthy leadership team able to have open, honest and direct conversation in a mature way, based on what's best for the organization rather than any individual's agenda. It is focused on your purpose and shared direction.

With your team you then prioritize the list, using as the main criteria what is of most value to your customers, and what will add most value to your business. By 'value' I mean what will give your customers the ability to do something they really want or need to do (whether they realized it beforehand or not), and what will help your business achieve its goals (such as growth or impact). You are looking for the top priorities, which currently represent the best fit with these criteria. These priorities will change over time, and with the ever-increasing disruption caused by Covid-19 and technology, this change will only accelerate. In Haymarket's case, the emergence of digital disruption in the last 10 years of the 20th century caused it to fundamentally revisit its priorities and to embark on a journey of digital exploration. Eventually, this led to the business shifting largely from paper to digital and to a range of non-print service offerings based on its core content assets.

Hence the emphasis in agile working on an iterative approach to developing new features in software, or, at an organizational level, an iterative approach to developing the organization's customer proposition (and the associated capability to deliver it better than anyone else). As the context changes around you, you need to be interpreting it and reviewing your backlog of tasks to check they are still relevant. This is disruptive thinking: being willing to reinvent the organization or business unit if necessary, to stay relevant in an ever-changing world. As competitors introduce substitute products and services, or pandemics change market structure, you may find your list becomes redundant, as happened to mainframe manufacturers in the 1980s and 1990s, when networks of personal computers offered a different way to use computing power for organizations large and small. The agile survived by reinventing themselves, such as IBM, rethinking how central computing power played a useful part in a customer's IT infrastructure, switching focus to services and the user interface, where the power was becoming most valued.

Once you have an agreed list, focus on the top tasks only, and define the outcomes you are looking for. In Scrum these outcomes are often defined in user stories, descriptions of what the customer will be able to do with the new features. This is a useful technique because it makes the outcome practical, and you will know when it has been done. When describing your vision, it is helpful to use examples, to tell stories about the outcomes you are looking to achieve. If it is a new customer experience, describe the specifics of someone having that experience. This will help others relate to it as well as understanding the outcome more vividly. An example might be: 'As a regular traveller, I want to see the location of my booked taxi on my mobile before it arrives, so I can avoid waiting around unnecessarily.' This is one of the features of Uber that helped make it so successful.

It is helpful, I believe, to recognize when goals need to change as context changes. When in 2011 Mark Zuckerberg realized that the future for Facebook was in mobile, he set this as the big goal, and reorganized the business to achieve that outcome. In 2013 it went mobile, and mobile advertising revenue reached 50 per cent of the total by the end of that year. This was in support of the ultimate vision for Facebook and was a critical shift in focus that moved the company into a winning position from what had been a losing one.

In line with that overall goal, you need to be clear on the priority in the next sprint period, which may at a business level be the next quarter. This is the top priority on the list you made with your team members earlier. In his book *Scaling Up*, Verne Harnish describes 'The #1 Priority... everyone is aligned with the #1 that needs to be accomplished this quarter to move the company forward' (Harnish, 2014). He suggests a disciplined approach to planning that reflects the rigour of agile, with a clear and shared plan that you communicate throughout your organization, with one priority in any given period. This leads to the acceleration of outcomes that Sutherland describes in Scrum, rather than the dispersed effort of people pursuing unrelated outcomes based on local or personal agendas.

A helpful approach is to agree the objectives and key results (OKRs) for the next period. Based on the work of Grove at Intel (Grove, 1983), OKRs comprise a clear objective and a small number of key results which can be specifically measured so that you know when they have been completed. This is aligned to the Scrum emphasis on the 'Definition of Done' which defines when an increment has reached the required quality standard (Schwaber and Sutherland, 2020). Clarity accelerates output and enables multiple teams to work in harmony towards complementary outcomes.

SIMPLE CLARITY

Six months into one of the most challenging years in business history [2020], simple clarity has become our most precious resource.

O'Keeffe (2020)

Your job is to create this level of joined-up understanding about the priority and how each team and individual contributes to it. Harnish suggests quarterly themes, which are fun ways to engage people in the priority, and to celebrate achievements along the way. By giving the priority a name, you give it an identity that encourages people to talk about it, make sense of it and stick to it. He also suggests a key question to be asked at the quarter-end celebration of success: 'How did you do it?' This question gets to the heart of agile, by asking people to learn from the experience. As they review what they did, what made it successful, and share this insight with others, they are defining lessons that can become part of how they work in the subsequent sprint. This learning drives improvement in the next quarter, increasing productivity and output.

The importance of context

In my doctoral research I interpreted data from the perspective of contextualism, which places emphasis on seeing actions, words or events in the context in which they happen. The standard of knowledge varies depending on the context. I mention this only to introduce the notion that the judgements we make when we choose priorities also need to be made in the context within which we are operating. Normally this means factoring into these judgements the changing priorities of our customers (or clients, patients or other service recipients), the overall purpose and strategic direction of our organization, and the external conditions affecting us in both the short and longer term.

When the Covid pandemic hit the world in early 2020, the context within which most organizations were operating changed suddenly, both from their customers' and colleagues' points of view. As the conditions changed, so did their priorities. The health and wellbeing of people became an immediate priority, as did survival for many organizations adversely affected by the lockdown of societies around the world. At Cirrus, our priorities switched to a) continuing to look after our people and b) enabling our clients to support their people (most working from home) with learning and assessments delivered online. Fortunately, 40 per cent of our delivery was already virtual, so we had deep experience to draw on. We switched all our resources into making this happen within 24 hours of the coronavirus lockdown in the UK and Australia – our people, our technology, our investment. The resulting virtualization of all service delivery was successful, and our clients were able to continue their learning, engagement, and assessment operations with minimal interruption. Consequently, the business continued to grow during the pandemic. As the context changed, so did our priorities and where we subsequently focused our effort and our resources. At no time, however, did we compromise on our purpose, direction and values, which remained at the core of our day-to-day decisions. The fact that we had clear purpose, direction and values in the first place made it easier to adapt to the rapidly changing context.

During the Covid-19 pandemic the benefits of ruthless prioritization became starkly clear. Many organizations adapted to the crisis with accelerating innovation to provide relevant products and services that customers valued in their new context. The crisis forced rapid decision making and focused action from governments, as well as from organizations such as Google which relaunched Meet in face of stiff competition from Zoom and Microsoft Teams. Enforced virtual working for many led to improved productivity (Dahik *et al*, 2020). And many individuals, who had to juggle working from home and a range of other priorities like caring responsibilities and parenting, had to focus their work time on the few tasks that mattered most.

Creating an obsession with simplicity

In my work as a consultant to some very successful organizations, one of the things I see people struggling with repeatedly is stopping doing things. The larger the organization, the more difficult this becomes, as so many activities continue because that is what has always been done. The legacy of processes, procedures, reporting and regulations can become a force in its own right. What we need is an obsession with simplicity that is intent on doing only what is necessary.

In larger organizations where economies of scale have been helpful in achieving a strong market position, there is often a danger that this same scale is now slowing them down and restricting their agility. The processes that have enabled them to deliver consistent quality reduce their ability to respond quickly to competitor activity. The complexity that often comes with operating in multiple geographies and sectors creates an internal industry of governance and negotiation. The structures that allow specialization in a new technology or customer segment cause silos that compete for resources and slow the organization down. All organizations, of whatever size, need appropriate levels of process and governance to operate effectively and efficiently. The problem is when these things have grown to dominate how you operate and slow down your ability to move quickly and easily.

The simplest way to achieve greater simplicity is to stop doing things. If you try to reduce complexity by fine-tuning processes or activities, you risk tinkering at the edges. You need to be bold. When Steve Jobs returned to a failing Apple in 1997, he cut the product lines radically so that it could focus on one platform and make it brilliant. Apple operates on the principle of 'extreme focus', focusing on a few innovative products that can dominate their market. When they brought out the iPhone in 2007 they made the iPod obsolete overnight, which was fine for Apple as they believed the iPhone would be the best product in the market. They said no to the iPod to make way for the iPhone, and the rest is history. Apple appreciates the importance of simplicity: in branding, in product design and in simple intuitive interfaces for its users.

Another example is at a major airline, where the CEO stopped all unnecessary reporting as a symbolic act of simplification. When each report was originally set up, there was almost certainly a valid reason for it, but what tended to happen was that when the reason disappeared the report continued. Layer after layer of reporting remained and gradually enveloped the organization, creating a small industry of reporting and review, much of which was obsolete. Cutting it out caused a positive ripple effect throughout the business, encouraging people to stop doing other redundant activities as well. As leaders we can either encourage or kill such acts in their tracks – can we do without the report, or do we hold on to it in case it's useful in the future?

A study by Accenture (Davies and Philipp, 2017) highlights the power of radical simplicity in the pharmaceutical industry, where complexity has too often been a by-product of the drug development and marketing process. The study recommends a 'zero-based' approach to process review, starting with a blank page to redefine the essential processes needed to achieve the priority goals. It recommends using technology to automate labour-intensive work and working with an 'entrepreneurial mindset' to challenge all assumptions and traditional ways of working, and to identify new ways to deliver customer or patient outcomes. It reflects on using data to drive change, analyse and manage risk and establish simple control methods. The study cites a 95 per cent reduction in complexity, which is radical indeed. It also illustrates how having an external view of your organization and how it operates can help you get to a simpler view of how it could operate. As pharmaceutical companies in 2020 battled to discover, test and release vaccines for Covid-19, the surge of simplification was impressive. Even regulators found ways to accelerate approval more rapidly than had ever seemed possible before the pandemic.

Simplicity is a mindset, a principle that it is worth investing effort in embedding across the organization. It is therefore important that you embody it first, so that you can provide a role model for others to copy. Make a list, prioritize, do one thing at a time, and then move on to the next task. If you focus on the main thing today, and get it done, you are embodying the spirit of agile working, and showing others the way.

Chopin, the illustrious 19th-century Polish composer and pianist, captured a key insight about simplicity, in that it is much more difficult to produce than complexity. 'Simplicity is the final achievement. After one has played a vast quantity of notes and more notes, it is simplicity that emerges as the crowning reward of art' wrote Chopin (Fost, 2007). Complexity springs up quickly where there is a lack of careful design. Simplicity, in contrast, takes effort, art and practice.

Performance improvement

Once you have agreed clear priorities with your teams it is time to shift your focus to supporting their performance improvement. You become the super-Scrum Master, in effect, focused on enabling teams to accelerate their velocity of output. According to *The Scrum Guide* (Schwaber and Sutherland, 2020), the Scrum Master is accountable for setting up and supporting agile teams to perform effectively across the organization. They are accountable for each team's effectiveness through enabling performance improvement.

THE SCRUM MASTER

The Scrum Master serves the Scrum Team in several ways, including:

- coaching the team members in self-management and cross-functionality
- helping the Scrum Team focus on creating high-value Increments that meet the Definition of Done
- causing the removal of impediments to the Scrum Team's progress
- ensuring that all Scrum events take place and are positive, productive, and kept within the time box.

Source: Schwaber and Sutherland (2020)

One leadership trait that is particularly helpful in supporting performance improvement is optimism. 'Optimism differentiates high-performing leaders from the rest', according to research by Newman (2008). Optimistic leaders keep their eye on their vision and have three traits that help improve performance, Newman states: they look for the benefit in every situation, they want to learn from every problem or challenge, and they focus on the task to be done. This mindset creates an environment of optimism: of always making progress and of improving through experience.

Team coaching

Enabling your team to achieve sustained performance improvement requires skills which are a combination of coaching and group facilitation – agreeing stretching goals, discussing regular feedback, asking insightful questions, listening, reading the group to know when to challenge or when to let the group take the lead, and bringing discussion to a helpful conclusion. These skills are typically built up over time, and there is no time like the present to practise. I have been facilitating executive teams for nearly 30 years, and I still learn new insights on a regular basis.

It may be helpful to consider whether this style of coaching is a regular experience for people in your team? Having weekly or even daily coaching conversations is a great way to drive performance improvement. The more you are asking people to reflect on what they are doing, and how they can improve it, the more quickly you will see them taking responsibility for it. The more you are asking rather than telling, the quicker they will learn to think for themselves. Clearly, there are situations where people will not know where to start, as they do not have the requisite knowledge and skills to perform a task effectively – such as someone new to role, where effective induction and training is critical. You would not want a mechanic to replace the brake pads on your car if they had not been trained to do the job well – the risk of error in such circumstances can be significant. But where you are working with experienced and competent people your role is to support and coach as often as it is helpful.

If you are leading a team of leaders of leaders, at a senior level typically, your perspective will be different to if you are leading a team of individual contributors. In the latter the focus will be on getting work done directly, on team cohesion, and on coordinating outputs to ensure you are on track with the customer priorities identified earlier. Whereas in the senior team your emphasis needs to be broader. You are coaching the performance of the team itself, as well as helping your colleagues to coach their teams, and so on. The emphasis shifts to creating a coaching culture, where the practices of coaching and being coached are embraced across the organization. The principles are broadly similar, but the content becomes more about the enterprise the more senior in the organization one goes. It is still important to have stretching goals, one plan and set of priorities, and a regular review of performance to stay on track and adjust as required by changing circumstances. But you also want coaching to become part of the culture.

Agile performance is essentially about team performance, and having a shared set of goals, with shared accountability for delivery, is appropriate at whatever level you are operating in the organization. Just as the individual contributor team review is not just about the individual performance of each team member, the senior team retrospective is not just about the individual functions or divisions represented in the room. The team is the focus with agile.

JURGEN KLOPP AND TEAM PERFORMANCE

When Jurgen Klopp arrived at Liverpool football club he said 'we must turn from doubters to believers'. He subsequently took them from 10th place in the UK Premiership when he arrived to European Champions in 2019 and Premier League champions in June 2020.

Klopp comes across as a warm and caring human being who raises the energy in the room and in the team. And almost without fail he has made players better, whether he signed them or inherited them. Their performance improvement has driven the team's performance, on the training ground and on the pitch.

He believes the training ground is where this difference is made. Drills and tactics are meticulously planned and executed with care. And he insists on the same meticulous attention to detail from others – meetings start promptly, for example. Before games he gathers a great deal of information and then condenses it into the essential details that enables him to make big decisions quickly. Before each game he presents the important information to his team, so they understand the opposition's strengths, and how to beat them, so they leave more confident, believing in their ability to win.

Feedback is fuel

My colleagues at Cirrus sometimes talk about the way we use feedback to drive improvement. We often share feedback after a significant client meeting, presentation or event, which often takes the form of my asking them how it went, what we did particularly well and what we could improve next time. For me it is intended to be a helpful conversation that allows us to give and receive feedback, and to identify how to improve for the next time we are doing something similar. However, I also recognize that for some of them, especially people new to the company, my questions can feel a little intimidating. I recognize that on occasions the opportunity for reflection and learning is being lost, so I have tried to adapt my style accordingly.

Feedback fuels learning and improved performance. If we can give and receive feedback based on facts that are explored with empathy, we can identify in any situation what went well and how to improve. This is at the heart of being agile, this plan–do–reflect–learn cycle in which we are constantly seeking to move faster and improve the quality of our outputs. However, feedback needs to be delivered in a positive way to enable the recipient to accept it easily. As humans we typically have two responses to feedback. If we perceive it to be negative, which feels like a threat, we want to get away from it and do not like to hear it. If we perceive it as positive on the other hand, we see it as a reward: it releases dopamine in the brain, and we move towards it.

Feedback has become an everyday norm of life in the digital age, with sensors on everything from erupting volcanoes to levels of spirits in optics in bars to improve service delivery. As we become more agile, we need to have similar feedback mechanisms in place to track customer responses to our products, their buying patterns, our competitors' activity, our colleagues' motivation, and our own behaviour (and its impact on others). To give and receive feedback well requires us to be receptive, to seek the information to improve, and to be able to distance ourselves from having a defensive reaction. We need to be able to process the information in a balanced way, seeking to understand what we can learn from it rather than seeking to justify why we are doing something.

It is helpful to separate the feedback from our identity as leaders. Feedback on how you are behaving, or how your products are performing for customers, is important data that gives you the opportunity to learn and improve. The data is about your behaviour or about your product's performance, not about you or your company's intrinsic value. If you have, or can establish, in your organization a culture where feedback is sought, valued, and acted on as a matter of routine, you will have more fuel to drive performance improvement.

The rituals and routines of agile working are at least in part designed to encourage regular feedback and learning for the team and its various stakeholders. The retrospective meeting, for example, helps the team to review what happened in the previous sprint, and to agree what is important learning to put into practice in the next sprint. The rituals create a cadence for feedback and regular improvement as well as celebrating successes (which in turn amplifies their impact on team performance). Rituals, whether face-to-face or virtual, are important in making agile ways of working habitual.

Much research into successful executives in this digital age focuses on learning agility (as I described in Chapter 5), and our ability to make sense of ambiguity and take good decisions in uncertainty. It is rooted in curiosity and the ability to assimilate incomplete information into a coherent picture that enables you to make high-quality decisions. 'People who are learning agile: seek out experiences to learn from; enjoy complex problems and challenges associated with new experiences because they have an interest in making sense of them; perform better because they incorporate new skills into their repertoire' (Hallenbeck *et al*, 2011). If we use feedback to fuel our desire to learn and improve, we will develop the muscles of learning and become more agile as a result. Feedback is one of the key sources of learning, so embracing it daily is a recipe for improvement.

PERFORMANCE IMPROVEMENT: JEAN-PHILIPPE COURTOIS, EXECUTIVE VICE PRESIDENT, MICROSOFT

When Jean-Philippe Courtois took control of Microsoft's global sales, marketing and operations in 2016, he launched a transformation initiative focused on harnessing the power of cloud computing to drive better results for customers. Involving over 40,000 employees, this was one of Microsoft's biggest ever change programmes. The first stage was a major restructuring. The second was all about transforming mindsets and behaviours. Courtois realized that Microsoft needed to move away from an 'inspection culture' towards one of coaching and learning (Ibarra and Jones, 2019).

The organization invested in developing coaching skills and deployed digital tools to provide greater insights into employees' ways of working to help managers have structured coaching conversations with their teams. Courtois pushed home the point that performance improvements are best achieved through coaching and feedback, advocating that the role of a manager is to 'pick, grow, and motivate the best capabilities to build customer success' (Ibarra and Jones, 2019).

The coronavirus pandemic effect on performance

Drawing on the agile team research I described in Chapter 3 (AMBS, 2020), we found some interesting insights into how working from home during the coronavirus pandemic had influenced individual and team performance. The data, drawn from an international pool of respondents, suggests that people found the experience to be roughly four times more positive than negative in terms of the impact on their individual performance. This included the use of technology to enable communication and workflow, freedom from close supervision to support greater autonomy, and their ability to plan their own work schedule. Personal productivity appears to have been improved through the experience of working from home, with more control over one's work priorities and less managerial oversight.

The coronavirus pandemic accelerated other changes in managerial approach significantly, with increased levels of trust in people to do a great job, more transparency of information and more flexibility in working arrangements. This is in line with the positive impact empowerment has on agile team performance, described in Chapter 8.

The research also suggests that the performance of teams that work with agile routines was not adversely affected by the pandemic and working from home. The team agility measure did not vary significantly between the February/March and September 2020 data collection stages. This suggests that the accepted wisdom of agile teams needing to be co-located is, at least in part, a myth. The agile teams in the research performed to the same levels before and during the coronavirus pandemic. Agile team rituals give teams the structure and process to continue to perform to high standards, whether co-located or not.

Working from home had a detrimental impact for many on mental well-being, however, as well as reducing social interaction and collaboration, which suggests that it is not a viable long-term approach by itself (QMUL, 2020). A more hybrid approach to working, with a flexible mix of working patterns which cater for both the organization's and the individual's needs, is likely to be preferable. What we must not lose is the increased trust, transparency and flexibility that emerged during 2020 around the world because of the coronavirus pandemic.

In the same research there was a clear link between the quality of relationship you have with your teams and their performance (AMBS, 2020). In Chapter 5 we explored this in more detail. This quality of relationships enables you to coach your teams with real purpose, based on trust and mutual respect.

Summary

We have explored how to plan for sustained performance improvement through ruthless prioritization and high-quality relationships with your teams. We have looked at the power of purpose to unite your people and how trust and feedback enable you to coach your teams to achieve great outcomes.

Now is a good time to take stock and think through how you define priorities. It is also a good time to think about where you focus your attention, and which bold decisions will help you and your people focus on the main thing.

References

AMBS (2020) Agile Team Research, Alliance Manchester Business School and Cirrus, Manchester

Bariso, J (2017) Sheryl Sandberg just gave some brilliant career advice. Here it is in 2 words, Inc, www.inc.com/justin-bariso/sheryl-sandberg-just-gave-some-brilliant-career-ad.html (archived at https://perma.cc/6K87-JR2T)

Cirrus/Ipsos (2017) Leadership Connections 2017, research paper, Cirrus, London

Collins, J (2001) *From Good to Great*, William Collins, New York

Covey, S (1988) *The 7 Habits of Highly Effective People: Powerful lessons in personal change*, Simon and Schuster, New York

Dahik, A, Lovich, D, Kreafle, C, Bailey, A, Kilmann, J, Kennedy, D, Roongta, P, Schuler, F, Tomlin, L and Wenstrup, J (2020) *What 12,000 Employees Have to Say About the Future of Remote Work*, Boston Consulting Group, Boston, MA

Davies, N and Philipp, M (2017) *Curing Complexity*, Accenture, Arlington, VA

Fost, J (2007) Chopin quotation in *If Not God, Then What?* Clearhead Studios, Luton

Grove, A (1983) *High Output Management,* Random House, New York

Hallenbeck, G, Swisher, V and Orr, J (2011) *Seven Faces of Learning Agility: Smarter ways to define, deploy and develop high-potential talent*, Korn Ferry Institute, London

Harnish, V (2014) *Scaling Up*, Gazelles Inc, Kansas City, MO

Hayward, S (2020) How to lead when you're forced to isolate, *Management Today*, www.managementtoday.co.uk/lead-when-youre-forced-isolate/leadership-lessons/article/1700793 (archived at https://perma.cc/W7JA-AWDQ)

Ibarra, H and Jones, A (2019) *Jean-Philippe Courtois at Microsoft Global Sales, Marketing and Operations: Empowering digital success*, London Business School Publishing

Newman, M (2008) *Emotional Capitalists: The new leaders*, John Wiley and Sons, Chichester, UK

Nieto-Rodriguez, A (2016) How to prioritize your company's projects, *Harvard Business Review*, 13 December

O'Keeffe, D (2020) *Retooling Strategy for a Post-Pandemic World*, Bain & Company, Inc, MA

QMUL (2020) London Poll, Queen Mary University of London, www.qmul.ac.uk/media/news/2020/hss/new-poll-reveals-that-nearly-half-of-londoners-who-worked-from-home-during-lockdown-said-it-impacted-negatively-on-their-mental-health.html (archived at https://perma.cc/R2U5-KMTV)

Rigby, D, Spits, J and Berez, S (2020) An agile approach to budgeting for uncertain times, *Harvard Business Review*, September

Rumelt, R (2011) *Good Strategy, Bad Strategy*, Profile Books, London

Schwaber, K and Sutherland, J (2020) *The Scrum Guide*, www.scrumguides.org/docs/scrumguide/v2020/2020-Scrum-Guide-US.pdf (archived at https://perma.cc/4657-ZH27)

CHAPTER EIGHT

Agile execution

Do less, obsess, and perform. HANSEN (2018)

Introduction

Agile leaders enable teams to decide and do – to make intelligent decisions and get work done, together. In this chapter we will explore the final two characteristics of agile leadership: thoughtful and devolved decision making, and collaborative achievement. Together they make the final quadrant – Execute – which is about looking across the team and across the organization to optimize performance (Figure 8.1).

QUESTIONS TO ASK YOURSELF

In this chapter you may find it helpful to consider the following questions as you read:

- Where should you be seeking step changes in execution?
- Where are silos slowing you down?
- What beliefs or assumptions do you need to reset to achieve change?

FIGURE 8.1 The agile leader wheel

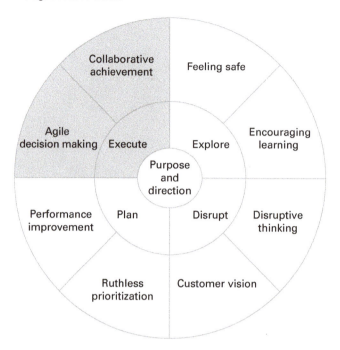

DEVOLVED DECISION MAKING: JACK MA, CO-FOUNDER AND FORMER EXECUTIVE
CHAIRMAN, ALIBABA GROUP

When Jack Ma announced his departure from multinational technology giant
Alibaba in 2018, he had already given his succession a great deal of thought.
Not only had he handpicked his successor, Group CEO Daniel Zhang, but he
also stated in his resignation letter that he had 'complete confidence in our next
generation of leaders'. Having built a culture of talent development, he
described Alibaba as no longer a company that relies on individuals (Hayward,
2018). Ma, who had been described as an autocratic leader early in his career,
adapted his leadership style as the company expanded and attracted more and
more highly qualified and talented people (Ee and Yazdanifard, 2015). He had
realized the value of devolving decision-making responsibility across the
business so that decisions could be made with speed and ease at a local level,
helping to build a more agile and customer-driven business.

Agile decision making

Making the right decision at the right time is the point at which your potential to be agile is put into practice. The decision to act is the start of execution and means you are committing yourself (at least at that moment) to a direction of travel. When the rugby player on the pitch decides to accelerate with the ball past an opponent, the next sequence of play is initiated. Of course, the way the sequence plays out is not known at the point of the move, but when the player moves to their left and seeks to pass the opposite player, they have decided *not* to pass the ball to a team mate. Consequences then play out on the pitch, just as they do in work. The player may lose the ball or create an attack from which a try is scored. It all started with the decision to accelerate.

As we learned from studies of top athletes in Chapter 1, being agile involves both cognitive and physical responses. We need to think agile and we need to act in an agile way. The transition from one to the other is the point of decision. Agility was defined as being 'a rapid whole-body movement with a change of velocity or direction in response to a stimulus' (Sheppard *et al*, 2006). This ability to move rapidly and change direction or speed at the same time is part of the attraction of becoming an agile leader and in creating an agile organization.

In this section we will explore two themes that will enable you and your teams to be more effective at agile decision making and putting the customer at the heart of your organization:

1 Thoughtfulness in making good decisions.
2 Devolution of decision making to enable the whole organization to make agile decisions.

By combining these elements of decision making you can accelerate agility in your organization and at the same time create more time for yourself, which in turn fuels agility. Like the rugby player above, the best leaders seem to have more time in critical situations to make the right call.

Clarity

Before we do, however, it is worth reminding ourselves of the importance of clarity in agile decision making. Providing clarity in an agile context is fundamentally about two things: clarity of purpose and clarity of customer priorities. The first is being clear why you exist, what you add to the world.

It is about what is important to your organization. The second is about understanding what is important to your customers. As we saw in the description of the Scrum ways of working in Chapter 3, being clear on what the customer (or end user, or patient, or student) values most is key to being able to define the priorities for the organization. These two areas of clarity are closely related, in that typically the organization exists to do something amazing for someone, and that someone has unmet needs now.

For example, Lego's ultimate purpose 'is to inspire and develop children to think creatively, reason systematically and release their potential to shape their own future – experiencing the endless human possibility' (Lego, 2008). What this purpose looks like now in terms of the product it sells is quite different to what it looked like 20 years ago, as it has been through a great deal of change in recent years, but it remains true to its purpose as well as being relevant to children today.

In the previous chapter we looked at ruthless prioritization, a corner-stone of agile decision making, which can be hard, especially in a large complex organization. The Lego example is a helpful one as it is focused on its purpose – there are many things that the Lego brand could be used to promote, but the company has remained focused on its core play system, with the bricks available in many formats and kits. Clarity enables connectivity between people across your organization, so that they can align their work effort in the same direction as the rest of the organization. It enables them to decide what is a priority and what is not. It allows people in teams to define shared goals, and for people across a process to align their outcomes.

One of my telecommunications clients was struggling with this idea in practice. The chief executive wanted to embrace agile ways of working, and yet he allowed many uncoordinated corporate initiatives to spring up across functions so that most were under-funded and doomed to become frustrating backwaters for determined but constrained middle managers battling to get organizational attention. Many of the initiatives required IT investment and support, creating a significant list of unfulfilled projects that clogged up the IT function's capacity.

To declutter the system, I facilitated some away-days for the executive team in which we went back to basics. We reviewed the purpose of the organization, its strategic direction and goals, its values that were irrefutable, its main customer priorities, and therefore the list of priority projects that the organization had to deliver. The team reviewed the list and agreed who would be the owner of which, and then agreed to stop the others until these were delivered. The managers who were leading 'stopped' initiatives were reallocated to the priority projects so that these were accelerated. The system soon got unblocked and as each priority was delivered to the minimum required standard, the executive team reviewed the priority list to see if it should continue or be replaced by a different priority on the backlog. Motivation had increased dramatically among executives and managers as they became more productive.

In one retrospective meeting with the executive team, I asked them about whether this was a sustainable way to prioritize the organization's activity. After some defensive speech making by some of the team members, the commercial director sat back and said, 'No, we can't carry on like this. We are now the bottleneck.' Silence, and then nodding rippled around the room. The commercial director continued, 'We need to rebuild this business, so it can do this for itself.' The next stage of the journey was set. Clarity of priorities had led to the need for devolved decision making.

There are a couple of tips I would add when you consider how best to provide clarity to your organization. The first is to involve people in the process so that a) you benefit from their insight and ideas, and b) they feel they have a stake in the outcome. Involvement drives engagement, which in turn drives discretionary effort in the workplace, which accelerates results. The second is to summarize this strategic clarity onto one page, what commentators have called a 'strategy on a page' or a 'one-page strategic plan' (Harnish, 2014). If you can simplify your strategy onto one page with no jargon, while keeping the particular meaning that makes it distinctive, there is a fair chance that others in your organization will be able to understand it – and this makes it more likely that they will take note of it and adapt their actions accordingly.

For the telecommunications client above, with such clarity came the ability to make joined-up decisions about, for example, what to invest in and what to stop doing. Once effective decision making was in place, with clear priorities, the organization could think about devolving this as close to the customer as possible. But before we explore devolution, let us dig a bit deeper into the thoughtfulness that underpins agile decision making.

Thoughtful decision making

Research into leading agile businesses highlights two aspects of decision making that mark them out from less agile ones. Firstly, they 'prioritize strategic decisions' (Accenture, 2017). Leading organizations ensure they give distinct focus to the bigger decisions that concern the company's strategic direction as well as creating an environment where the decisions that affect day-to-day operations are made at the appropriate level in operations. Secondly, they accelerate decision making. They have built a culture of 'making critical decisions at speed – always ensuring that those decisions are tuned to market conditions'. This became even more important as many organizations emerged from the Covid-19 pandemic into dramatically different market conditions. So, you need to be strategic and fast, and for these to be effective you need to be thoughtful.

Going back to the successful athletes, their ability to react quickly and intelligently to create advantage is key to their competitiveness. They read the situation and decide on the appropriate response, supported by their learning agility.

High-performing CEOs do not necessarily stand out for making great decisions all the time; rather, they stand out for being more decisive. They make decisions earlier, faster and with greater conviction. They do so consistently, even amid ambiguity, with incomplete information and in unfamiliar domains. Data shows that individuals described as 'decisive' were 12 times more likely to be high-performing CEOs, as reported by Botelho *et al* (2017) who described their analysis of assessment data for 2,000 CEOs, which revealed what made the most successful CEOs more successful than others. The other behaviours that described the most successful leaders were engaging with stakeholders, adapting to changing circumstances, and reliability.

This decisiveness involves five steps which can help us act quickly in an intelligent way. The five steps are:

1 Pause, to create space to think.
2 Consult with trusted advisers and experts to draw on their insight and experience.
3 Decide, once you have assimilated as much relevant information as possible.
4 Move quickly to execute the decision with confidence.
5 Review and check what is happening.

These elements, shown in Figure 8.2, describe a thoughtful yet rapid approach, one that helps ensure your business has a strong sense of direction, and the ability to act quickly and with a clear shared goal, in response to what has changed. This ability to slow down your thinking to allow you

FIGURE 8.2 Thoughtful decisiveness

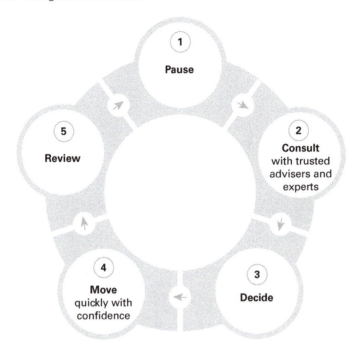

to make a quicker and better decision is a key skill for agile leaders to develop, creating space and time for reflection in the heat of the moment. It leads to intelligent decisions, based on a balanced interpretation of the information available. It can also lead to disruptive decisions if the circumstances require a break with the current norm.

Research into those organizations that emerged most effectively from the immediate effects of the Covid-19 pandemic reinforces the view that decisiveness is key to gaining competitive advantage. 'Turbulent times favour companies that prepare well and that take bold steps despite uncertainty... The ability to spot signals of change and respond to them quickly is how the best companies stay relevant year after year, come what may' (O'Keeffe, 2020).

Interestingly, research suggests that being decisive is not linked to having a particularly high IQ (Botelho *et al*, 2017). In fact, the study showed that this sometimes gets in the way of rapid decision making, as very bright leaders are prone to hold on to greater complexity, wanting the perfect answer to the problem before making the decision to act. This behaviour can lead to bright leaders becoming bottlenecks in their organizations, slowing down their own decision making and that of those around them, thus slowing down the whole organization, making it less agile. Being decisive is therefore not a function of IQ per se; sometimes the opposite is true. But it is a function of your mental agility, of how you approach the need for a decision in the first place. We looked at mental agility in Chapter 5.

If you do have a high IQ, however, all is not lost, as you can learn the five steps above and train yourself to be more decisive. Pausing to breathe, to reflect, to sense what is happening around you and thereby to give yourself the opportunity to understand, is a key skill that agile leaders possess in spades. How often have you come back from a holiday or a trip involving long-haul travel with fresh ideas and a better understanding of the opportunities and threats around you? Certainly, my colleagues at work confess to being a little wary when I come back from a trip with some big new ideas. The key thing for me to do then is to consult with trusted advisers and internal experts to help refine my thinking and gain their insight so that between us we can build a more robust picture of the options. And then decide.

If we can simplify the idea so that we can explain it to someone with no knowledge of the business we are in, then we have probably got a good handle on the nature of the opportunity or threat to which we are responding. We are then in a better place to make the right call, to decide on what ideas to pursue, and how. Notice how we have moved from 'my' idea to 'our' decision, which is a helpful way to gain commitment to act, but ultimately the responsibility for the decision is with the person accountable for the decision area. Getting others involved helps with the fourth stage, which is the confident execution of the decision. Diffident action, slowed down by caution and a lack of conviction, will tend to be less effective. Finally, there is a need to review regularly and to be willing to fail fast if the judgement turns out to be either poor or inaccurate given changing circumstances.

Intelligent speed is our goal here. The champion fencer, for example, is responding to stimuli constantly, as well as moving with agility, to outwit and ultimately outmanoeuvre their opponent. The cut and thrust of the fencer embody this 'read and respond' approach in dynamic glory, with such speed and ease of movement, and yet with such care and attention to the competitor. In the 17th century a lack of cognitive ability could end in death, whereas in the modern sport of fencing the consequences are somewhat less fatal, but the drama is still real, and the way each fencer reads the other is key to victory. The stages of this thoughtful response happen quickly: perception of the stimulus from the opponent, interpretation, and analysis of the options of how to respond, and finally a decision to act. Then the physical agility of the fencer takes over and balance, strength and speed all play their part in success, or failure.

It is helpful to focus for a moment on the interpretation and analysis stage in the fencer's response, as though we are watching them in slow motion. In his book *Thinking, Fast and Slow*, Nobel laureate Daniel Kahneman (2011) describes how in our minds there are two modes of thought and judgement going on, as illustrated in Figure 8.3. He defines them as System 1, which is fast, instinctive and emotional, and System 2, which is slower, more logical and takes more conscious effort.

Kahneman describes how these systems affect our cognitive biases as we seek to make sense of what is going on around us. The fencer, for example, is taking in data about their opponent and seeking to outwit them (using System 2 thinking), while also relying on instinctive responses in the moment to protect themself from attack (drawing on System 1 memory). We tend to default to System 1 as it is easier, automatic and quick, which is fine in predictable circumstances. In unpredictable or complex situations however, where we need to be more agile, we also need to be using our System 2 mode to make more reasoned choices based on more critical thinking. Kahneman describes several decades of academic research that suggests people place too much confidence in their human judgement. If we are to make intelligent decisions in uncertain situations, we need to make the effort to slow down, gather facts and evidence, think more consciously, and maintain a level of sceptical detachment from our instincts and feelings.

Interestingly, it is the System 2 mode of thinking that can maintain a paradox, such as the agile leadership paradox where we need to be enabling others to connect and make sense and yet at the same time challenging the basis of this connection and shared understanding. It takes considerable mental effort to live in this space, rather than the easy, instinctive world of

FIGURE 8.3 Thinking, fast and slow

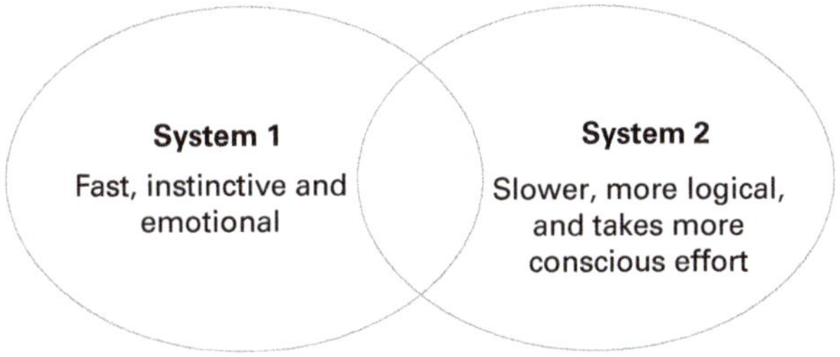

System 1	System 2
Fast, instinctive and emotional	Slower, more logical, and takes more conscious effort

Source: Daniel Kahneman (2011)

System 1 confidence. The effort is worth it when we can make better decisions than our competitors – 'seeing around corners', as one of my clients puts it.

As you develop a more agile organization it is helpful to maintain a balance between thoughtfulness and pace, so that you are achieving better-quality decisions without losing competitive speed. In some clients I have seen two types of paralysis that really slow down the organization and render it unable to compete with disruptive competitors, whether it is in financial services, airlines or retail. First is *analysis paralysis*, where leaders' desire for ever-more detail and analysis of the data causes the business to slow down to a grinding halt. This is often motivated by the leaders wanting to get to a perfect decision, when competitors are experimenting and learning what works for customers in real time. Second is *approval paralysis*, where people in the organization seek approval from their senior managers before acting, often because they fear making a mistake and the consequences of such failure. Decisions take longer than is necessary as they are delegated upwards, drawing senior leaders into getting involved in detail that is better left to the experts they employ to make such decisions in the first place. If you sense either of these types of paralysis apply to you and your organization, it is worth considering this further to identify the real issue, as they are corrosive cultural factors that resist agility and slow you down.

Creating mental space for the System 2 cognitive response to major strategic issues is essential if you are to make agile decisions quickly and yet with the degree of thoughtfulness of the champion fencer. This needs you to be able to slow things down, in the moment very often, and to give yourself calmness to think. A great technique to help you do this is to practise mindfulness through meditation, which trains you to focus your attention on the immediate.

Mindfulness has become popular in the Western world in recent years, and it originates from Buddhist teachings, where it helps to develop self-knowledge and wisdom, leading gradually to what is described as enlightenment or ultimate freedom from suffering. A typical starting form of meditation to build mindfulness might be a 10-minute morning routine when you awake: sit on the side of your bed or in a chair, focus on your breathing and empty your mind of other thoughts. Repetition makes the process of emptying your mind of thought easier. Key to it is having a non-judgemental approach, accepting of the situation and returning to focus on your breathing when your mind wanders.

At the end of such a routine you might frame your day, thinking about how you want to show up at work, how you want to make others feel, and how you want to feel during the day. This creates a helpful reference point for the day, so that you can go back to these small decisions and refresh your mind with their intent. The non-judgemental approach to yourself can also be a helpful approach to others, as we know from authentic leadership theory that having a balanced, non-judgemental approach to processing information improves your ability to make thoughtful decisions that others are more likely to trust (Walumbwa *et al*, 2008).

It is not unusual to see sports people preparing for a big match or tournament listening to music on headphones, getting into the zone where they are focused and calm, with 'blue heads' as the All Blacks would say. In 2010 James Kerr had unprecedented access to the New Zealand rugby team to learn how they had rebuilt themselves as world champions after their premature exit from the 2003 World Cup (Kerr, 2013). They wanted to overcome their habit of seizing up at critical moments and focused on keeping 'blue heads'. 'Red head' is a state in which you are off task, easily panicked and ineffective. 'Blue head', on the other hand, is an optimal state in which you are on task, focused and performing to your best ability. Using personal triggers such as stamping feet, the players were able to recall their 'blue head' mindset so they could achieve clarity and accuracy, and so perform consistently well under pressure. There had never been any question about their ability and commitment. What they needed was the mental space to think clearly and to make great decisions – individually and as a team – throughout the intensity of a rugby test match.

Meeting madness

One change you can make to create time for high-quality decision making is to reduce the volume of time you spend in meetings. In my experience, there is a direct correlation between the size of an organization and the concentration of meetings leaders attend. In many smaller, more entrepreneurial organizations, meetings are as short as possible, focused on key topics, and with only those present that need to attend. In larger organizations, too often managers are in back-to-back meetings throughout the day, with little time for thinking properly or on a longer-term basis. Without time to think it is difficult to make progress and to see clearly where the big decisions for your organization are.

One CEO I have worked with in retail has moved the main business meetings to a Monday, so her team is all together for that day, and delegated other meetings where she is not really needed to others. She has created time out of the office to listen to colleagues and customers around the stores and distribution centres and has a monthly half-day meeting with her wider leadership team to discuss and make sense of the challenges facing the business and how to resolve them. She is listening, consulting, learning and involving others.

She has also started to create mindful moments, points in the day when she can refresh her mental agility, reconnect with what is important, and give her brain time and space to be still. She starts with the first few minutes when she gets up in the morning, pausing to breathe, to focus on how she wants to be today, how she wants to feel and what she wants others to feel like as they interact with her. She breathes deeply and slowly, allowing her mind to be present in a purposeful way. On Mondays on the way into work she makes sure she has thought through each meeting she will attend and what is the important discussion or decision that the meeting needs to focus on. She is clear about the purpose and how she can best engage her colleagues into a fruitful discussion. She thinks about the one or two questions that will be most helpful in focusing on the right issue.

She makes time for connecting with others with lunch or a call while she walks around the block. She is seeking all the time to be present, and thus able to reflect on what is important in each conversation, asking the best question, listening for what is said or not said, seeking to learn each day and to have a similar effect on her colleagues, so that they are also creating mindful moments to allow themselves to be thinking effectively rather than being busy. She is using deliberate techniques to slow things down, to slow her own thinking down, rather than being in a rush. By slowing down, she can speed up what matters and she can focus on the few decisions that matter most to the business.

Ultimately, she and the board will make the strategic decisions that are their responsibility, and do so with confidence and appropriate speed, but she has reduced this list to the minimum necessary and consults experts widely in the business to get a balanced set of insights. This CEO has found a helpful balance between the rhythm and routine she and the business need for goal achievement with the strategic space to think longer term. She recognizes the need to balance reliability and agility, delivering results consistently while being open to trends in the market and adapting to meet them. This delivery gives her and her team the space to think ahead and make well-formed decisions that adjust the direction of the business in line with seizing emerging opportunities or responding to competitive threats or shifts in technology. Then they execute the decisions with the greater conviction that their thoughtful approach has given them.

Devolution works

One of the factors from the connected leadership research that underpins agility is the devolution of decision making to be as close to customers as possible, increasing your organization's responsiveness to changing trends and market conditions (Hayward, 2016). As I mentioned in Chapter 1, devolving decision making at Waterstones, the leading UK bookseller, helped to save the company. By putting control back in the hands of local store managers and their teams, the company regained a trusted relationship with its local book-reading consumers who wanted local relevance in the world of uniform digital delivery created by the Kindle.

I find that this approach is often misunderstood by senior managers who think that devolving decisions means creating an adhocracy, where there is little order, more a hope that managers and teams will make the right decisions. Ad hoc decision making is not coherent decision making, and it is likely to lead to reduced performance, because it is essentially random. You are more likely to produce predictable and positive results if you manage the process of devolving decision-making responsibility in a planned, careful and supportive manner.

The concept of empowerment has had a mixed press over the last 20 years, sometimes seen, in my experience, as either a unilateral decision by well-intentioned individual managers to delegate responsibility to others, or a sign of 'power to the people' inspired by left-wing politics. Neither is remotely true. Empowerment relates to how people perceive their work (Spreitzer, 2008). It is a psychological state that encompasses four aspects of how people feel:

1 *Competence* – an individual's belief in his or her capability to be effective.
2 *Impact* – the degree to which an individual can influence outcomes at work.
3 *Meaningfulness* – the value people see in a work goal, judged in relation to their own standards or ideals.
4 *Self-determination* – an individual's sense of having choice in initiating and regulating action.

Empowerment is primarily driven by line managers (supported by the organizational culture created by senior leaders), as they create the psychological climate in which people are making these judgements every day. What climate do you create? What climate do your line managers create? Is it a safe one where people believe in their capability, where people feel that their role is valued, that they have influence and a sense of discretion about what they do? Or is it one where they feel diminished, impotent or with little control? The climate you create will be the most important determinant of whether efforts to devolve decision making closer to the customer are successful.

A planned approach to devolution has several important components, which taken together will lead to a successful devolution of decision making closer to the customer. Here is a seven-point checklist of what you need to do:

1 *Climate of trust* – create a climate where people feel trusted to take risks by their leaders, without the threat of punishment.
2 *Definition* – agree which decisions should be made at each level in your organization and with what frequency.
3 *Training* – provide training and coaching for managers to be able to engage their teams in this process and to support them to make effective decisions together.
4 *Information* – provide accurate, relevant, and easy to interpret management information to managers and teams at each level so they can make informed decisions on a regular basis.
5 *Letting go* – senior leaders and managers throughout the organization let go of decisions that are allocated closer to the customer.
6 *The system* – adapt the processes and systems to support more localized decision making in practice.
7 *Feedback* – give consistent and transparent feedback to everyone so they know what is happening, how they are performing, and where to focus on improvement.

This list suggests that it does take time to build the climate and the supporting infrastructure to make devolved decision making a reality. In practice it can take years to embed a more empowered organization, where decisions are made as close to the customer as possible. But the benefits are worth the effort: faster decision making, brilliant service recovery, increased customer loyalty and advocacy, improved engagement and greater agility.

Collaboration and agile teamworking

Teamwork is at the heart of both devolved decision making and agile execution. An agile team is a multi-skilled collaborative unit of production, empowered to decide how it will achieve its goals, in line with your customer-centred strategy.

Creating a collaborative environment requires both trust and a quality of relationship that is unusually high. The alternative is a siloed environment with an emphasis on tribal loyalties first, which is too often the case in larger organizations, according to research and my own experience. 'Stripping down of silos is the key to profitability', according to a 2016 report by PwC (Staak and Cole, 2016). This global survey of more than 300 retail and consumer goods chief executives found that only 18 per cent had eliminated operational silos to deliver seamless omnichannel shopping experiences. 'Those who had eliminated silos expressed greater confidence in revenue growth (59 per cent compared with 48 per cent average for all chief executives) and profit growth (63 per cent against 43 per cent for those still siloed).'

Customers tend to expect a seamless experience when working with different parts of an organization, but internal barriers and poor inter-departmental relationships mean that often this is not delivered. As an agile leader, it is your responsibility to set the tone and to be a role model for changing this situation where it occurs, especially in the post-Covid-19 world where customer expectations are even higher than before.

SPACE TO THINK TOGETHER

When we built our new Centre for Scientific Excellence in Hull, we created a very open-plan environment to encourage collaboration. We used the new centre to accelerate transformation, breaking down silos, improving cross-functional working, and creating connections. Even when we work remotely, we have maintained that collaboration because it has become the norm. We can respond to change very quickly. Communication and openness have improved, and we can leverage the new networks we have built.

Bruce Charlesworth, Chief Medical Officer, Health, RB

Build strong team foundations

Strong teams tend to outperform collections of talented individuals, as was demonstrated in Belbin's famous team experiments, which showed that the key difference between the most successful teams and others was not intelligence but behaviour (Belbin, 2011). Successful teams in Belbin's research had a complementary blend of different team-oriented behaviours, whereas the groups of talented individuals tended to compete, resulting in sub-optimal performance overall.

These team behaviours tend to start with developing a shared sense of purpose and shared goals. A study of team performance in over 30 companies showed that members of high-performing teams share a meaningful purpose and experience high levels of commitment and satisfaction from being part of and working with the team (Katzenbach and Smith, 1992). Teams with shared purpose are also good at solving their own problems, as there is mutual accountability and a willingness to act, which in turn leads to quality results.

In an agile context, teams are empowered to operate with a high level of discretion about how they achieve the goals defined by the product owner. For this to work in practice, the team needs agreed ways of problem solving, making decisions and reviewing performance. These attributes help to build trust between team members, and an appreciation of the contribution each member can make, so that they can value the differences between each other. Trust underpins an inclusive culture within the team, which in turn encourages all members to contribute fully to the team's effectiveness.

As I said in Chapter 5, trust in a business context is about having a real confidence in others, in their capability to deliver and their character to do so reliably and honestly. Building trust in your teams is an essential foundation if you want them to work together in agile ways, and it starts with creating an environment where they feel safe, and therefore confident to take risks. As Sutherland (2015) states, 'the absolute alignment of purpose and trust [in teams] is something that creates greatness'. This requires dedicated effort from the team and the team leader to build this confidence through creating time and space for honest conversations, team reviews and reinforcement of positive behaviours.

The absence of trust is the first dysfunction of a team cited by Lencioni (2005) in his review of the barriers to effective team performance. He describes progressive levels of team functionality that is a helpful checklist you can use to evaluate your own team's behaviours:

- Team members trust each other so strongly that they can be completely open with each other about their fears, weaknesses and mistakes.
- They can therefore engage in healthy and challenging dialogue about how to make the team perform better.
- This in turn leads to genuine commitment from all team members to important decisions, which may involve disagreement and debate, so everyone's views have been listened to, but leads to a unanimous decision.
- Team members can then hold each other accountable for performance versus these decisions and standards of behaviour and will challenge each other where appropriate to step up.
- Ultimately, team members can put their own needs and agendas to one side and focus on what is best for the team to achieve optimal results together.

Ask yourself: to what extent can you truly say each of these sentences is true of how you and your team work together? Where are you deficient and how can you address it?

Developing great team working requires time, courage and sustained reinforcement. Time for reviews of performance in retrospectives to explore what worked well and where there are opportunities for improvement in the next sprint. Courage to give honest feedback and to accept feedback as information intended for improvement. Courage to resolve interpersonal conflict to build stronger relationships. And sustained reinforcement to keep the bonds of trust and respect strong, growing and healthy. Just as a gardener tends to their garden with a regular diligence to keep it in a healthy state, the team leader and team members need to invest time to review, discuss and agree how to keep improving.

COLLABORATIVE ACHIEVEMENT: CHRISTINE LAGARDE, PRESIDENT, EUROPEAN CENTRAL BANK

Lagarde has described her leadership style as one of fostering change and bringing people together to spark new ideas (Ignatius, 2013). She has often spoken of the economic benefits of greater inclusion, of encouraging greater female representation at board level, for example, particularly during times of crisis. Accepting a Distinguished Leadership Award from the Atlantic Council in 2019, her speech recognized others who had influenced her, stating that, 'We are all in this together' (IMF, 2020). Her inclusive ethos helps to drive greater economic collaboration.

Self-managing teams

Once you have strong teams in place you can accelerate the way they manage their own work and outputs. Your teams need to have the skills and confidence to define together how to deliver the outcomes for the next sprint or period. This can mean getting support from the outside, from an agile coach for example, to facilitate discussion about issue resolution and to create greater honesty and transparency between team members, so that they really do get to a decision to which they are all committed. Agile coaches provide informal 'enabling leadership' and help to 'accelerate innovation' at companies such as Spotify (Backlander, 2019). They support teams to improve 'team dynamics and performance'. Great teams that really take responsibility for their performance tend to have regular and sometimes difficult discussions about individual and collective performance, as well as problems that need solving, and this requires a strong foundation of trust and respect. Without it, the team risks breaking up under the pressure these conversations create.

I used to be a keen rower. There are a couple of insights from rowing that relate to self-managing teams. The first is that we needed a good routine to perform well. This related to our training sessions as well as our race day activities. In training we needed short bursts of intense activity to build capability, and then an opportunity to debrief. On race days we had an almost obsessive approach to setting up the boat correctly, warming up well and getting to the start smoothly. In business teams the same is true – we need to work in short sprints, with clear outcomes, and an opportunity to stop and review to improve the next time. We need a ritual for setting up projects or new priorities, with clearly defined stages of briefing, planning and execution.

The second insight from rowing is that it takes a range of skills to make up a balanced and effective team. Some were big and strong and rowed towards the back in the 'engine room'. Some had excellent technique and rhythm and sat towards the front. One of them was stroke, setting the pace and rhythm in the boat. Some were suited to be trainers, working with the crew to coach and identify the opportunities to make the boat go faster. Some were lighter and became coxes, steering the boat and managing the crew on the water. Even in a sport like rowing, there was a need for a multi-skilled team. In a professional work context, this need is often greater, and yet too often we see teams built in the image of the leader, with superficial harmony based on a shared outlook, but lacking trust and challenge to perform well.

Size matters

It is also important to ensure that each team is not too large (or small), and the received wisdom is the rule of 'seven plus or minus two'. Too large and the numbers get in the way of dialogue and decision making, too small and the team is likely to lack key skills and experience. Once a team gets into double figures the number of different communication channels becomes too complex to manage easily and the quality of dialogue will diminish rapidly. I have been asked more than once to 'do team building' with executive groups that have numbered from 15 to 25. I have had to decline, as it is not possible to develop a strong executive team on this scale, when their role in the organization is to think together, plan together, decide on strategic options together, review organizational performance together and create a winning culture together. So, size does matter.

Fluid team structures

In an agile context there are two types of team that you need if you are going to create a more agile enterprise. The first is the stable team that, for example, develops software or product innovations, and that will develop a depth of mutual understanding over an extended period. These teams need to be multi-skilled and well supported. Clearly, team structures change, as the organization adapts to changing circumstances and strategic priorities, but these teams are essentially stable.

The second type of team is the short-life team that forms for a specific piece of work, drawn together from across the organization and having a finite period in which to achieve a particular outcome. These short-life teams should have an appropriate diversity of capability and experience to achieve the outcome, often requiring a blend of cross-functional expertise that can be quite educational for everyone involved. They also need strong organizational sponsorship to give them the influence they need to succeed, as they will often be working across traditional functional boundaries and potentially challenging existing power dynamics.

MIXED TEAMS FOR DIGITAL CHALLENGES

I'm inspired by the thought that we have 19th-century institutions facing 21st-century problems. Our existing tools, practices, approaches are largely insufficient, if not broken; we must make new ones. We need to address

---

21st-century issues with a more flexible toolkit. Hybrid solutions emerge from the synthesis of disciplines into something new. I've led project teams that contain designers, architects, artists, coders, economists, filmmakers and sociologists. These transdisciplinary teams are extremely well-equipped to tackle the kind of complex, interdependent challenges we face today, and tomorrow. We know that new knowledge and new practice – new ideas and new solutions – emerge through the collision of disciplines, at the edges of things, when we're out of our comfort zone.

Dan Hill, Director of Strategic Design, Vinnova (Swedish government's innovation agency), and Visiting Professor, UCL Institute for Innovation and Design Academy, Eindhoven

Team meetings

There is one type of meeting that needs to be protected in an agile environment and that is the team meeting. Daily huddles, regular planning meetings and retrospective meetings at the end of sprints are all part of the team rhythm and routine that helps the team function at its most productive level.

The key thing in all these meetings is that there is a rhythm and discipline to ensure that you are focused on the right topics at the right time – the daily huddle, for example, is not the time to discuss strategic priorities, so if a significant issue emerges it should be taken offline for when you have time to explore it effectively, such as in a monthly planning meeting. The daily huddle is a powerful way to bring the team together, stay on track and address operational issues as they arise. It is short, focused and practical.

When you have distributed team members (working from home or spread geographically) it is particularly important to maintain a drum beat of regular meetings in which the team can connect, build relationships and have time to understand each other's priorities and issues.

The team leader's role is to facilitate these discussions effectively. Where some people are working from home and some are in the office, it is important to maintain a geographically neutral approach, so that there is no sense that people in the same location get more airtime or attention than those in remote locations. A helpful technique is to agree with the team certain ground rules, such as each person's contribution can only last for a set period of time, and that everyone is invited to contribute regularly wherever they are located. Virtual teams often need to work harder to develop the levels of trust and mutual understanding needed for agile working to work well, which in the early stages of a team coming together may require more time to be invested in meetings to allow this to build. Ideally, bring the team together in one location at the beginning of their working together, to accelerate building mutual understanding and trust between geographically dispersed team members. Annual face-to-face meetings or conferences become important ways to reinforce the team's shared purpose, goals and mutual trust. Following the lockdowns caused by the Covid-19 pandemic, this is likely to be more important than ever, where feasible.

Another helpful tip with virtual teams is to communicate extensively using multiple channels, so people in various locations can receive information and be part of dialogue in ways that suit them. Synchronous video meetings are now ubiquitous, but it is also helpful to use asynchronous channels (like Teams or Yammer) for recorded audio or video messages or written updates, and WhatsApp or similar group apps to share daily news. Encourage the team to own these channels to maximize ownership of the communications. The more dispersed your team the more various communications channels can be helpful to build and maintain a sense of shared purpose and accountability for shared results, although it is worth remembering that too much of a good thing is also not helpful.

Finally, in all team settings, it is helpful to bear in mind the value of personal moments, when individual or team achievements are celebrated, and when personal challenges are recognized by the team and support is provided. Increased levels of social interaction helped to protect team performance during the pandemic-related lockdowns in 2020 (AMBS, 2020). It is great to see how people rally around a colleague when they receive a call from school to say their child is ill and needs picking up, or when they celebrate someone mastering a new technique in their work, or when they stop to console a colleague when they have had a bereavement. These moments knit people together, creating bonds of commitment that can often outlive the team for many years.

Summary

You can accelerate your organization's agility through more thoughtful and devolved decision making and developing purposeful teams to execute the decisions with determination. Ramping up agility in this way will enable faster and more effective responses to digitization and global disruption.

You need to pause and keep a cool head to deal with complex and uncertain situations and carefully devolve decision making throughout your organization so that decisions are made thoughtfully and quickly as close to the customer as appropriate.

Teams are at the heart of agile working and need a clear purpose, commitment to shared goals, and a depth of trust that allows for robust debate and direct feedback without anyone taking offence. This takes time, courage and sustained reinforcement. Self-managing teams that decide how to achieve their goals need both the authority to make these decisions and the coaching support to operate effectively.

As an agile leader, you may wish to reflect on this chapter both for your own team and for teams across your organization. Where are you seeing success, and where is there scope to improve teamworking in practice? Investing your time and effort in these areas will pay significant dividends in terms of accelerating agile working and the ability to deliver customer outcomes faster and more efficiently.

References

Accenture (2017) *Traits of an Agile Business: Accenture strategy*, available at www.accenture.com/gb-en/insight-traits-truly-agile-businesses (archived at https://perma.cc/8PZG-TLTD)

AMBS (2020) Agile Team Research, Alliance Manchester Business School and Cirrus, UK

Backlander, G (2019) Doing complexity leadership theory: How agile coaches at Spotify practise enabling leadership, *Creative Innovation Management*, Wiley Online Library, London, doi.org/10.1111/caim.12303 (archived at https://perma.cc/PXX9-ZN9A)

Belbin, M (2011) Management teams: Why they succeed or fail, *Human Resource Management International Digest*, **19** (3)

Botelho, EL, Rosenkoetter Powell, K, Kincaid, S and Wang, D (2017) What sets successful CEOs apart, *Harvard Business Review*, May–June

Ee, CTJ and Yazdanifard, R (2015) The review of Alibaba's operation management details that have navigated them to success, *Global Journal of Management and Business Research*

Hansen, M (2018) *Great at Work: How top performers do less, work better, and achieve more*, Simon and Schuster, New York

Harnish, W (2014) *Scaling Up*, Gazelles Inc, Kansas City, MO

Hayward, S (2016) *Connected Leadership*, Financial Times Publishing, Pearson, London

Hayward, S (2018) What can Alibaba's Jack Ma teach us about succession planning?, *Management Today*, www.managementtoday.co.uk/alibabas-jack-ma-teach-us-succession-planning/leadership-lessons/article/1493063 (archived at https://perma.cc/8EWN-GB3T)

Ignatius, A (2013) I try to spark new ideas, *Harvard Business Review*, Boston, MA

International Monetary Fund (2020) A personal view on leadership, www.imf.org/en/News/Articles/2019/05/06/sp043019-a-personal-view-on-leadership (archived at https://perma.cc/7XE5-7HWB)

Kahneman, D (2011) *Thinking, Fast and Slow*, Farrar, Straus and Giroux, Macmillan, New York

Katzenbach, J and Smith, D (1992) *The Wisdom of Teams: Creating the high-performance organization*, Harvard Business Review Press, Boston, MA

Kerr, J (2013) *Legacy: What the All Blacks can teach us about the business of life: 15 lessons in leadership*, Constable, London

Lego (2008) Lego brand framework, available at www.lego.com/en-us/legohistory/mission-and-vision (archived at https://perma.cc/MR86-449Y)

Lencioni, P (2005) *Overcoming the Five Dysfunctions of a Team*, Jossey-Bass, San Francisco, CA

O'Keeffe, D (2020) *Retooling Strategy for a Post-Pandemic World*, Bain & Company, Inc, MA

Sheppard, JM, Young, WB, Doyle, TLA, Sheppard, TA and Newton, RU (2006) An evaluation of a new test of reactive agility and its relationship to sprint speed and change of direction speed, *Journal of Science and Medicine in Sport*, **9**

Spreitzer, M (2008) Taking stock: A review of more than twenty years of research on empowerment at work, *Handbook of Organizational Behaviour*, Sage, London, pp 54–72

Staak, V and Cole, B (2016) *Reinventing Innovation: Five findings to guide strategy through execution*, PwC Innovation Benchmark, London

Sutherland, J (2015) *Scrum*, Random House Books, London

Walumbwa, F, Avolio, B, Gardner, W, Wernsing, T and Peterson, S (2008) Authentic leadership: Development and validation of a theory-based measure, Management Department Faculty Publications, Paper 24, University of Nebraska, Lincoln, NE

PART THREE

Making it happen inside and out

CHAPTER NINE

Creating an agile enterprise

We place the highest value on actual implementation and taking action. FUJIO CHO, PRESIDENT, TOYOTA (2004)

Introduction

Throughout this book I have drawn on agile principles and ways of working and sought to describe how you can embrace them as a leader so that you can create agile teams and an agile organization. An agile organization can adapt quickly to changing market conditions, such as during the Covid-19 pandemic, as well as radically improving productivity, the pace of innovation and improving your customer experience.

In this chapter I will describe how you can take people with you on the journey and inspire them to exploit opportunities more rapidly. In the post-Covid-19 world, the winners will often be those organizations which reacted more quickly, more boldly, more collaboratively, and with greater strategic clarity (de Smet *et al*, 2020).

As we have explored, however, becoming agile is not a trivial change: it is a radical shift for many leaders and organizations. For them it will need to be a metamorphosis – both personally and collectively – if it is to have the benefit of creating an agile organization able to succeed in our digital world. So, if you want to take people with you, you need to create a movement in which others choose to believe.

QUESTIONS TO ASK YOURSELF

In this chapter you may find it helpful to consider the following questions as you read:

- Are you a brilliant role model for agile ways of working?
- How can you coach your team to embrace agile?
- Where are the most fertile areas to introduce agile working in your organization?

As the authors of a Boston Consulting Group paper on leading digital transformation wrote: 'In the age of agile, CEOs can't expect their teams to sprint if they just keep jogging' (Danoesastro *et al,* 2017). You need to be a role model and to have some committed supporters who will start the movement going with you. At parties and weddings around the world, some brave person will typically try to get the dancing started, but it is the second person who joins them on the dance floor, and then the third and fourth who follow, who turn it from a solo demonstration into a real dance. So, it starts with leadership – your leadership. Here are five tips to help you get the dance going:

1 Articulate the vision.
2 Flip managers.
3 Build the muscle.
4 Light fires.
5 Embed the process.

As the ultimate product owner, your role starts with articulating the vision for transformation in service of the customer. It continues with getting other leaders around you who can carry the story to a wider audience, and who can move away from the rules of the past to embrace new ways of working. As you widen the management involvement you can also start to deepen organizational capability to think and work in agile ways.

Throughout this process you need to be lighting fires as pockets of agile working appear around your organization. These fires will create breakthrough moments, innovations that attract customers, and accelerated outputs that attract more people to want to get involved. Over time you will build a community of agile thinkers who embrace the new ways of working, and then you can embed them in the core processes of your organization, such as hiring and promoting, and reporting and management information.

In this way you create a movement, one that after a while can become self-sustaining, so that you can spend more time thinking around the corner, anticipating market shifts and new technologies and their application in ways that we have not yet seen.

1 Articulate the vision

Creating a sense of opportunity for people is inherently motivating, so aligning what becoming more agile will mean for the organization and individuals is key. Engaging people in the agility vision, the purpose behind it, and the priorities for action, is a necessary precursor to rapid change. It is helpful to articulate the principles of how you want to work in your own words, in a way that will resonate with the people in your organization. You might want to take the principles in the Agile Manifesto as a starting point, as we saw at the end of Chapter 3, and edit them down to a few key principles that capture your intent for your organization in particular. Describe the movement you want to create, and how you need everyone to be part of it.

It is important to help people make emotional connections with the movement to build and sustain momentum. 'Human behaviour is complex. Organizations don't adapt to change; their people do. But this human element is overlooked again and again. About 75 per cent of all organizational change programmes fail, largely because employees feel left out of the process' (Dawson and Jones, 2015). It is therefore vital to involve people at all stages, and to articulate what agile means for each person, the benefits to them of working in this way – like the pride in meeting customer needs more rapidly, the satisfaction of working in a highly productive team, or the career opportunities from introducing new ways of working to drive organizational success.

An underlying benefit of agile working relates to the first agile value – people over processes and tools. Agile working puts people at the centre of everything, as they learn and adapt and accelerate together in cross-functional teams. Once people have tasted agile working, they are unlikely to want to go back to more traditional working patterns. At Cirrus, our development team has been working with agile methods for several years, and now this has spread to the rest of the business. People in other teams have seen the developers' enthusiasm for the Scrum approach and are now embracing these ideas in a practical way through a major overhaul of processes and ways of working. We have moved to a quarterly business cycle, with monthly reviews, and we are focused on delivering the best customer experience in our sector.

A key aspect of this has been the people emphasis at the heart of agile working. The advance of digitization, accelerated by the coronavirus pandemic, has too often been at the cost of human intimacy and respect. As humans we value the friendly smile, the reassuring pat on the arm, the hug of an old friend when you need comfort, the nod across the room of someone you know will always be at your side, however tough the circumstances. Agile working brings this level of trust and interdependence back into work in an exciting way. In this post-Covid-19 world, with significant social disruption as well as ever-increasing digital connectivity, we are at risk of losing our sense of human connection, which is too high a price to pay. Agile teams turn this on its head. If you can connect with your people in this way you will get them involved and emotionally invested from the start, which will accelerate progress in time.

2 Flip managers

For managers in many digital-native organizations such as Uber, Airbnb and Spotify, agile ways of working are familiar. For many managers in organizations that are not digital natives, this is less the case, except in perhaps the IT function or the development teams. They are likely to be used to more traditional management practices, with a more hierarchical approach and with linear timelines and dates for outputs set for workers. If you are in the latter group, you will find much of this chapter (and this book) helpful in getting your head around the flip needed to embrace and support successful implementation of agile working. 'The success of a transformation depends on the organization's leaders, especially the CEO, due to the scale and complexity of the changes required' (Danoesastro *et al*, 2017).

Agile leadership is not a very traditional style of leading. Getting managers to 'flip the way they work' is the first big challenge (Rigby and Sutherland, 2016). This requires a mindset shift among managers at all levels in the organization, starting with the most senior, reframing their role from control to enabling, and from hierarchy to support. As we saw with the elite athletes earlier, if you learn to think differently, you can learn new levels of skill and movement that make you more agile and competitive. Just learning the skills or movements alone will not give you the peak performance required to compete with the best. In my experience this is best achieved by using a multifaceted approach, involving several elements at the same time:

- *Outside-in learning* – learn from the successes of the digital natives and meld it with your organization's core strengths and culture, such as learning how to understand your customers more intimately through analysing big data trends.
- *Shorter planning cycles to be more adaptive* – adopt shorter plan and review cycles (monthly or quarterly) and stay flexible in between to flex with changing market forces; set the vision (or product goal) to drive alignment and step back to give autonomy to others in achieving the vision.
- *Experiential development to challenge deep-seated habits* – take your leaders into uncomfortable experiences that challenge their assumptions about control, trust and delegation and support them with coaching and organizational encouragement to change. This can be done by using external consultants to design such experiences and to facilitate them effectively (eg providing a safe environment for leaders to work in small teams with little time to achieve challenging tasks).
- *Create advocates by getting leaders to teach others* – involve leaders in training people across the organization so that through the articulation of the 'why', 'what' and 'how' of agile they embody it more deeply; leaders can run workshops, for example, with their teams and with wider groups of people to train them in agile prioritization and decision making.
- *Senior role modelling of letting go and supporting mistakes* – visibly support mistakes as learning opportunities and ensure you and senior leaders are constantly getting feedback about your behaviour so that you do not inadvertently disrupt agile initiatives.
- *New team skills* – learn the skills of collaboration, feedback and review, empathy, and continuous improvement, through skills development, coaching and sharing with your own teams.

If it were easy, everyone would have done it by now. Much of this transformation in leadership capability will be difficult to adopt for managers in traditional organizations. It is likely to be disorientating for some and will challenge underlying assumptions about whether they can trust others by empowering them and leaving them to get on with tasks.

The coronavirus lockdown measures in 2020 accelerated flexible working practices around the world, and productivity tended to stay the same or increase as a result (Dahik *et al*, 2020). For some managers, this greater flexibility may still prove too much, and if they self-select out of your organization then it is probably best for everyone. The worst outcome is for those who do not believe in the agile approach to remain as passengers or terrorists. They will hold you back and be unhappy in the process. So be alert, but give managers time to adapt, and do not judge too easily or soon, as it is a challenging journey and will take time to make real progress.

3 Build the muscle

You are looking to create new sustainable organizational muscles, or capabilities, in agile ways of working. What is an organizational capability? According to Ulrich and Smallwood (2004):

> Organizational capabilities emerge when a company delivers on the combined competencies and abilities of its individuals. Organizational capabilities enable a company to turn its technical know-how into results.

To develop agility as a company-wide capability you need to engage all your people in the journey – but where do you begin? There are two muscles that you need to build systematically among colleagues if you are to set up agile working to succeed: 1) agile process and skills – agile ways of working such as prioritization, planning, sprint review, and visualization of progress; and 2) team skills – working collaboratively in the team, respecting different skills and experience from cross-functional colleagues, giving and receiving feedback as fuel for improvement, and empathy. These two muscles are complementary and can be strengthened through formal training, coaching support and ongoing development, as described in the Scrum ways of working in Chapter 3.

Building agile leadership capability is another key step, and the more pervasive the better. The more the ability to read and respond quickly is permeated throughout your organization, for example, the more the whole enterprise can move quickly in a balanced and coordinated way. The coordination then does not need to come from the top, as this will slow you down. It is better when it comes from the self-organizing teams across the organization, each responding intelligently to those around them and in line with the organization's long-term vision and short-term priorities.

Once we are thinking agile we can behave in an agile way.

In my experience, there are a few simple rules that help to set things up for success in developing such skills and behaviours across large groups of people (see Table 9.1). All this needs to be supported by coaches who help teams to put agile mindset and skills into practice on a day-to-day basis, so that they gradually increase velocity and deliver beneficial results.

TABLE 9.1 Developing agile capability across the organization

Rules	Description
1. Mean it	If you and your leadership colleagues do not mean it, then it will not work (and it is better not to start). So, discuss this change carefully and commit as a leadership team to embark on the journey. Actively support the training across all levels to demonstrate your commitment and desire to learn.
2. Be disruptive	To change mindset and behaviour you need to challenge preconceptions and help people reframe their assumptions. So, design challenging learning experiences that take people out of their comfort zones and give them the opportunity to experience new ways of working in practice.
3. Make it enjoyable	Learning works best when it is engaging and enjoyable, so use imaginative ways to get people involved and create a shared memorable experience.
4. Build momentum	Change takes lots of energy at the beginning, as well as time and regular reinforcement to build momentum, so be willing to invest time and effort early on and repeatedly. Nudges help build momentum, so use a campaign over time to increase action and learning.
5. Make it two-way	Help people to make sense of agile through dialogue and reflection during any training and afterwards in implementation. Involve people in the design and delivery of all training activity so they feel a sense of ownership.
6. Celebrate progress	Measure progress through feedback loops focused on what people are learning and what they are doing with it in practice. Make the feedback visible and simple, and review it as key management data to celebrate shared progress wherever possible; and recognize people when they make breakthroughs to encourage more.

(continued)

TABLE 9.1 (Continued)

Rules	Description
7. Be persistent	Persistence is vital as it takes time and repetition to make changes of this nature permanent. Keep telling the vision story, like a broken record, gradually changing the language people use. Build new habits.

A final insight from Toyota, whose investment in people is a key ingredient in its sustained success. Toyota sees its people as 'knowledge workers who accumulate *chie* – the wisdom of experience – on the company's front lines' (Takeuchi *et al*, 2008). The company invests heavily in developing people and organizational capabilities, and it is constantly seeking to learn from people across the organization. In the world of lean and agile working, the 'chie' of your people becomes a core organizational asset, providing the insight to accelerate improvement and drive innovation.

4 Light fires

So far, much of this has made it sound like a grand company-wide change initiative, and in many ways, this is what you may need to establish. In practice, it is also helpful to start lighting fires across your organization wherever you find complex problems that need agile teams to generate creative breakthrough. In this way you can build bottom-up momentum, a movement from within the organization, that attracts others so that they want to join in. Create multifunctional teams and nudge them regularly to be bold, to challenge old ways of doing things, and to achieve real innovations through an iterative process. Engage them through asking their views on how to solve a problem, listen to their insight and encourage them to develop their ideas into actions.

When fires are lit and teams are set free to work in agile ways, one of your roles is to ensure that other managers do not interfere or inadvertently scupper the new ways of working. Make sure managers understand the agile process, and that their role is to set vision and support the team to deliver. The decisions on how to deliver are with the teams. From the teams' point of view, they will find the experience challenging but quickly experience a sense of control and responsibility that is invigorating for most. Once they have been through a couple of sprints, experienced the excitement of self-management, the satisfaction of achieving a 'done' product, and the insight from a retrospective session to identify how to go faster next time, they will not want to revert to more traditional methods. Through these teams you also accumulate evidence of impact, and this in turn fuels curiosity and uptake elsewhere. So, it is important to nurture the early adopters, without smothering their autonomy, to help them get into their stride and achieve breakthrough results.

> We need enhanced communication capabilities at every step. For managers this means learning to have interactive conversations, to employ authentic narratives, to pose open-ended questions that energize and inspire, and to engage in attentive listening, and encourage horizontal communications to enhance learning. ... a shift from the model of, 'I've got something to tell you and I'm hoping you're going to see it the way I see it, and if you do that, I'll pay you for it,' into 'I've got a spark: let's build a fire together.'
>
> Stephen Denning, 2005

It is helpful to know where to focus your efforts. There are likely to be areas of your organization where agile ways of working are less urgently needed, where, for example, planning horizons are two years out, with predictable customer needs and stable conditions that are unlikely to change this situation. It is better to focus where there is greater opportunity for breakthrough innovation and allow the more predictable areas to adopt what is helpful to them at the right time (see Table 9.1 for further information).

5 Embed the process

It is important to embed agile thinking into your organization's ways of working, including institutionalizing it in core processes such as in Human Resources and Finance. Changing your people and financial processes will reinforce a more agile and flexible mindset across the organization. Equally as important is creating a community of agile advocates, who will make the process changes work well in practice through their own enthusiasm and experience.

People processes

Let us look first at creating more agile people processes to support agile working. We know that technology is driving change at an ever-increasing rate. We also know that people would rather work for a cause than a company (Cirrus/Ipsos, 2017), and have a more detached view of their employer than was prevalent historically. We know we have a changing demography in the workforce, with five generations present, altering retirement practices and an increasing need for 24/7 working to satisfy global working. And the Covid-19 pandemic has only accelerated these changes. Research by the Agile Future Forum (Cannon, 2017) has identified four areas in which you can introduce more flexible practices to aid agile working:

1 **Who is employed?** For example, consider fixed-term contracts, sharing the pool of labour and hiring freelancers.
2 **When do they work?** Can you use more voluntary reduced time, overtime, shift working, part-time working and job sharing?
3 **Where are they working?** Would you benefit from more home working, mobile working and working across multiple sites?
4 **What do they do?** Can you do more multi-skilling, job rotation, skills-based allocation of tasks and rapid retraining?

As we have seen during the Covid-19 pandemic, agile teams can work in flexible ways to accommodate changing conditions such as home working and changing team make-up. If you keep the discipline of each team's rhythm and routine – planning, daily stand-ups, retrospectives and so on – and provide clear goals and coaching support, in my experience these teams can adjust to changing working arrangements and maintain productivity. It is also important to be creating flexible capacity that gives the organization the ability to dial up skills in high-demand areas quickly and dial them down when needed.

Hybrid working has accelerated rapidly because of the pandemic and HR has the opportunity to shape a new style of work which can be of enormous benefit to both the enterprise and the individual worker. Based on a foundation of trust and mutuality between the employer and the worker, hybrid working will support improved productivity *and* personal flexibility, allowing people to balance their care responsibilities, for example, with their team responsibilities.

Learning in the flow of work (Bersin, 2018) is another example of how people processes can be adapted to accelerate agile performance. Giving people the learning when they need it, often through the system they are using for their work, gives people and teams the opportunity to implement improvement immediately and to see the benefit in real time. Bersin also describes the need 'to create learning business partners, Capability Academies, and strong performance consulting skills to help identify performance issues clearly and continuously' (Bersin, 2020). By building the ability in your learning and development teams to sense and adapt, you are more able to align your investment with your future strategic capability requirements.

There are other practices that I would recommend you add to your list of ways to support agile working, such as hiring for willingness to think independently and having a diversity of people working across your agile teams. I would recommend that you encourage your HR colleagues to start hiring for 'creativity, collaboration and curiosity'. For agility to flourish you need diversity of thinking and experience. You also need people who are willing to challenge, to ask awkward questions in the pursuit of improvement, so seek out 'the non-conformists – the candidates that don't easily fit into a box. These are the generalists with an entrepreneurial spirit' (Gothelf, 2014).

The message is: creating more fluidity and diversity of labour, hiring and promoting those who think differently and are willing to speak up, and developing a team-oriented culture, will all encourage agile working in practice. And this can apply in the HR function as much as it does in HR policy across the organization. HR needs to operate with greater flexibility, adapting quickly to changing circumstances, and supporting shifting team structures based on changing customer requirements. When HR understands the customer vision and works with leaders to focus people on the key priorities, agile can accelerate as a result.

Finance processes

Similarly, if we look at the Finance function, the traditional approach to financial control and return on investment or capital is not going to help embed agile ways of working. The assumption of predicted value outcome is not easy in an iterative, experimental world, where the value is incrementally added and customer needs evolve through changing customer experiences within and outside your own market. What is needed is a shorter cycle of funding, with a more flexible view on value as each project develops. The principle of getting funding approval is still valid, but with a different emphasis.

In a *Harvard Business Review* article, Gothelf draws an interesting comparison with a more entrepreneurial business approach. He takes a steer from the start-up world, recommending that the Finance team works with business teams as if they are an 'in-house start-up – a group of people tasked with solving a business problem'. Each business problem needs to have an objective, which is measurable, and which defines the team's success. Then at the end of each funding period, the teams 'must present their cases to the finance office for re-funding' (Gothelf, 2014). The Finance team becomes a partner in discovery, which requires them to understand the project's goals and to work collaboratively, while still maintaining a duty of care to the organization and its shareholders as stewards of funds. Reporting and management information can then be aligned with this new perspective.

Implicit in the iterative design and development approach is a level of managed uncertainty that traditional 'waterfall' methodologies seemed to remove. Complex project plans with clear deliverables over a two- or even five-year period are common in the waterfall approach, with an apparent certainty of return on investment that is very attractive to those investing the money. Agile working lacks this certainty, which creates problems when you are trying to convince your Finance team about a business case for investment. So, we need a Finance function that understands this shift and is willing to fund projects on the same iterative basis. Working with your Finance colleagues is therefore key to getting agile working in place – they need to buy into it if they are to adapt their own ways of working to support its less predictable financial profile.

Agile with a small 'a'

I hope that through this book I have shown you how the principles of agile working can be used to great effect more widely across the enterprise in areas which are not developing products like software. Let us take the Scrum approach and see how it can work in different parts of the organization. The 2020 *Scrum Guide* states: 'Scrum is a lightweight framework that helps people, teams and organizations generate value through adaptive solutions for complex problems' (Schwaber and Sutherland, 2020).

In project teams, for example, the main elements of Scrum working relate well but may need to be adapted to varying periods that suit the work being done. The focus is still on collaborative working to solve complex problems in a structured cycle of planning, doing, gaining frequent feedback and improvement. Team resources may not be dedicated to the team (which in more formal Scrum environments is helpful in maintaining quality and efficiency). This is a world where cross-functional teams work flexibly but with a consistent rhythm and routine. Strategic innovation, for example, may need the discipline of agile but also the freedom and flexibility of this new way of working.

Agile principles also apply in areas of the organization which need to be built on consistency and reliability to ensure economies of scale and quality delivery to customers such as manufacturing operations. In Table 9.2 you can see how the main elements of Scrum apply in both project teams and stable manufacturing-type environments. The emphasis in the latter is on continuous improvement rather than solving complex problems to produce new products. *The Scrum Guide* states that 'Scrum is founded on empiricism and lean thinking.' We learn through experimentation and empirical experience, which allows us to improve our decision making. In lean thinking we focus on reducing waste and keeping things simple.

TABLE 9.2 How Scrum works in different situations

Scrum	'Project teams'	'Manufacturing'
EVENTS		
The sprint – a container for work, one month or less	Agreed period to organize work in regular sprints, eg a month or two	Agreed period for review and continuous improvement
Sprint planning – max eight hours planning session	Regular team planning meeting at start of each period	Regular team improvement planning meeting
Daily stand-up – 15-minute team check-in to stay on track	Daily or regular team stand-up to stay on track	Daily or regular team stand-up to stay on track
Sprint review – max four hours review of sprint outcomes with key stakeholders	Regular review of work outcomes with key stakeholders at end of each period	Regular review of improvement outcomes with key stakeholders

(continued)

TABLE 9.2 (Continued)

Scrum	'Project teams'	'Manufacturing'
Sprint retrospective – max three hours review of sprint working	Regular review of team working to identify improvements at end of each period	Regular review of team working to identify improvements
ARTEFACTS		
Product backlog – ordered list of what is needed to achieve the product goal	Priorities list agreed by team for next 6–12 months (or appropriate duration)	Agreed goals for improvement in quality and efficiency over time
Sprint backlog – work to be done and plan to achieve the sprint goal	Team plan of work to be done in next period	Agreed short-term goals and plan for improvement with visuals of progress
Increments – concrete usable output satisfying the definition of done	Concrete usable output satisfying the definition of done	Incremental targets for improvement

The opportunity created by the shift to working from home and more varied patterns of work that emerged during the Covid pandemic is for agile ways of working to be used more widely across the enterprise, wherever the balance of work is focused on collaboration, innovation and continuous improvement. Scrum events and artefacts provide a structure for teamworking which can enable teams to maintain social connections as well as robust outputs, whether they are working virtually or together in one place. Social connections will continue to be an essential ingredient in team performance, whatever office or hybrid working arrangements you select in the future.

CASE STUDY   Transforming service: Yodel

The UK delivery company Yodel has transformed its service by creating a more agile enterprise, resulting in a more efficient and profitable business where employees are engaged and customers are satisfied.

Yodel delivers millions of parcels every week to every postcode across the UK. It operates in a highly competitive, rapidly changing market. Customers are increasingly demanding and expect high levels of service. When chief operating officer Carl Moore joined Yodel in 2018, he could see the company had opportunities to develop: 'We were spending too much money, losing too much money, and our service wasn't best in class.' A major restructuring programme was launched.

Articulate the vision

Carl joined a business where staff turnover hovered around 40 per cent across the business. 'The first thing we did as part of our restructuring was to establish an executive team that were all experienced in their own fields but could also work together and were strong enough to deal with the challenge we faced,' says Carl. The new executive team also introduced a completely new ethos, moving away from the previous style of leadership towards one which was more inclusive.

Light fires

The new leadership team actively involved others in the planning process, introducing concrete planning around Yodel's services and locations. 'We involved colleagues in devising a plan. We encouraged openness and honesty. We provided a sanctuary where people felt safe to share information, which they had not always been open to. That was a massive cultural change. When we discuss issues today, the openness is astounding.'

Yodel wanted to create a culture of continuous learning, where feedback, challenge and reflection are encouraged. Managers are proactive about regularly reviewing performance and identifying improvements within their teams.

'Plans are regularly reviewed,' says Carl. 'Some of this happens informally, with managers taking time to walk around sites, talking and listening to colleagues. Feedback is actively encouraged. Healthy challenge is encouraged. Some of the reviewing is more formal, where plans are adapted in response to changing circumstances if necessary.'

Building the muscle

Carl could also see that there was a great deal of talent across the organization just waiting to be unleashed. 'We already had all the ingredients we needed to turn the company around, and we gave our people the tools they needed to learn and develop within their roles.'

Yodel invested in a learning and development programme which built the capability of operational managers to devolve people management responsibility more widely across the organization. It helped to create behavioural change, encouraging managers to be more proactive and to take more responsibility for efficiency and service improvement. Development opportunities are now more widespread and there are formal, recognized career paths open to all colleagues.

Flip managers

More regular communication now includes daily team huddles and regular one-to-ones between managers and colleagues. There is a culture of coaching and many managers are taking on new tasks such as group presentations, communicating and engaging with colleagues more widely. Team members now have a greater understanding of business priorities, performance issues, and what is expected of them. Managers are delegating more and are more confident about handling poor performance issues.

Senior leaders are powerful role models for new behaviours. 'Our managers are more approachable,' says Carl. 'We are relaxed. We don't panic, even in the toughest of operating theatres, and we let people do their job. We employ the best people, we get a great team together, we get them to help each other and support each other and we let them do their thing. I like them to be free to concentrate on the key objectives we set between us.'

'Management capability is so high now, compared to what it was,' says Paul Graham, who looks after the North of England. 'This enabled us to tackle the major challenge of Covid-19 which we just wouldn't have been able to do in the past.'

Embed the process

Yodel has succeeded in creating a more agile culture with a focus on continuous improvement. Customer satisfaction is at a record high, employee retention has improved, and sickness absence has reduced. Working conditions have improved. Sites are well maintained and cleaned more regularly to make them safer and more pleasant places to be. Carl also notes other benefits: 'Our compliance is so much better than what it was. Our health and safety scores are so much better. It's incredible.'

Paul is enthusiastic about the cultural transformation Yodel has achieved. 'We've flipped from top-down management to bottom-up management, which is the way it should be. That has enabled people across the business to draw on their expertise and to thrive.'

'I genuinely believe people work at Yodel now because they're proud of Yodel and they want to turn up every day and make a difference,' says Carl. 'We now have many colleagues planning their careers with Yodel over the next five to ten years. We've turned eight years of losses into profit. But our success is not all about profit – we have created a positive environment which makes success sustainable.'

Engaging your teams in the conversation

As you engage your teams on the agile journey you may find it helpful to use a simple diagnostic questionnaire to gauge current levels of team agility. This will help to open the conversation with each team about where to focus their initial improvement efforts. The checklist below will help you do so. It is designed to reflect the content of this book from a team's perspective. Ask your team members to complete the survey individually and then in a team meeting ask them to share their scores and comment on the differences – both within their own scores and between all the team members.

Agile team checklist

Please score your main team against each descriptor on the list below using a scale of 1 to 5, based on the following definitions:

1 – we never work like this
2 – we rarely work like this
3 – we sometimes work like this
4 – we often work like this
5 – we always work like this

Add up each section as you go and record the score in Table 9.3. Please be as honest as you can, neither too optimistic nor too pessimistic.

1. FEELING SAFE

- We feel confident to experiment.
- We are consistently supported to take intelligent risks.
- We feel respected by colleagues in different teams.
- We appreciate each other's views and opinions.

2. LEARNING AGILITY

- We are always curious to learn more.
- We try new things to learn and improve.
- We have a range of diverse skills as a team.
- We focus on work that plays to our strengths.

3. DISRUPTIVE THINKING

- We welcome challenges to our assumptions.
- We like to think the unthinkable.
- We learn lots from outside our organization.
- We quickly spot and act on new opportunities.

4. CUSTOMER VISION

- We focus our resources on increasing customer value.
- We scrutinize the problem we are solving for our customers.
- We engage with our customers regularly and deeply.
- We always seek input and feedback from our customers.

5. RUTHLESS PRIORITIZATION

- We make tough choices about what to focus our time and resources on.
- We focus on the few things that will have the biggest impact on our customers.
- We stop doing things to free up resource.
- We review priorities and adjust them to respond to changes.

6. PERFORMANCE IMPROVEMENT

- We regularly receive coaching to help us improve pace and quality.
- We have ambitious goals.
- We have regular reviews to identify how to go faster in future.
- We track progress to review our performance.

7. AGILE DECISION MAKING

- We are thoughtful when making decisions.
- We are empowered to decide how we achieve our goals.
- We are clear about our roles and responsibilities.
- We act boldly as a team once a decision is made.

8. COLLABORATIVE ACHIEVEMENT

- Teamwork is our natural way of working.
- We have daily huddles to stay aligned as a team.
- We work with other teams to improve process efficiency.
- We care about how our work impacts other teams.

Please transfer the sub-totals to Table 9.3. This will be a helpful basis for a discussion with your team and with your team coach or leader – explore the scores both in absolute terms and relative to each other, so you can identify priorities for team development.

TABLE 9.3 Agile team score table

Agile leader characteristic	What this means for the team	Total score
1. Feeling safe	A climate of psychological safety where people feel confident and supported to take intelligent risks.	
2. Encouraging learning	People are universally committed to learning through experimentation so they can perform better, in a diverse and multi-skilled environment.	
3. Disruptive thinking	There is widespread openness to the opportunities created by technology to improve performance and customer value. Disruptive ideas and innovations from outside are welcomed and explored in a balanced way.	
4. Customer vision	There is a shared understanding of and commitment to the vision of what customers want, which guides people's work and priorities in a practical way.	
5. Ruthless prioritization	The direction and priorities are clear and aligned with customer vision. People review a backlog of activities and focus on delivering the top priorities with quality and pace.	
6. Performance improvement	Performance improvement is a shared priority. Coaching is common for both individuals and teams to accelerate performance improvement in line with stretching goals.	
7. Agile decision making	Decisions are made thoughtfully and executed with speed and determination. People feel comfortable to make shared decisions on how to achieve their goals. They have the information, tools and skills needed to do so.	

(*continued*)

TABLE 9.3 (Continued)

Agile leader characteristic	What this means for the team	Total score
8. Collaborative achievement	Teamwork is the norm. People commit time and energy to improve their team's performance. They embrace working across teams on shared goals to achieve outcomes quickly and effectively. Team processes are consistent and efficient.	
	TOTAL TEAM SCORE	

Summary

Many young organizations, so-called digital natives, are naturally agile in many ways, as they have grown up in a world where digital was the obvious choice for doing business. Many operate with some or all of the characteristics in this book already in place, at least in parts of their organization. Creating an agile enterprise is harder for those who pre-date the internet. It represents a transformation of well-established ways of thinking and working for most, in a counter-intuitive shift away from predictable patterns of production, distribution and service. In this chapter I have laid out some ways to get this transformation going and to sustain it so that the benefits of agility can permeate the way you operate. I hope they are of value to those that are digital natives and those that are not.

Start by articulating (or refreshing) your vision for the transformation, in terms everyone can understand, and create a sense of the opportunity for everyone in making this shift. Flip managers from control to enabling, from hierarchy to self-managing teams, from risk aversion to experimentation. Build the muscle of capability across the organization, so that teams in all divisions and functions are aligned with the new ways of working and support each other in putting them into practice. Light fires of agile teams creating breakthrough innovation where the need is greatest, and build out from there, with increasing levels of interest and desire to be part of the movement. Embed agile in your core processes, so that they support rather than inhibit agile working.

References

Bersin, J (2018) A new paradigm for corporate training: Learning in the flow of work, joshbersin.com/2018/06/a-new-paradigm-for-corporate-training-learning-in-the-flow-of-work/ (archived at https://perma.cc/RLB3-EW9S)

Bersin, J (2020) A new model for corporate training: The adaptive learning organization, joshbersin.com/2020/11/a-new-model-for-corporate-training-the-adaptive-learning-organization/ (archived at https://perma.cc/L8XZ-CANA)

Cannon, F (2017) *The Agility Mindset*, Palgrave Macmillan, Basingstoke

Cho, F, quoted in Liker, J (2004) *The Toyota Way*, McGraw-Hill, New York

Cirrus/Ipsos (2017) Leadership Connections 2017, research paper, Cirrus, London

Dahik, A, Lovich, D, Kreafle, C, Bailey, A, Kilmann, J, Kennedy, D, Roongta, P, Schuler, F, Tomlin, L and Wenstrup, J (2020) *What 12,000 Employees Have To Say About the Future of Remote Work*, Boston Consulting Group, Boston, MA, August 2020

Danoesastro, M, Freeland, G and Reichert, T (2017) A CEO's guide to leading digital transformation, in *BCG Perspectives*, Boston Consulting Group, Boston, MA

Dawson, M and Jones, M (2015) *Human Change Management: Herding cats*, PricewaterhouseCoopers, London

De Smet, A, Mygatt, E, Sheikh, I and Weddle, B (2020) *The Need For Speed in the Post-COVID-19 Era, and How To Achieve It*, McKinsey, MA

Denning, S (2005) *The Leader's Guide to Storytelling: Mastering the art and discipline of business narrative*, Jossey-Bass, San Francisco, CA

Gothelf, J (2014) Bring agile to the whole organization, *Harvard Business Review*, November

Rigby, D and Sutherland, J (2016) Understanding agile management, *Harvard Business Review*, April

Schwaber, K and Sutherland, J (2020) *The Scrum Guide*, www.scrumguides.org/docs/scrumguide/v2020/2020-Scrum-Guide-US.pdf (archived at https://perma.cc/4657-ZH27)

Takeuchi, H, Osono, E and Shimizu, N (2008) The contradictions that drive Toyota's success, *Harvard Business Review,* June

Ulrich, D and Smallwood, N (2004) Capitalizing on capabilities, *Harvard Business Review*, June

CHAPTER TEN

Agility and the network society

Anything not built for a network age – our politics, our economics, our national security, our education – is going to crack under its pressures. RAMO (2016)

Introduction

This final chapter reflects on the way agile leadership is relevant to the wider society in which we live, with the impact of coronavirus, technology and political change challenging the nature of organizations as they currently exist. We live in an increasingly connected and yet disrupted world. There is a growing need for more networked organizations that are able to adapt to varying situations around the world and yet maintain a coherent strategy and culture. The agile leader embraces this challenge, and the chapter ends with views on how the agile leadership paradox can help us understand the political and social changes going on around us in the world today.

> **QUESTIONS TO ASK YOURSELF**
>
> In this chapter you may find it helpful to consider the following questions as you read:
>
> - Do you currently embrace an open or closed view of society?
> - Where could your organization create more effective networks?
> - Where else in your society could you provide more agile leadership?

Accelerating change

We live in 'the age of connected acceleration', according to Ramo, in which our knowledge is soon to be obsolete and we are increasingly reliant on our instincts (2016). Research from EY in 2012 found that while most global companies understood the need to adapt to the evolving use of technology by their customers, the majority did not realize how little time they had to address these changes. After all, it took 10 years for the internet to become part of everyday life. EY pointed out that the pace of technological change was increasing rapidly and that in a world where everything was becoming digital, businesses would have to innovate in order to disrupt their own industries before competitors did. 'There is no time to lose,' predicted the researchers (EY, 2012).

Fast forward even five years and the challenges of leading in a digital world had shot to the top of the organizational agenda. Bersin found that 90 per cent of organizations in 2017 believed their core business was threatened by new digital competitors, while 70 per cent believed they did not have the right leadership, skills or operating models to adapt (Bersin, 2017). Gartner research showed that 42 per cent of global CEOs had embarked on digital business transformation (Gartner, 2017). In the third decade of the 21st century, when the coronavirus pandemic accelerated digitization even more rapidly, industries such as retail and travel experienced traumatic change. The percentage of organizations working on a digital transformation is now over 80 per cent (Gartner, 2019) and rising.

The implications of this situation push us towards more agile ways of working. Organizations no longer control the customer relationship; disruptive competition is enabled by accelerating technological possibilities, which also drive supply chain transformation and the increasing risk of commoditization. Add to this the changing global context, with the shift of economic power from West to East, rising populist political leadership, the range of politically unstable areas around the world, and we see a level of unpredictability that suggests the VUCA world is only going to get more volatile.

Many advisers start their response to these changes with a digital perspective. They recommend increasing use of technology across the enterprise, in a digital transformation that will solve the problems of long-standing organizations seemingly buried in legacy systems and processes. I believe this is the wrong starting point. Yes, digital transformation is needed by many organizations seeking to cope with new digital market entrants, and technology will continue to drive many of the changes around us. Many retailers, for example, are still trying to catch up with their digital competitors, with inadequate online resources to provide a competitive customer experience. However, starting with technology will not lead to agile competitiveness. Starting with people will.

As we have seen throughout this book, the key to unleashing agile innovation and improvement is fundamentally about 'people over processes and tools' (from the Agile Manifesto, Highsmith, 2001). It is what people believe that is important. How they interact, what they focus on and how open they are to learn, is what will ultimately make the difference between success and failure. Digital transformation can work if it is led by leaders who understand this. We have repeatedly seen examples in this book where success is predicated on culture, teamwork and agile ways of working. These in turn make investment in technology and new target operating models more likely to succeed.

Networked organizations

Social media and the internet have created consumer networks that are outside the control of organizations. We see a level of global device connectivity where control of digital networks belongs to no particular enterprise. Artificial intelligence and machine learning are creating learning systems that can take control of themselves and therefore be unaccountable to human intervention. Crowd-sourcing has changed how we buy services and gain funding for our businesses. Blockchain has made transactions transparent and will disrupt global industries where trust is key, potentially cutting out intermediaries such as banks in the process. In this context, the need to create learning organizations has never been more apparent. Agile working is a route to this that is now well-established, and based on a successful history of lean manufacturing and continuous improvement.

Part of the challenge to making this a reality, however, is the need for organizations to collaborate with others to succeed. This applies, for example, in rapidly evolving markets such as communications, with app developers fuelling smartphone supply, and financial services, where big-tech companies are providing services direct to customers and driving a cashless open banking environment. The ubiquitous application programming interface (API) is a symbol of this networked organization, an ecosystem of supply and demand working through defined protocols and tools to communicate and collaborate for mutual benefit.

In the car industry and its associated markets such as car hire and car finance, for example, the changes that autonomous vehicles will bring will be seismic, and require organizations to rethink their whole commercial model. As we see Transportation as a Service (TaaS) gather pace, with consumers booking autonomous transport via apps, and car ownership as we know it possibly disappearing, the ripple effects across public and private transport systems will be significant. The movement of people and things will become a seamless process managed by intelligent systems that use public and private facilities, giving consumers the best experience based on their preferences and user history. Payment will be managed through an integrated commercial model. The way the various organizations involved in any journey interact will determine the winners and losers – the best networked integrators will have a lead, and those whose heads have been in the sand will fail.

In *Hit Refresh* Nadella of Microsoft talks about 'building partnerships before you need them… When done right, partnering grows the pie for everyone – for customers, yes, but also for each of the partners' (Nadella, 2017). You can take many of the agile lessons from this book and apply them to building partnerships and to managing relationships and work at the interface between organizations in a network. Short cycles of activity, for example, with regular huddles to test whether progress is meeting the needs of all participants, are helpful to stay close to the priority deliverables in the partnership. Mixed teams bringing expertise from all partners can greatly accelerate progress if the people involved are free to be transparent, share knowledge and solve problems together. Retrospective meetings to review the last sprint and identify how to work faster in the next one will drive improved benefits for all parties. For these ways of working to succeed between organizations it needs leaders to set up the ground rules with collaboration in mind, so that people working in the teams are empowered by their employers to work in ways which otherwise seem naïve.

Many of these ecosystems are currently based on commercial pragmatism – Apple is famous for its closed operating environment that precludes collaboration unless it suits Apple. Yet Nadella describes the first time he stood up at a conference and took an iPhone out of his pocket to demonstrate the Microsoft products running on it – 'the crowd erupted in applause'. New generations of consumers seek better experiences as well as greater meaning in life and expect their suppliers to collaborate to deliver them. This combines the needs for organizations to have a clear sense of customer value as well as explicit societal purpose. The same applies to networked ecosystems, made up of various partners, operating in an API world of agreed protocols that facilitate creating greater value for customers than their competitors. These systems need to articulate why consumers should trust them and what they stand for. This will enable them to be sustainable beyond a convenient moment in time when a smartphone maker needed software applications to make the device useful, or a bank needed software to respond to big-tech competitors. This in turn will need leaders capable of creating shared purpose, shared goals and shared outcomes – leaders with the ability to connect beyond boundaries, to engage competitors in collaborative ventures, and to create trust where it did not exist.

What sort of society do we want?

The power of prejudice and fear was clear when Hutus and Tutsis killed each other in Rwanda's civil melt-down. But it was also clear when Mexicans at the US border were seen as not deserving basic human rights under the Trump administration.

In our increasingly polarized world, with exclusive right- and left-wing views growing in popularity, increasing social division, and accelerating climate change, we need leadership which can rekindle public preference for freedom, respect and inclusive politics. We seem to lack strong leaders who can inspire the majority to advocate for inclusion and a fair society. In this void it is not surprising that strident populist voices are often heard more readily.

In a world where we see ever-increasing connectivity and yet more walls being built, we are faced with a choice. Do we go forwards or backwards? Do we embrace an open world or a closed one? My sense is that agile leaders will be clear and decide to move forward towards a more open and collaborative world, both at the micro level of their organization, and on the wider macro-economic stage.

In his annual lecture at the Royal Society of Arts in 2020, Matthew Taylor called for the dawn of a 'reflexive age', in which greater self-awareness for individuals and in society as a whole leads to a more humane liberal democracy (Taylor, 2020). What does he mean by a reflexive era? 'It is what could result from cultivating a deeper and shared awareness of *ourselves*, our nature and the social patterns that result from that nature.' He argues for a more intentional balance between three key motivators of human agency:

- the caring authority of the state
- the responsible autonomy and happiness of the individual
- social cohesion based on respect for differences as well as belonging.

The principles of agile leadership will, I believe, create a more reflexive work environment, balancing clear vision and direction, shared purpose, team belonging, autonomy and choice, and regular reflection and holding ourselves to account. This in turn will create conditions for greater mental health and wellbeing in the workplace. The Covid crisis has created, Taylor believes, the opportunity for populism, consumerism and cynicism to be replaced by a new, reflexive enlightenment, which is aligned with the agile leadership characteristics discussed in this book.

Taylor's motivators are also in tune with the three functions of complexity leadership theory we reviewed in Chapter 4 (Uhl-Bien *et al*, 2007). The administrative, adaptive and enabling functions combine to create balance in the organization so that it can succeed in unpredictable and constantly changing environments. Similarly, in a healthy society we need a balance between state authority, individual autonomy and social cohesion. Agile leadership describes an approach to leadership which is highly consistent with these themes – shared vision, purpose and direction yet with devolved decision making, individuals feeling safe to experiment and learn, and collaborative achievement to maximize shared outcomes.

The Scrum Alliance is founded on five principles which illustrate the inherent bias in agile thinking: 'Commitment, Focus, Openness, Respect and Courage' (Schwaber and Sutherland, 2020). As agile leaders we might find it helpful to consider to what extent we demonstrate these principles in how we behave day to day. Are you a role model for these principles in practice? If you are, you are more likely to be creating the environment where reflexive agility can flourish. Does your organization demonstrate these principles in the societies in which it operates? Is it focused on learning, societal purpose and the greater good of all stakeholders, or only on profit?

Talking about all stakeholders, research of nearly 2,000 executives around the world showed, 'It's no longer an option to see the people you employ, the people you sell to and the people who live in the world around you as three distinct groups. Not if you want to compete in today's global economy' (Fujitsu, 2018).

FASHION AND THE PLANET

The British Fashion Council (BFC) is accelerating sustainability across the fashion industry. In February 2020, just before the pandemic hit, it launched a platform called the Institute of Positive Fashion (IPF). The IPF aims to revolutionize the British fashion industry by bringing it in tune with the needs of the planet. It is focused on global collaboration and local action. It unites experts from across the fashion industry, government and academia.

'This is not just another platform,' says Caroline Rush, CEO of the BFC. 'We have put the IPF at the heart of our strategy. We have set a new bar of accountability for us and for the industry as a whole. It has created a focus for global collaboration to accelerate change.'

In recent years, many in the fashion industry have been reflecting on their purpose – the impact they have on the planet, and how they can be a more effective force for good. More consumers want to shop in a responsible and sustainable way. Both business and consumers are thinking more about the role they play in climate change. 'The fashion industry has an opportunity to reinvent itself,' says Caroline. 'The consumer can play a part in that.' The IPF is a bold stand and an opportunity for a whole sector to change its impact on society.

The agile leadership paradox in society

As we saw in Chapter 1, digitization continues to accelerate in all areas of life. We therefore need to embrace a leadership paradox. Great leaders connect people, customers and nations, and yet they also challenge the status quo, disrupt thinking and break well-established norms such as the regulation of taxis in our cities, the concept of car ownership, or the office as the place of work.

To be agile leaders in a digital world we need to be both enablers and disruptors, creating a joined-up society and at the same time challenging how it operates at the most fundamental level. We need to embrace both sides of the agile leadership paradox – the need to connect and yet the need to disrupt – creating cohesion and yet being reflexive by questioning the assumptions that underpin it.

The upsurge in populist leaders in many parts of the world is one example of how our society is changing and in a way that is antithetical to the principles of agile working. The four values of agile in the original Manifesto resonate today: 'people over processes and tools, prototypes over documentation, responding to change over following a plan, and customer collaboration over rigid contracts' (Highsmith, 2001). The emphasis is on people, experimentation to learn, adapting and collaboration. These are not the words of xenophobia and walls: they are the words of bridge building, partnership and openness to others.

When I describe disruption as one side of the agile leadership paradox (Figure 10.1), I mean disruption for innovation, for bold improvement and for reinvention. This is balanced with the need to enable people to connect, to learn and to work together to accelerate outcomes for customers and for society. Agile working is essentially not about ego, but about working as an inclusive team in which the differences are valued and drawn into the discussion as a source of challenge and insight. This takes trust between people, and trust from leaders to empower others to get on with making things

FIGURE 10.1 The agile leadership paradox

Enabler	Disruptor
• Clear purpose and direction	• Looking out
• Create a safe place	• Close to customers
• Trusted and trusting	• Ruthlessly prioritize
• Coach for improvement	• Challenge the status quo
• Devolve decision making	• Bold and determined
• Collaborative	

happen. As a model for a healthy society it has many merits. Taylor suggests we need more disruptive thinking in our mainstream politics focused on establishing a new enlightenment, or what I would call a connected society (Taylor, 2020). This is an open society, where differences are valued and the balance between good governance, individual achievement and societal cohesion is robust.

The type of disruption that we see in the upsurge in popular politics is not conducive to an agile and connected society that is open to equal opportunity. We need to recognize that the underlying frustration it shows with a capitalist system that is biased towards the wealthy minority is unsustainable.

The principles of agile working are fit for wider application, as a basis for creating a more connected society where respect for each other means we need to reframe our assumptions about how rewards are allocated, with a more equal approach tied to a drive to empower people to make as full a contribution to our collective wealth and happiness as they can. If, as a society, we enable more people to contribute, we can share more of the economic gains more widely. This in turn will help to reverse the feelings of frustration and injustice of many. The agile mindset and ways of working provide us with an approach that can contribute to this shift away from power and resources being held by the few, towards a more egalitarian society where inclusion, trust and contribution are at the fore.

If you are a leader with vision, I hope you will embrace the insights in this book about enabling agile working where you work. I also hope that you will see the value in taking these principles and applying them more widely, to other organizations in your personal ecosystem. We face choices every day about whether to collaborate, whether to trust others to do a good job, and whether to take risks and learn from the outcomes, whatever they are. By embracing agile leadership, you can drive improved productivity and innovation as well as making a big difference to those around you at work, at home and in our wider society.

References

Bersin, J (2017) *Predictions for 2017: Everything is becoming digital*, Bersin by Deloitte, Deloitte Consulting, London

EY (2012) *The Digitization of Everything*, EY, London

Fujitsu (2018) *Co-creation for Success. Unlocking creativity, knowledge and innovation,* Fujitsu Corporation, Japan

Gartner (2017) *CEO Survey: CIOs must scale up digital business,* Gartner Group, Stamford, CT

Gartner (2019) *2019 CEO Survey: The year of challenged growth,* Gartner Group, Stamford, CT

Highsmith, J (2001) *History: The Agile Manifesto,* available at agilemanifesto.org/history.html (archived at https://perma.cc/M5XZ-ZG7H)

Nadella, S (2017) *Hit Refresh,* William Collins, London

Ramo, JC (2016) *The Seventh Sense,* Little, Brown and Company, New York

Schwaber, K and Sutherland, J (2020) *The Scrum Guide,* www.scrumguides.org/docs/scrumguide/v2020/2020-Scrum-Guide-US.pdf (archived at https://perma.cc/4657-ZH27)

Taylor, M (2020) The Reflexive Age, RSA annual lecture, The Royal Society for Arts, Manufactures and Commerce, London

Uhl-Bien, M, Marion, R and McKelvey, B (2007) Complexity leadership theory: Shifting leadership from the industrial age to the knowledge era, *The Leadership Quarterly,* **18**

Index

Note: Numbers are filed as spelled; acronyms and 'Mc' are filed as presented. Page locators in *italics* denote information within a figure or table.

CPSIA information can be obtained
at www.ICGtesting.com
Printed in the USA
JSHW031948190123
36531JS00007B/217

9 781398 600713